Emerging Markets

Emerging Markets
Strategies for competing in the global value chain

Robert Grosse

KoganPage

LONDON PHILADELPHIA NEW DELHI

First published in Great Britain and the United States in 2016 by Kogan Page Limited

2nd Floor, 45 Gee Street
London
EC1V 3RS
United Kingdom

1518 Walnut Street, Suite 1100
Philadelphia PA 19102
USA

4737/23 Ansari Road
Daryaganj
New Delhi 110002
India

© Robert Grosse, 2016

The right of Robert Grosse to be identified as the author of this work has been asserted by him in accordance with the Copyright, Designs and Patents Act 1988.

ISBN   978 0 7494 7449 2
E-ISBN   978 0 7494 7450 8

British Library Cataloguing-in-Publication Data

A CIP record for this book is available from the British Library.

Library of Congress Cataloging-in-Publication Data

Grosse, Robert E., author.
   Emerging markets : strategies for competing in the global value chain / Robert Grosse.
      pages cm
   ISBN 978-0-7494-7449-2 – ISBN 978-0-7494-7450-8 (ebk)   1. Developing countries–Commerce.
2. International business enterprises–Developing countries.   3. Strategic planning–Developing countries.   4. New products–Developing countries. I. Title.
   HF1413.G687 2016
   658.4′012–dc23
                                                                                          2015033995

Typeset by Graphicraft Limited, Hong Kong
Print production managed by Jellyfish
Printed and bound by CPI Group (UK) Ltd, Croydon CR0 4YY

CONTENTS

Introduction

What to expect in Chapter 1

Global economic growth will centre on China, India and probably Brazil, Russia, Indonesia, South Africa, Mexico and a handful of other emerging markets in the next 25 years. Why? How should we think about and what should we do about this reality? The challenge is that if you can't fit your business into this reality, you will face decline. The opportunity is that if you look at emerging markets, you will find attractive markets and supply sources, as well as networks to join.

Chapter 1 places these challenges into a framework for thinking about companies as participants in global value-added chains or networks, in which they buy inputs from suppliers and sell their products and/or services to customers. The goal for the company's management is first to identify where the company is in global value-added chains, and then decide on how to expand into additional activities or places and also how to defend its position in the existing configuration of value chain participants. Emerging markets fit as both sources and target markets in these networks.

Examples are given of the value-added chains into which Triad companies fit (Apple, Exxon, Hoffmann-La Roche, Accenture and Morris International Group) and emerging market companies fit (Cisneros Group, Crescent Petroleum and FEMSA). By sketching out the range of activities and locations of the company, you can see opportunities for expansion (or contracting out) to build more sustainable competitive positions.

The Chinese economy has grown at an average of about 10 per cent per year for the past quarter-century. It is now about 60 per cent of the size of the US economy, and is projected to pass the United States in national income by the year 2018. Is this a concern?

Employment in the business process outsourcing sector in India has grown at an annual rate of about 15 per cent during the past 25 years. This sector directly employs about 2.8 million people in India today (and indirectly about 9 million people), particularly in call centres, and includes literally hundreds of thousands of jobs outsourced from US companies to lower their costs. Is this a positive development?

US companies such as Chrysler and Levis, not to speak of Apple and Microsoft, have moved a significant part of the production of their cars, jeans, hardware and software to China. Are these jobs lost to Americans, or should they be viewed in some other way?

These examples illustrate the huge importance of these two emerging markets to people and companies in the United States and other industrial countries, whose economic livelihood has been challenged by the threat of job losses to lower-wage countries and then by the 2008–09 financial crisis and subsequent slow growth in all of the Triad areas of North America, the European Union and Japan. The underlying fear is that with lower-wage competition from China and India, and from many other emerging markets, jobs and lower unemployment rates may not return to the United States and the European Union. Is the first major crisis of the 21st century going to leave the Triad countries in a slow-growth, high-unemployment state of paralysis, or is there a light at the end of the tunnel?

The book shows how emerging markets are the opportunity of today and the future, and how firms and individuals from the industrial countries should view this opportune environment in order to benefit from it. Beginning with several examples of Triad-based companies that have incorporated emerging markets into their global operations, the discussion demonstrates the fit of these companies into global value-added chains. Likewise, examples of companies based in emerging markets also demonstrate how they fit into global value-added chains, sometimes different from the Triad companies (particularly in high-tech industries) and sometimes similar to them (particularly in natural resources industries and in many services). Along with the analysis of international companies in global value-added chains, the book talks about the history of emerging markets over many centuries, and about the importance of innovation.

A fundamental driver of business success in the 21st century, as in the past, is *innovation*. Innovation involves the creation of new knowledge and the launching of products and services based on that knowledge in the marketplace. Companies that are able to follow paths of innovation stand a much greater likelihood of success than those that fail to pursue innovation.

Countries that are able to offer conditions that attract and foster innovation will have a major competitive advantage over those that are not able to achieve such conditions. The United States remains the lead country in providing these conditions – so there is no risk that the United States will simply be overwhelmed by the low-wage competition from emerging markets. Unless, of course, innovation migrates to emerging markets – or better stated, unless emerging markets are able to create favourable conditions for innovation – the United States and other high-innovation countries such as Germany and the United Kingdom should retain a key place in the world economy through this century.

Consider again the statement that China's economy is growing at a rate such that it will pass the US economy in overall size by the year 2018, according to *The Economist* magazine.[1] Even if this projection is overly optimistic from the Chinese perspective, there is still no doubt that the Chinese economy, with about 1.4 billion consumers, will be larger than the US economy, with about 320 million consumers, within another decade. Still, per capita income, or average family income, is projected to be higher in the United States for several decades to come. Chinese per person annual income in 2013 was just $US 6,800, compared to US per person income of $US 53,100.[2] So living standards are expected to be much higher in the United States (and other industrial countries) than in China for quite a while. Even so, China is estimated to have already moved more than 300 million people from poverty into middle-class income levels during 1985–2005 (United Nations and People's Republic of China, 2008), so that the market in China already is approaching that of the United States in terms of the number of consumers/clients that companies can serve with many of their products and services.

The same cannot be said of India. Even with over 1.2 billion consumers, India's economy is not expected to exceed the size of the US economy until perhaps 2050 at the earliest. In India, per capita income in 2013 was about $US 1,500 (or $US 5,400 in purchasing power parity terms), with far fewer middle-class consumers than in China. While this picture is less compelling than that of China, even so, India's market is becoming more and more important to the overall world economy – and consequently to companies that want to see growth in their sales and profits in the years ahead. India is particularly attractive to US companies, because of the fact that English is the main language of the country's 1.2 billion potential customers/employees, and because it is a democracy where rules of the game are more similar to those in the United States.

The lesson of these two comparisons, of India and China with the United States, is to point out that the two countries are not just low-cost labour havens for industrial-country companies, but that they are themselves extremely attractive markets for many of the products and services sold in the Triad countries today.[3] Seeking out growth for a medium-sized or large company today really requires the consideration of China and/or India as a target market now and into the future.

Are the Chinese and Indians taking jobs away from US citizens? This is not at all an easy question to answer. The simplistic view that every manufacturing job that migrates to China is a job lost in the United States is of course wrong. If US companies did not move some of their production to China, companies from Germany and Japan and elsewhere still will do that, and the US firms will still end up with a big cost disadvantage. But even more important than that logic is the fact that the US companies who move parts of their production abroad are also hiring more US employees – even though not for the same jobs. That is, US companies that succeed in creating, producing and selling products or services are able to divide up their activities, so that some production may be moved to China – at the same time as the company may increase its employment in purchasing, shipping, R&D, opening more stores or points of sale, and maintaining customer relations.[4] China and India are vital parts of the overall value-added chain for firms in the 21st century.

Value-added chains, networks and global competition

Another key element of competition in the 21st century is the use of *networks* of companies to carry out parts of a supply chain or value-added chain. Just as IBM contracted with Intel for supplying processor chips and with Microsoft to design and build the operating system of its PC in the past century, so today do thousands of large and small firms use alliance partners to carry out parts of their supply chains.[5] The network may involve large companies, such as Exxon or Apple, or it may be just among small and medium-sized companies – but the arrangement of sharing costs and risks is very common today. In the case of the Apple iPhone, for example, production of components and assemblies is carried out in four countries: United States, Japan, Germany and Korea; and then these inputs are assembled in China. Table 1.1 shows this multinational production process.

TABLE 1.1 Apple iPhone

Manufacturer	Multi-source probability	Component description	Cost	Country
Toshiba	High	Flash Memory NAND, 16GB, MLC	$24.00	Japan
	High	Display Module 3.5" Diagonal, 16M Color TFT, 320 × 480 Pixels	$19.25	
	Medium	Touch Screen Assembly Capacitive, Glass	$16.00	
Samsung	Low	Application Processor ARM Core, Package-on-Package	$14.46	Korea
Infineon	Low	Baseband HSDPA/WCDMA/EDGE Dual ARM926 and ARM7Core	$13.00	Germany
	Medium	Camera Module 3 Megapixel Auto-Focus	$9.55	
Samsung (with Elpida die)	High	SDRAM—Mobile DDR 2GB Package-on-Package (Mounted on Application Processor)	$8.50	Korea
Broadcom	Low	Bluetooth/FM/WLAN Single Chip, WLAN IEEE802.11b/g, Bluetooth V2.1+EDR, with FM and RDS/RBDS Receiver	$5.95	United States
Numonyx	High	Memory MCP 128MB NOR Flash and 512MB Mobile DDR	$3.65	United States

TABLE 1.1 *continued*

Manufacturer	Multi-source probability	Component description	Cost	Country
Infineon	Low	RF Transceiver Quad-Band GSM/EDGE, Tri-Band WCDMA/HSDPA, 130nm RF CMOS	$2.80	Germany
Infineon	Low	GPS Receiver Single Chip, 0.13μm, with Integrated Front-End RF, PLL, PM, Correlator Engine and Host Control Interface	$2.25	Germany
Infineon	Low	Power IC RF Function	$1.25	Germany
Murata	Low	FEM Quad-Band GSM, Tri-Band UMTS Antenna Switch and Quad-Band GSM RX RF SAW Filters	$1.35	Japan
Dialog	Low	POWER IC Application Processor Function	$1.30	Germany
Cirrus Logic	Low	Audio Codec Ultra Low Power, Stereo, with Headphone	$1.15	United States
		Rest of bill-of-materials*	**$48.00**	
Various		**Total bill-of-materials**	**$172.46**	Various
Foxconn	Medium	**Manufacturing costs***	**$6.50**	**China**
Grand total			**$178.96**	

SOURCE: Adapted from Rassweiler (2009), courtesy of IHS, Inc

FIGURE 1.1   Exxon value-added chain

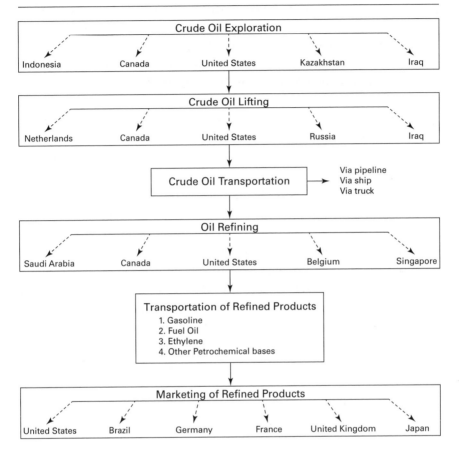

SOURCE: constructed by the author; countries are examples of where Exxon operates

While the iPhone bears Apple's logo, the actual phone itself is the product of a global supply network in which German, Korean, Japanese, Chinese and US companies provide inputs. The various suppliers/participants in the value-added chain each compete in independent markets for their products against other competitors, at the same time as they contribute to the value-added chain of the iPhone. The final assembly of the components into an iPhone is done by Taiwan-based Foxconn (Hon Hai), in factories located in mainland China.

In the case of Exxon's oil-industry activities, the supply chain (Figure 1.1) goes from exploration for new oil deposits (some of which is carried out in-house, and some contracted from third parties); extraction of the oil from the ground/ocean (mostly carried out by Exxon or by joint ventures with local state-owned oil companies); transporting the crude oil to refineries, mostly done by Exxon; refining (also done mostly in-house today); transporting petrol to service stations and other refined products to markets (done largely by Exxon in-house); and finally operation of petrol stations (with most of these retail points of sale contracted out by Exxon to franchisees).

The Exxon supply chain spans the world, as oil and natural gas deposits are located in countries from Saudi Arabia to the United States, from the North Sea to Brazil, and in African and Asian countries as well. Refining tends to be done near the sources of the raw material – but not necessarily so. Marketing of petrol and other refined products is done largely in places with lots of consumers, such as the Triad countries of North America, Europe and Japan. Over time Exxon has been more or less involved directly in all of the various stages of the production process. For example, in the 1980s the company sold much of its refining capacity to third parties, when the margins in refining had dropped to single-digit levels. Then when that business became more profitable again in the 1990s, Exxon re-invested in refining, such that it now refines more than half of its own oil production.[6]

An alternative oil-industry supply chain exists in the Middle East and Far East context. Saudi Aramco produces several million barrels a day of crude petroleum in Saudi Arabia. This company operates much like Exxon, with activities at every stage of the value-added chain. Focusing rather on other participants in Aramco's supply chain, smaller, more focused companies can be identified. Saudi Aramco contracts with Bahri, an independent Saudi Arabian oil shipping company, to transport some of its crude oil to the Philippines. There the local company Petron (owned by the San Miguel conglomerate) receives the crude oil and refines it into petrol. And then Petron sells the petrol under its own brand name through its network of service stations, as well as to independent service stations that operate under the Petron brand name. So this supply chain includes four separate companies from extraction of the oil to sales of petrol to consumers. In each case the participants in the value-added chain are emerging market companies, some large and some small.

In each of these examples, the key point is that the firm, whether it be Apple or Foxconn, Exxon or a petrol-station franchisee, is operating in a network of supply chain participants. And the goal is to optimize the firm's fit into that supply chain – including even the rearrangement of the chain to better suit the firm's view of an optimal supply chain in the particular business sector/activity. When amazon.com perceived a supply chain for store-less delivery of books and other products to consumers, it had to invent a new variant of the supply chain, cutting out the personal visits to stores and replacing them with online views of the products and low-cost, rapid delivery of these products from centralized warehouses.[7] When emerging market entrepreneurs perceived a demand for rapid and inexpensive telephone service, they had to implement virtual (ie mobile phone) phone service to replace the traditional slow, expensive fixed-line telephone service that was the only choice before that (eg **http://news.cnet.com/Emerging-markets-fuel-cell-phone-growth/2100-1039_3-6159491.html** and **http://ijoc.org/index.php/ijoc/article/viewFile/216/179**).

It is not that all firms need to create new supply chain structures, but rather that they need to understand their fit into existing structures and to be alert for shifting arrangements that may benefit or hurt them. When commercial banks faced the threat of virtual banking more than a decade ago, it appeared that they might lose their ability to compete with the footloose, low-cost virtual providers of financial services. That outcome has not happened yet, but the electronic banking phenomenon has produced a huge increase in online services provided by the traditional banks, as well as huge drop in the use of personal cheques to carry out payments in the United States.[8] New market niches have arisen as well – for example, the ability to pay bills via a mobile phone; and the idea of crowd funding, with many providers of credit channelling their funds through an internet-based consolidator. Financial service providers have to decide what their core business is, and then fit themselves into networks of strategic allies to be able to survive in this competitive market.

So, the approach of this analysis regarding business strategy is to place a firm into its overall supply chain, identifying suppliers, customers, competitors, facilitators and so on, and then to construct strategies based on this network of interacting participants. Figure 1.2 depicts this approach for a Swiss firm that produces proprietary pharmaceuticals, F Hoffmann-La Roche Ltd.

Hoffmann-La Roche was founded in 1896 by a Swiss chemist whose name remains as the company name, lately shortened to Roche. The company's initial products included a thyroid drug and a wound antiseptic, Airol. These were soon followed by the heart medicine Digalen, the cough syrup Sirolin and a pain reliever, Pantopon. Over time the portfolio of pharmaceutical products changed strikingly, to a focus on vitamins in the 1920s and 1930s, to anti-depressants and pain relievers along with vitamins in the 1940s, to cancer therapies in the 1960s. The sedative Valium was introduced in 1962. Cosmetic fragrances were another major product line introduced in that era. By the end of the 1960s Roche had entered into the diagnostic instruments and testing business.

After a number of major divestitures in the early 2000s, and the full acquisition of Genentech in 2009, the company today has two main lines of business: proprietary pharmaceuticals and diagnostics. We will just focus

FIGURE 1.2   Hoffmann-la Roche in its global supply chain

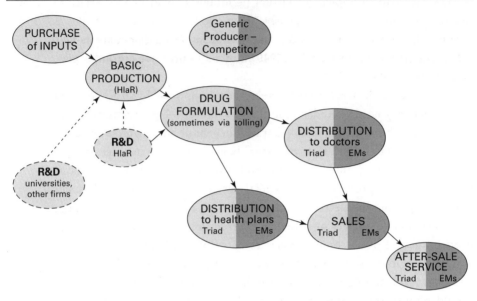

KEY: light shading indicates activity in a Triad country; dark shading indicates an emerging market.

on the first of these. Roche's industry is changing greatly in the 21st century, with sales to doctors being replaced in many countries by sales to medical plans. And some of the R&D traditionally done by a major drug company such as Roche is being done today by independent companies and universities. Generic (non-branded) products are forcing prices down as soon as they go off-patent, and the process of obtaining a patent easily takes up more than half of the typical 20-year life of protection offered by this legal structure.

Roche has chosen today to focus primarily on cancer-related drugs. It is the largest producer of such products for breast cancer, colon cancer, cervical cancer and lung cancer. Roche operates three major research programmes, in cancer, diabetes and central nervous system diseases (such as Alzheimer's, multiple sclerosis and schizophrenia). It also seeks out external research through 150 different alliances with universities and other companies. Fully one-third of Roche's total sales come from drugs licensed or purchased from other companies or research facilities. In 2012 alone the company signed 43 R&D collaboration agreements and licensed 9 products from other companies.[9]

The challenge for Roche in the 21st century is to continue to invest in expensive R&D while competing with both generic drug producers and competitors who are also investing in cancer-related treatments. The solution to Roche's challenge is to build links to other companies and universities that can provide inputs such as R&D, to distribution channels such as hospital chains and health plans, and even to competitors for the purpose of formulating drug products in shared facilities. This solution does not completely solve Roche's challenge, but it does spread the risks and costs among a much broader range of participants in Roche's value-added chain.

Switching focus to a very different business, a service industry, look at Ireland-based Accenture's fit into a global supply chain for software implementation services. This company originated as part of the accounting/auditing company Arthur Andersen, as a consulting arm in the 1950s. It was established as a separate division in 1989. With the demise of the accounting firm in 2001,[10] Accenture became an independent organization. Today it has three main business areas: management consulting; technology consulting; and business process outsourcing. The focus in this discussion is on the technology area, where Accenture is the world's largest provider of systems integration consulting (Figure 1.3).

Accenture provides implementation service for software such as the SAP and Oracle enterprise resource planning systems. Its services are aimed at businesses, generally large ones that want to implement large-scale software

FIGURE 1.3 Accenture's fit in a global supply chain for ERP

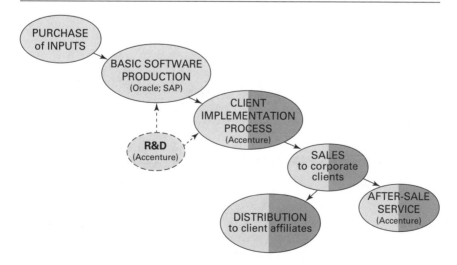

to manage their data, including sales and client-related records, production and transport information, internal salary and HR information, and so on.

Note that in this instance, the company (Accenture) depends heavily on the suppliers of the initial enterprise resource planning (ERP) software, namely SAP and Oracle. Those independent companies also offer implementation service, but Accenture has discovered that the market niche is large enough for them to occupy along with the original software providers – and clients often find that Accenture's ability to carry out the implementation is superior to that of the software providers. Accenture's dependence leaves the company quite exposed to the risk of competition from its two key suppliers. Nevertheless, the bilateral relationship has lasted for over a decade, and there is no specific threat to its continuance.

Accenture is an excellent example of a company that clearly fits into a global supply chain of enterprise resource planning, in which it occupies an intermediate role between the software producer and the corporate client. So, Accenture has to be looking for opportunities to protect its position against incursions by the software suppliers, develop new client relationships to provide its ERP service, and at the same time evaluate the overall value chain to see if they want to move upstream or downstream, or to apply the implementation skills and knowledge to another supply chain (say, implementation of other IT packages or programs).

FIGURE 1.4   Morris Group International in its supply chain

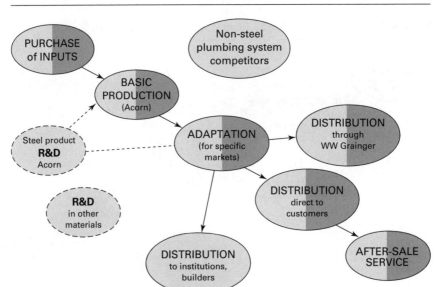

As a final example, consider a medium-sized, privately owned US company, Morris Group International (Figure 1.4). This company traditionally manufactured stainless steel restroom products as well as safety products (namely, fire extinguisher cabinets and emergency drench equipment) for building contractors. Around 1990 the company began to see growth opportunities outside the United States, and it looked to Canada, Europe and Mexico as logical target markets. Then with US construction activity dramatically reduced in the 2008–09 financial crisis, the firm began to concentrate more carefully on overseas sales opportunities, particularly in emerging markets.

Morris Group Intl is not large relative to the institutional clients it serves, such as governments, construction companies and schools. Morris's own sales force goes directly to client organizations to propose the purchase of their (primarily steel) fixtures, while the potentially lucrative opportunity to build new customer relationships through the internet is passed on to WW Grainger and other internet purveyors, who offer Morris products to clients who shop on their websites. Morris does not market its products directly on the internet, since it has an agreement with the purveyors to sell and distribute for it, so Morris depends on them for third-party sales.

As far as the full value-added chain is concerned, Morris Group focuses on high-quality production of steel fixtures such as sinks, toilets and fire extinguisher cabinets, purchasing steel from large US suppliers, and selling to clients through direct visits of salespeople and internet sales through their purveyors. Morris Group's Potter Roemer division began using a brass foundry in Taiwan about 10 years ago. It purchased fire protection products from the Taiwanese supplier as a check and balance to its original Italian supplier. As time went on, the Taiwanese supplier began making some products for only Potter Roemer. Today Morris Group has its own machine shop, and as it keeps expanding this foundry connection has become a vital casting supplier. With all divisions utilizing this foundry, Morris Group has become one of the largest customers for this Taiwanese company. This gives Morris Group a tremendous amount of leverage with the Taiwanese company.

Morris Group's fit into the global supply chain has evolved from simply a supplier of steel fixtures such as sinks and toilets to an international supplier of a range of institutional fixtures with production and sales in emerging markets. The dependence on internet purveyors for third-party sales is a weakness in that Morris does not control the marketing done through them; but at the same time it is not a threat, because the purveyors do not have interest in moving into the manufacturing activity that is Morris' fundamental business.

Value chains of emerging market-based competitors

The kinds of example presented here are not limited to traditional companies from Triad countries. For example, Grupo Diego Cisneros (now Cisneros Group of Companies, CGC) from Venezuela is a quintessential emerging market company that also can be viewed as part of a global supply chain. Since its founding in 1929, the Cisneros Group has demonstrated a great capacity for switching industries, running a diverse portfolio of businesses, and keeping government support (or at least avoiding government condemnation). When founded by brothers Diego and Antonio Cisneros, the company offered transport services for construction materials and then also passengers around Caracas, the capital and largest city in Venezuela.

In 1939, the Venezuelan government decided to put passenger transport into a public monopoly business, and pushed out the Cisneros. The brothers then opened a car parts importing business, bringing these parts from the United States. In 1940, Antonio Cisneros decided that it would be a viable business to sell Pepsi-Cola in Venezuela, and the brothers entered into that activity.[11]

The Cisneros Group entered the television business in 1961, when the Venezuelan government asked Gustavo Cisneros to take over the bankrupt Television Independiente (Canal 4) and Venevisión was launched. This step was really a transforming one, since the Cisneros then proceeded to build additional media and entertainment businesses, ultimately exiting virtually all of their other activities.[12] By the early 2000s the Cisneros Group was comprised primarily of media companies such as Venevisión, Venevisión International (throughout Latin America), the Miss Venezuela pageant, and production of Spanish-language TV content that is presented on Venevisión and other Spanish-language channels in the United States and Latin America. In 2013 the group was reorganized into three divisions: media; interactive (including mobile advertising services, digital publishing, gaming and e-commerce); and real estate (including a major tourist development, Tropicalia, in the Dominican Republic).

The Cisneros Group's development over time is a classic emerging market success story. The company began in local transportation, entered into franchises of foreign (US) products such as colas, hamburgers, pizza and even computers, and then shifted largely into television and other media. In 2013 it entered into real estate (actually tourism) development and e-commerce as well. The group has been flexible, quick to react to challenges

FIGURE 1.5   Grupo Cisneros value-added chain

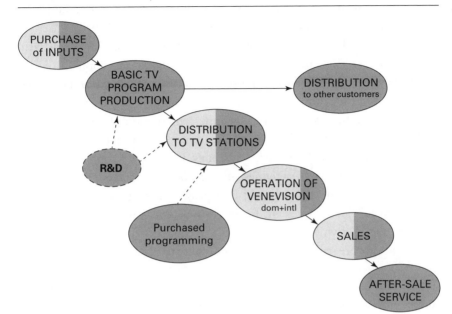

in one or another of its businesses, and ready to ally itself with international partners from Pepsi-Cola to DirectTV.

Cisneros Group's fit into its principal global value chain today largely focuses on television service and programming, as shown in Figure 1.5. While the company is seeking to expand its presence in the television programming and service provision activities in Latin America and the United States, it is simultaneously building new core activities in the other two divisions (interactive media and real estate). So in this case, as in many emerging market companies, the strategy is to evaluate various value chains and to put attention and money into those that offer greatest returns in the current environment.

Another emerging market group with growing international exposure is the Crescent Group, which encompasses the Crescent Petroleum oil and gas company that originated the group in the 1970s, along with Crescent Enterprises, which incorporates a range of other businesses into the group, including ports and logistics, aviation, real estate and construction, project implementation, IT commerce, healthcare and private equity.

Crescent originated as an oil exploration and production company in the United Arab Emirates in the early 1970s. The company received an exploration concession from the government of Sharjah (a province in the UAE) in 1969, then discovered oil in the offshore Mubarek field and began production in 1973. Crescent has stayed in the upstream range of the petroleum industry since the beginning, selling its oil to international oil companies for downstream refining and sales to ultimate clients.

Crescent decided to enter the business of natural gas production as well, obtaining concessions in Egypt and Iraq in the 1990s. The company established Dana Gas as its dedicated subsidiary to focus on the natural gas business. Its main production comes from deposits in Egypt and Iraq. In addition to producing natural gas, Dana has led the construction of two natural gas pipelines between production and distribution locations in the Middle East.

As the businesses developed, Crescent's leaders saw opportunities to expand into other related activities such as port management and logistics, as well as real estate development and project management (Figure 1.6). A separate subsidiary, Crescent Enterprises, was set up to manage and co-ordinate these activities. In recent years the company has expanded further into the healthcare sector and into private equity to invest in other companies.

A final example that helps to illustrate this point about the fit into global supply chains is FEMSA (Fomento Económico Mexicano, SA) in Mexico. This company has operated for over 100 years, with its origin in the beer business operating as the brewer Cerveceria Cuauhtémoc Moctezuma in Monterrey, Mexico. Actually, the group started as Cerveceria Cuauhtémoc (Cuauhtémoc Brewery) in 1890, and only acquired competitor Moctezuma in 1985. During the early years of operation, the brewery found a need for a reliable source of high-quality glass bottles, and decided to produce them itself, establishing the Vitro glass company in 1909. Likewise, for shipping

FIGURE 1.6   Crescent's value-added chain

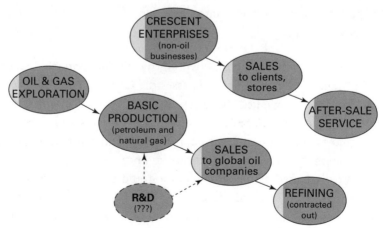

the bottles the company needed high-quality packing material, and ultimately decided to make its own, establishing Titan packaging company in 1936. Further diversification into related packaging, shipping and financing activities resulted in establishment of Banca Serfin, the Hylsa steel company, and the VISA holding company, which eventually spun off the non-beer businesses into the Alfa holding company in 1974. The beer business was renamed FEMSA in 1978.

FEMSA expanded into other beverages in 1979, by becoming the principal distributor of Coca-Cola products in Mexico and later in several other Latin American countries. Coca-Cola FEMSA (KOF) is today the largest Coca-Cola bottler in the world. At about the same time, in 1978, FEMSA expanded into convenience stores, under the OXXO brand. Today OXXO has more than 10,000 stores throughout Mexico. In 2010 FEMSA sold its brewing business to Heineken, in exchange for 20 per cent of the shares of Heineken and two seats on the board of that company.[13]

Looking at FEMSA's fit into a global value chain (Figure 1.7), the situation is much like that of Accenture. That is, if we look at FEMSA's business of soft drink bottling and distribution (called KOF), it is a business in which FEMSA depends heavily on the soft drink supplier (Coca-Cola) and occupies a value chain location between producer and consumer.

This brief story of FEMSA gives a glimpse of the kind of strategies pursued by emerging market multinationals, similar to Cisneros and Crescent, which ebb and flow in their core businesses due at least partly to the global demand

FIGURE 1.7 FEMSA's KOF value-added chain

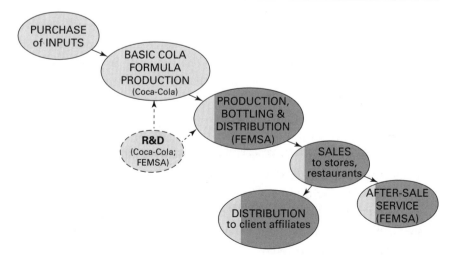

for their products and the competition from other companies. At the same time these emerging market firms look for opportunities to insert themselves into international supply chains, in this case initially through beer distribution in Latin America and the United States, and then through the link with Coca-Cola to provide bottling and distribution of Coke products throughout Latin America. OXXO thus far is largely a domestic business, not linked with any international partner, although it has expanded with a few dozen convenience stores in Colombia.

Whether the leaders of FEMSA view things this way or not, they are plotting a course through global supply chains, in beer, in colas and other beverages, and even in convenience store operation. They are tightly linked to global Triad branded producers (Heineken and Coca-Cola), and they are constantly searching for additional value-added activities to pursue.

In each of the examples presented above, the company needs to understand its fit into the global value-added chain(s) where its products or services fit, and then to develop ways to get the best results from its participation in the overall chain. Perhaps more striking for all of these companies, future growth seems to be concentrated in emerging markets, from Argentina to Vietnam, with most emphasis on the nearby markets in Latin America and Eastern Europe, plus the Big Two: China and India.

Innovation and competitiveness

How does *innovation* relate to all of the above? The challenge of creating jobs in the 21st century depends heavily on markets (numbers of customers or clients and their purchasing power) and on costs (the ability to get production and distribution costs down in order to become or to stay competitive in the market). It also depends on the ability to create new products and services to fill people's needs and wants. The genius of Steve Jobs was to perceive consumers' wants before they themselves recognized them, and then to produce products and services such as the iPod and the iPhone, not to speak of iTunes and the iStore, to supply music, communications and other features to them through beautiful instruments.[14] This is not to say that all companies should try to copy Apple – but that innovation is a source of competitive advantage that will enable companies to survive global competition wherever the company may originate. Companies in the Triad countries tend to be the innovators;[15] and this capability may enable them to stay competitive despite what we will see are the major advantages that emerging markets possess today.

Ultimately we are interested in opportunities for companies to grow and prosper. Emerging markets offer rapidly growing markets for consumer and industrial products and services. (See Table 1.2.) Emerging markets also offer possibilities for reducing production costs, by providing low-cost labour in many instances, and also access to other factors of production that may be less expensive than in the Triad countries, such as agricultural land, natural mineral and metal resources, and sometimes (subsidized) funding.

TABLE 1.2   Emerging market per capita incomes and GDP growth rates

		Brazil	China	India	Indonesia	Mexico	Russia	Africa
1980	GDP/capita (US $)	7,565	524	881	1,371	10,009	NA	8,763
	Growth rate (%)	9.1	7.8	6.7	8.7	9.2	NA	6.6
1985	GDP/capita (US $)	7,136	814	1,013	1,615	9,955	NA	8,255
	Growth rate (%)	7.9	13.5	5.3	3.5	2.6	NA	−1.2
1990	GDP/capita (US $)	7,175	1,101	1,217	2,073	9,785	12,626	7,975
	Growth rate (%)	−4.3	3.8	5.5	9	5.1	−3	−0.3
1995	GDP/capita (US $)	7,714	1,849	1,417	2,785	9,524	7,851	7,490
	Growth rate (%)	4.4	10.9	7.6	8.4	−6.2	−4.1	3.1
2000	GDP/capita (US $)	7,906	2,667	1,741	2,679	11,406	8,613	7,641
	Growth rate (%)	4.3	8.4	4	4.9	6.6	10	4.2
2005	GDP/capita (US $)	8,502	4,115	2,234	3,141	11,723	11,853	8,597
	Growth rate (%)	3.2	11.3	9.3	5.7	3.2	6.4	5.3
2008	GDP/capita (US $)	9,573	5,712	2,672	3,581	12,406	14,767	9,605
	Growth rate (%)	5.2	9.6	3.9	6	1.2	5.2	3.6
2009	GDP/capita (US $)	9,456	6,207	2,861	3,695	11,522	13,616	9,357
	Growth rate (%)	−0.3	9.2	8.5	4.6	−6	−7.8	−1.5
2010	GDP/capita (US $)	10,079	6,819	3,122	3,873	11,979	14,182	9,516
	Growth rate (%)	7.5	10.4	10.5	6.2	5.3	4.5	3.1
2011	GDP/capita (US $)	10,264	7,418	3,277	4,072	12,291	14,731	9,730
	Growth rate (%)	2.7	9.3	6.3	6.5	3.9	4.3	3.5

TABLE 1.2   *continued*

		Brazil	China	India	Indonesia	Mexico	Russia	Africa
2012	GDP/capita (US $)	11,939	8,391	3,855	4,634	14,296	21,565	10,620
	Growth rate (%)	4.8	9	8.2	5.36	4	4.6	2.67
2020*	GDP/capita (US $)	15,347.16	13,937.94	5,813.01	6,179.40	17,793.66	29,249.48	12,720.27
	Growth rate (%)	3.93	5.91	6.08	4.72	4.12	2.86	3.44
2030*	GDP/capita (US $)	21,032.64	21,174.34	9,289.91	8,556.33	23,300.95	40,390.44	17,425.15
	Growth rate (%)	3.99	3.41	6.15	4.5	3.79	2.46	4.31
2040*	GDP/capita (US $)	29,267.98	30,202.92	14,844.2	11,731.40	29,511.86	53,478.75	23,969.55
	Growth rate (%)	3.65	3.45	5.47	3.93	3.22	1.81	4.03
2050*	GDP/capita (US $)	39,891.70	43,154.60	21,899.14	15,735.43	36,718.38	67,111.63	31,492.51
	Growth rate (%)	3.33	2.75	4.63	3.78	2.86	1.27	3.58

*projected values GDP at PPPs (constant 2009 dollars)

SOURCES: World Bank GDP data up to 2012 [http://data.worldbank.org/]; PwC forecasts of GDP for subsequent years from http://www.theguardian.com/news/datablog/2011/jan/07/gdp-projections-china-us-uk-brazil; UN data for population from United Nations, Department of Economic and Social Affairs, Population Division (2013) [http://www.un.org/en/development/desa/population/] World Population Prospects: The 2012 Revision, DVD Edition

And finally, emerging markets offer multinational enterprises (MNEs) the opportunity to learn about operating in such countries, where the market ranges from large percentages of people in low-income, even poverty segments, up to wealthy consumers with tastes often similar to those in the Triad.

Most of the time emerging markets are not a source of new technology in the traditional sense of patented inventions of new products. Even so, there are emerging market MNEs that are indeed filing patents and gaining visibility as technology leaders (such as Huawei electronics in China and Mahindra automotive in India). And these tentative steps into world-leading innovation will only increase in the near future, just as they did in the catch-up processes of the United States, Japan and Korea in earlier decades (Kennedy, 1989; Olson, 1984).

This book suggests that that best way to view the threat/challenge of emerging markets today is to look at the company as a part of a global continuum of companies and customers, searching for opportunities to reduce costs, raise revenues, obtain technology and skills, and even reduce risk by operating in emerging markets. As shown above, even mighty Exxon contracts out for the vast majority of service stations that sell its branded petrol. Exxon also obtains support from outside firms in emerging markets and elsewhere in the process of exploration for new deposits of oil and natural gas. Indeed in many emerging markets Exxon is only allowed to participate in the industry through contractual agreements or joint ventures with a local firm. And in the middle of the supply chain, Exxon contracts out the shipment of oil and refined products to pipeline operating companies such as Kinder Morgan in the United States. Other firms from small businesses to multinationals likewise need to think through the value-added chain in their industry, and choose a path including emerging markets that will provide the best returns for their sets of capabilities.

The value-added chain itself has components such as management of the inputs into each stage – and also financing, technology, human resources and even risk management – that can be either carried out by the firm itself or contracted to [more capable] third parties as shown in Figure 1.8. A company's management team has to decide which functions and which products/services to produce inside the firm, and which ones to obtain from outside, through alliances and/or contracting with other companies.

The value-added chain for a particular product may stretch across several countries, involving large and small companies from Triad countries and

FIGURE 1.8 The value-added chain including emerging markets

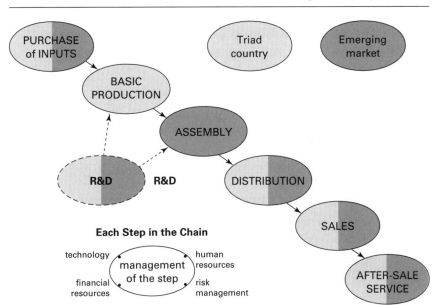

FIGURE 1.9 Apple and Samsung mobile phone production and sales

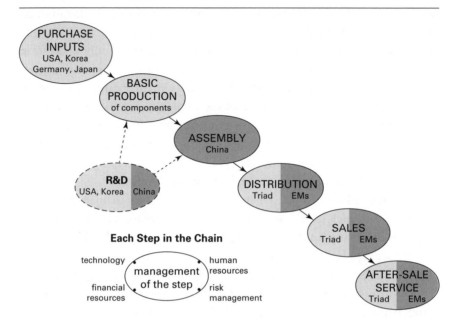

emerging markets. The view here takes the value-added chain as the unit of analysis, showing how the firm fits into that chain, and identifying opportunities and challenges that arise from this interconnectedness.

Recall the example of Apple's production of the iPhone. If we look at the mobile phone value chain in more detailed terms, we see that it involves many participants, large and small, but particularly in emerging markets (Figure 1.9).

In both cases, design of the mobile phones takes place in-house, and actual assembly of the final instrument is contracted out to third parties, particularly to Foxconn (Hon Hai) in China. The emerging market presence in this value-added chain appears in a major way on the supply side, in the assembly process. But if the market also is considered, it turns out that the demand for Apple and Samsung mobile phones is more than 50 per cent from emerging markets, as described in Table 1.3.

The growth potential for mobile phone sales in emerging markets is enormous, based on the very low percentages of the populations of these countries covered by current mobile phone use (as shown in column 6 of Table 1.3).

TABLE 1.3 The top 10 mobile markets by number of subscriptions

Country	Mobile subscriptions in millions	Population in millions (source: World Bank)	% of population	3G/4G subscriptions in millions	% of population	Sources (subs; 3G subs)	Last update
World	6,835	6,973.7	98.0	2,096	30.1	ITU Informa WCIS	Feb 2013 Dec 2012
1 China	1,155.3	1,344.1	85.9	293.0	21.8	China Mobile; China Unicom; China Telecom	April 2013
2 India	active: 699; total: 906.6	1,241	73.1	70.6	6	TRAI Informa WCIS	Sept 2012 Dec 2012
3 United States	321.7	311.6	103.3	256.0	81	CTIA Informa WCIS	June 2012 Dec 2012
4 Indonesia	260	242.3	107.3	47.6	19	BuddeComm Informa WCIS	May 2012 Dec 2012
5 Brazil	259.3	196.7	131.8	65.5	33.3	Anatel/Teleco Anatel/Teleco	Oct 2012

TABLE 1.3 *continued*

Country	Mobile subscriptions in millions	Population in millions (source: World Bank)	% of population	3G/4G subscriptions in millions	% of population	Sources (subs; 3G subs)	Last update
6 Russia	227.1	141.9	160	27.0	19	Wireless Intelligence Informa WCIS	June 2012 Dec 2012
7 Japan	128.4	127.8	100.5	104.4 (Mobile Internet subs)	81.7	TCATCA	Oct 2012
8 Pakistan	120.5	176.7	68.6	N/A	N/A	PTA	Sept 2012
9 Germany	112.7	81.7	137.9	53.2	65	Bundesnetzagentur Informa WCIS	Q1 2013 Dec 2012
10 Nigeria	active: 106.9; total: 143	162.5	65.8	10.5	6	NCC Informa WCIS	Sept 2012 Dec 2012

Note: Informa 3G stats are forecasted estimates for Dec 2012.   **Data compiled by:** © mobiThinking

SOURCE: http://mobiforge.com/research-analysis/global-mobile-statistics-2014-part-a-mobile-subscribers-handset-market-share-mobile-operators#topmobilemarkets, courtesy of mobiforge.com

Samsung has become a world leader in the development of new mobile phones, and not just in assembly of these instruments, despite its base in the formerly emerging market of South Korea. It can be expected that mobile phone technology will advance in the future based on innovations from emerging markets such as China, and possibly others such as India, Russia and Nigeria, which are large emerging markets that could develop such innovations to serve their large populations. It is already clear that the Chinese firms Huawei and Zhongxing Telecommunications Equipment (ZTE) are making major inroads into mobile phone design and production.

Some conclusions

Competition around the world is involving more and more companies from emerging markets, as well as focusing increasingly on emerging markets for sales growth opportunities. This reality can be seen as a threat or an opportunity. The examples discussed above demonstrate how a company, large or small, can benefit from recognizing the global supply chains that exist and finding ways to fit itself into these networks of companies. And most importantly, we see that including emerging markets in a company's strategy is becoming more and more necessary, as they provide low-cost inputs, attractive markets, and even innovations that can be applied elsewhere in the world.

Next, we will look at a handful of major emerging markets that provide great opportunities for Triad companies and increasing numbers of locally based international competitors. Subsequently, attention turns to a longer-run view, considering the trajectory of emerging markets from the time of the Roman Empire until today – noting that the United Kingdom and United States have been emerging markets along the way. After that we will turn to a focus on specific company experiences going in both directions – into and out of emerging markets.

Notes

1 http://www.economist.com/blogs/freeexchange/2012/03/china-will-overtake-america-within-decade-want-bet. This competition of economic size has already been won by China, if you consider national income adjusted for local price differences for the same products. According to the IMF, in 2014 China's economy reached the purchasing power parity (PPP) size of $US 17.6 trillion, while the US GDP in PPP terms was estimated at $US 17.4 trillion.

2 This is according to the IMF. According to the *CIA World Factbook*, US per capita GDP for 2013 was $US 52,800, and China's per capita GDP was $US 6,800. Measured at a PPP exchange rate, the Chinese per capita income would be a higher $US 11,800 according to the IMF and the World Bank. In all cases there remains an enormous gap between Chinese personal incomes and those of the United States and other industrial countries, and this gap will not be eliminated in less than decades into the future.

3 Tarun Khanna (2008) explores the challenges and opportunities in China and India in his book, *Billions of Entrepreneurs: How China and India are Reshaping Their Futures – and Yours*.

4 The overall impact of offshoring on US employment is still under debate. See, for example, Ottaviano *et al* (2012); Ebenstein *et al* (2009); Harrison and McMillan (2011).

5 Arndt and Kierzkowski (2001) call this phenomenon 'global fragmentation'; Hanson *et al* (2005) call it 'vertical production networks'. Fundamentally, we are looking at the global disaggregation of supply chains, across countries and generally across companies.

6 In 2013 refining profits had again dropped precipitously, and it would not be surprising to see Exxon again outsource more refining to third parties. See, for example, http://www.bloomberg.com/news/2013-10-31/exxon-third-quarter-profit-declines-as-refining-slumps.html

7 And now it is fascinating to see amazon.com preparing to offer a drone delivery service, through a fleet of drone aircraft that are intended to deliver packages directly to amazon.com customers in many locations. See for example http://www.amazon.com/b?node=8037720011

8 This phenomenon is far more advanced in EU countries and elsewhere in the world, where checks never achieved the high level of acceptability that they did in the United States. Electronic banking today is a reality worldwide, despite the remaining concerns about the security of such virtual activities.

9 Roche 2012 annual report, p 47. http://www.roche.com/investors/annual_reports/annual_reports_2012.htm. Also see Roche 2013 annual report, p 30. http://www.roche.com/gb13e.pdf

10 Accenture is the name of the renamed consulting business of Arthur Andersen, one of the Big Eight accounting/auditing companies worldwide at the turn of the century. With the Enron scandal, Andersen was criminally penalized by the US government for fraudulent auditing service, and the company went bankrupt in 2002. Andersen Consulting was spun off from Arthur Andersen a few months before the scandal, and changed its name to Accenture in the following few months.

11 The Cisneros Group remained the sole importer of Pepsi-Cola until 1995, when it abruptly dropped its Pepsi franchise and began a relationship with Coca-Cola in the same Venezuelan market. This dramatic change occurred mainly because the Cisneros wanted capital to expand the business, and Pepsi decided that it did not want to invest the required new funds in Venezuela. Coca-Cola had not been able to enter the market previously, so this window of opportunity greatly appealed to them.

12 Cisneros sold its share of Panamco, the Coca-Cola bottling company, to FEMSA from Mexico in 2003, thus ending the group's presence in soft drinks after 63 years.

13 In principle this 20% could give FEMSA the opportunity to take control of Heineken at some point; however, the Heineken family owns 50.1% of total shares, so FEMSA is likely to remain as an influential portfolio investor.

14 This is an overstatement, since Jobs not only perceived the consumer desires, but he also was able to orchestrate a team that produces aesthetically attractive instruments. Identifying the needs and subsequently producing the products are two separate but hugely important aspects of Jobs' brilliance.

15 Companies in the Triad countries are the predominant innovators in the sense that they file the vast majority of patents that are registered with the US Patent and Trademark Office (http://www.uspto.gov/patents/stats/index.jsp). Interestingly, Taiwan and South Korea, as well as China, have become major sources of US patents in recent years.

References

Arndt, S and Kierzkowski, H (2001) *Fragmentation: New production patterns in the world economy*, Oxford University Press, Oxford

Ebenstein, A *et al* (2009) Why are American workers getting poorer? Estimating the impact of trade and offshoring using the CPS. *NBER Working Paper #15107*, June

Hanson, G H, Mataloni, R J and Slaughter, M J (2005) Vertical production networks in multinational firms, *Review of Economics and Statistics*, 87, pp 664–78

Harrison, A and McMillan, M (2011) Offshoring jobs? Multinationals and US manufacturing employment, *The Review of Economics and Statistics*, 93(3), pp 857–75

Kennedy, P (1989) *The rise and fall of the great powers*, Vintage Press, New York

Khanna, T (2008) *Billions of Entrepreneurs: How China and India are Reshaping Their Futures – and Yours*, Harvard Business School Press, Boston, MA

Olson, M (1984) *The rise and decline of nations*, Yale University Press, New Haven, CT

Ottaviano, G, Peri, G and Wright, G (2012) *Immigration, offshoring and American jobs*, CEP Discussion Paper No 1147, London School of Economics, London, May

Rassweiler, A (2009) iPhone 3G S carries $178.96 BOM and manufacturing cost, iSuppli teardown reveals, http://www.isuppli.com/Teardowns/News/Pages/iPhone-3G-S-Carries-178-96-BOM-and-Manufacturing-Cost-iSuppli-Teardown-Reveals.aspx, 24 June

UNCTAD (2013) Global value chains: Investment and trade for development, *World Investment Report*, United Nations, New York, http://unctad.org/en/publicationslibrary/wir2013_en.pdf

United Nations and People's Republic of China (2008) *China's progress towards the Millennium Development Goals: 2008 report*, Ministry of Foreign Affairs, Beijing

Why emerging markets are the place to be

02

What to expect in Chapter 2

There are two fundamental reasons why emerging markets are the place to be in the 21st century. First, they are markets that are growing, on average, significantly faster than the Triad countries, and thus offer opportunities to companies for growth in their sales. And second, they are often, but not always, sources of lower-cost production than in the Triad countries, so they present opportunities for companies to reduce their costs of producing goods and services – or at least to place part of their value-added chains in such countries.

Seven emerging markets are examined in some detail here: China, Brazil, India, Indonesia, Mexico, Russia and South Africa. These are all relatively large countries in terms of population, and their GDP growth rates have exceeded those in the Triad countries during the 21st century. In each case the country is described in terms of its strengths in market size, availability of natural resources and costs of production – as well as in terms of government policies towards domestic and international business.

All of these large emerging markets are major sources of raw materials, from oil and gas to gold to coal, as well as agricultural production. Thus, multinational companies based locally or elsewhere have attraction to those resources and towards the use of these emerging markets as sources of the raw materials. Also, several of the countries (China, India and Mexico in particular) are targets for offshore production of goods and services by multinationals, owing to their relatively low-cost labour and their accessibility to the target Triad markets via physical or electronic transportation. And finally, all of these countries are growing in importance as markets, as their middle classes grow and per capita incomes rise.

Government policies are quite open towards business in Mexico and South Africa, quite restrictive in China, India and Russia, and somewhere in between in Brazil and Indonesia. This means that entry and local operations are more based on competition in the first group of countries, and more based on successfully dealing with the government in the second group. In all cases relative to the last century, business in each of these countries faces fewer restrictions and more opportunities today than in that same country previously.

Why are emerging markets the place to be in the 21st century? For two fundamental reasons. First and foremost, their markets are growing much faster than those in the traditional countries of the Triad (United States, Europe, Japan). While per capita incomes are lower in emerging markets, and often much lower, still there are many consumers who are able to buy the goods and services produced by Triad companies. In China alone, the middle class is estimated at over 300 million people – a market as large as the United States.[1] And second, emerging markets are great sources of raw materials and production capabilities, to expand the access of Triad companies to these materials and to lower production costs across a wide range of products and services.

In this chapter we will look at seven emerging markets in more detail, describing some key aspects of their economies, some of their key industries, the way in which foreign firms are permitted (or not) to compete there, and also analysing some features of the likely direction of each country in terms of sectoral growth, the government's role in the economy, and other broad aspects of the business environment. We will start with the largest one, China, and finish with a smaller but key country, South Africa, covering Brazil, India, Indonesia, Mexico and Russia in between.

Emerging markets as markets

Think first about the emerging market countries as target markets for products and services of all kinds. Table 2.1 shows the economic growth rates of a set of the most important emerging markets, and compares them to the United States, Germany and Japan.

TABLE 2.1 GDP/capita and GDP growth rate, selected countries and years (in current $US and in annual percentage rates)

Country/year		Brazil	China	India	Indonesia	Mexico	Russia	S Africa	USA	Germany	Japan
1980	GDP/capita	7,565	524	881	1,371	10,009	NA	8,763	25,510	20,861	17,835
	Growth rate	9.1	7.8	6.7	8.7	9.2	NA	6.6	-0.3	1.4	2.8
1985	GDP/capita	7,136	814	1,013	1,615	9,955	NA	8,255	28,562	22,497	21,265
	Growth rate	7.9	13.5	5.3	3.5	2.6	NA	-1.2	4.1	2.3	6.3
1990	GDP/capita	7,175	1,101	1,217	2,073	9,785	12,626	7,975	31,899	25,881	26,523
	Growth rate	-4.3	3.8	5.5	9	5.1	-3	-0.3	1.9	5.3	5.6
1995	GDP/capita	7,714	1,849	1,417	2,785	9,524	7,851	7,490	33,874	27,809	28,026
	Growth rate	4.4	10.9	7.6	8.4	-6.2	-4.1	3.1	2.5	1.7	1.9
2000 old	GDP/capita	7,906	2,667	1,741	2,679	11,406	8,613	7,641	39,545	30,298	28,889
	Growth rate	4.3	8.4	4	4.9	6.6	10	4.2	4.2	3.1	2.3
2005 new	GDP/capita	11,095	4,843	2,898	5,101	14,643	18,589	11,328	47,744	31,816	29,478
	Growth rate	-0.7	10.5	8.2	-4.6	4.3	-3.6	3.0	3.4	4.1	4.9

TABLE 2.1 *continued*

Country/year		Brazil	China	India	Indonesia	Mexico	Russia	S Africa	USA	Germany	Japan
2008	GDP/capita	11,069	6,010	3,057	4,182	14,778	20,432	10,892	48,372	36,985	33,522
	Growth rate	-1	3.7	-2.5	-8.5	0.1	2.6	-2.2	-0.3	3.4	1.8
2009	GDP/capita	10,440	6,541	3,153	4,072	13,229	18,702	9,974	46,064	35,878	32,496
	Growth rate	-4.83	9.5	4.5	-1.3	-9.3	-8.5	-7.3	-3.9	-3.2	-3
2010	GDP/capita	11,104	7,156	3,374	4,259	13,627	19,647	10,181	46,936	36,848	33,471
	Growth rate	7.3	10.1	8.4	6	4.3	5	3.2	2.8	2.5	3
2011	GDP/capita	11,497	7,745	3,611	4,458	13,932	20,566	10,440	47,776	37,501	33,959
	Growth rate	4.5	8.9	8.5	6.1	3.6	4.5	3.6	2.7	1.6	1.4
2012	GDP/capita	11,939	8,391	3,855	4,634	14,296	21,565	10,620	48,828	38,193	34,604
	Growth rate	4.8	9	8.2	5.4	4	4.6	2.7	3.1	1.7	1.8
2020*	GDP/capita	15,347	13,938	5,813	6,179	17,794	29,249	12,720	55,175	44,264	40,923
	Growth rate	3.9	5.9	6.1	4.7	4.1	2.9	3.4	2.2	1.5	1.8

TABLE 2.1 *continued*

Country/year		Brazil	China	India	Indonesia	Mexico	Russia	S Africa	USA	Germany	Japan
2030*	GDP/capita	21,033	21,174	9,290	8,556	23,301	40,390	17,425	64,966	51,763	50,354
	Growth rate	4	3.4	6.2	4.5	3.8	2.5	4.3	2.5	1.1	1.5
2040*	GDP/capita	29,268	30,203	14,844	11,731	29,512	53,479	23,970	78,445	64,454	60,430
	Growth rate	3.6	3.5	5.5	3.9	3.2	1.8	4	2.5	1.8	1.2
2050*	GDP/capita	39,892	43,155	21,899	15,735	36,718	67,112	31,493	92,993	81,578	75,232
	Growth rate	3.3	2.8	4.6	3.8	2.9	1.3	3.6	2.2	1.6	1.5

SOURCES: World Bank GDP data up to 2012 from World Bank website: http://data.worldbank.org/; *PwC forecasts of GDP for subsequent years from http://www.theguardian.com/news/datablog/2011/jan/07/gdp-projections-china-us-uk-brazil; UN data for population from United Nations [Website], Department of Economic and Social Affairs, Population Division (2013). World Population Prospects: The 2012 Revision, DVD Edition.

The numbers are quite striking. As noted in Chapter 1, China's growth rate has been exceptional for a long time, and the overall Chinese economy will exceed the size of the US economy in the near future. But per capita income in China will take a very long time to catch up to the US level, indeed not achieving that level until well after 2050, according to the estimates in the table here. Other emerging markets are not as large as China, and per capita income is quite varied, but almost all are growing rapidly compared to the Triad countries. According to these estimates, Russia will be the first of the emerging markets in the list to approach the Triad countries in per capita income, sometime after 2050.

These numbers indicate that for firms looking to expand their sales and market shares, it may often be the case that emerging markets are a more attractive target than Triad countries today. Clearly, the United States, European Union and Japan offer much higher per capita incomes, and thus more affluent potential consumers for a company's products or services. At the same time, per capita incomes are growing more rapidly in many emerging markets, and with their billions of people, they too are producing more and more potential consumers for high-income as well as lower- and middle-income products and services.

Before entering into country discussions, some background on emerging markets is in order. These countries can be seen as sources of products and services, ranging from natural resources to call centre back-office services. They can also be seen as target markets, with their high growth rates in recent and future years, relative to Triad countries. And most importantly for our context, emerging markets can be seen as parts of global supply chains for a huge range of products and services, becoming every day more important as they consume the majority of global GDP.

Emerging markets as sources of production

With respect to products and services, emerging markets were seen in the past century largely as a source of raw materials (particularly oil), and in the last half of the century as locations for carrying out inexpensive assembly operations for manufactured goods such as cars, electronics and clothing.[2] Looking at production of raw materials, Table 2.2 shows the rankings of various countries in industries from oil to agriculture.

It is clear that emerging markets dominate the production of these commodities – and most others as well. Note that China is among the top three producers of all of these commodities except oil, where it ranks fourth.

TABLE 2.2 Commodity production by country, 2012

Product/country	Oil	Coal	Iron ore	Copper	Wheat	Corn	Cattle
1	Saudi Arabia	China	China	Chile	European Union	United States	India
2	Russia	United States	Australia	Peru	China	China	Brazil
3	United States	India	Brazil	China	India	Brazil	China
4	China	Australia	India	United States	United States	European Union	United States
5	Iran	South Africa	Russia	Australia	Russia	Ukraine	European Union
6	Canada	Russia	Ukraine	Zambia	Canada	Argentina	Argentina

SOURCES:

Oil – http://www.mapsofworld.com/minerals/world-crude-oil-producers.html

Coal – http://www.mapsofworld.com/world-top-ten/world-map-countries-by-coal-production.html

Iron core– http://www.mapsofworld.com/minerals/world-iron-ore-producers.html

Copper – http://www.mapsofworld.com/minerals/world-copper-producers.html

Wheat production – http://www.indexmundi.com/agriculture/?commodity=wheat&graph=production

Corn Production – http://www.indexmundi.com/agriculture/?commodity=corn

Cattle – http://www.indexmundi.com/agriculture/?commodity=cattle

Indeed China is the largest producer of commodity products overall, despite the attention being paid to that country's voracious appetite for commodity imports, particularly from Africa, in recent years.

The fact that emerging markets produce more raw materials and other commodity products than Triad countries is perhaps not surprising, because this is the kind of activity that many people attribute to the low-skill, resource-rich countries of the world. This fact has to be tempered with the reality that emerging markets today have achieved many advances in manufacturing and services, such that they are becoming global leaders in these other sectors as well. Next, take a look at these other key parts of modern economies.

As far as services such as utilities and banking are concerned, production is somewhat more based in Triad countries, but even here, the emerging markets are coming to dominate overall production. Table 2.3 shows this activity in selected service sectors.

This makes sense in that these services are generally consumed locally, so with the majority of world population living in emerging markets, it is not surprising that they produce the majority of these key services. Note that *ownership* of the service production is not separated out here, so that the activity – for example in electricity generation – may be carried out by Triad-based multinational companies through their local affiliates in emerging markets.

Looking finally at *manufacturing* of clothing, cars, electronics and so on, the leading countries are shown in Table 2.4. This activity focuses on the process of producing final products, using inputs that may come from local and/or imported sources. Even though this manufacturing activity is the one most subject to shifting to low-labour-cost locations, such as Mexico and China, the rankings are quite similar to those for service production.

In fact the table shows that manufacturing activity remains more in the Triad countries than the other two sectors; this is due to the fact that technological innovation is located much more extensively in the Triad countries, which thus tend to launch new products first. The amount of offshore assembly of manufactured goods is quite large, but overall manufacturing still remains to a greater extent located in the Triad than the other two broad economic sectors of commodities and services.

A quick glance at the previous two tables, along with this last one, shows that in fact emerging markets are leading the world economy in most kinds of economic activity today.[3] And the ownership of this economic activity is sometimes in the hands of Triad MNEs, sometimes local firms in emerging markets, and often in combination.

TABLE 2.3 Service production by country, 2012

Service/ country rank	Telephone service*	Electricity√ generation	Banking+	Hospitals#	Construction◊	Transport (road)Δ
1	China	European Union	China	China	European Union	United States
2	United States	China	United States	India	China	China
3	Japan	United States	United Kingdom	Vietnam	United States	India
4	Germany	Japan	Australia	Nigeria	Japan	Brazil
5	Russia	Russia	Canada	Russia	Korea	Japan
6	Brazil	India	Japan	Japan	Brazil	Canada

SOURCES:

* = number of main telephone lines in use, *CIA World Factbook*, data for 2011.

√ = electricity – production in billions of kilowatt hours, from http://www.indexmundi.com/g/r.aspx?t=10&v=79

+ = assets of largest banks, from http://www.relbanks.com/worlds-top-banks/market-cap

= hospitals – http://www.mapsofworld.com/world-top-ten/world-top-ten-countries-by-hospitals-map.html

◊ = top construction company home countries, based on http://www.constructionweekonline.com/
pics-23037-pictures-the-25-biggest-contractors-in-the-world/10#.UyuOeYWmaOl

Δ = transport – https://www.cia.gov/library/publications/the-world-factbook/rankorder/2085rank.html

TABLE 2.4 Manufacturing value by country and sector, 2012

Mfg sector/ country	Car* production	Cell phone√ production	Clothing+ production	Shoe# production	Electronics◊ production
1	China	Korea	China	China	China
2	European Union	China	Hong Kong	India	United States
3	United States	United States	Italy	Brazil	Japan
4	Japan	Finland	Bangladesh	Vietnam	European Union
5	Korea	Japan	Germany	Indonesia	Korea
6	India	Canada	India	Pakistan	Malaysia

SOURCES:

* Cars: http://www.oica.net/category/production-statistics/

√ Cell phones: http://just4bloggers.blogspot.com/2013/04/top-10-biggest-mobile-phone.html (based on the largest companies)

+ Clothing: largest exporting countries: http://asicentralblog.com/blog/2013/06/03/top-10-apparel-exporters/

Shoes: http://www.apiccaps.pt/c/document_library/get_file?uuid=7200889f-26E8-4329-855d-5bdb268eb49a&groupId=10136

◊ Electronics: www.statista.com/statistics/268398/market-size-of-the-global-electronics-industry-by-country

To understand the distribution of these economic activities, the value-added chain provides a helpful perspective, demonstrating the links of each stage of the process to each other and to firms from a variety of countries (as with the Apple iPhone value chain described in Chapter 1).

Emerging markets as sources of knowledge

A final subject of attraction in emerging markets is to gain access to *knowledge* there. This is different from the traditional focus on knowledge-seeking in the form of industrial technology. In that instance, firms flock to Silicon Valley to get access to the latest knowledge in computing, or to Cambridge, Massachusetts, to do pharmaceuticals research, or to Korea (and more recently Taiwan) for flat-panel displays for computers and phones, or to Tokyo for R&D on all manner of consumer products, from next-generation mobile phones to digital toilets.

In the case of emerging markets, the knowledge is much more likely to be market related or customer related. For example, a major strength of companies in China in general is their ability to obtain Chinese government support (or non-interference) for their business; a foreign company must be present in China to try to gain access to that kind of support. Likewise, in Mexico successful local firms have long-term knowledge of local distribution channels and of ways to deal with customers/clients. A foreign firm will need to be present in some form in order to gain access to that knowledge.[4] Even though the knowledge that is key to competing in many emerging markets is not the traditional R&D-based kind, it still provides a strong basis for competitiveness to the possessor firms. And for foreign firms to gain access to that market/customer knowledge, they need to be present in the emerging markets.

This emerging market knowledge is largely institutional, that is, understanding of how institutional features such as regulators and customer preferences operate in the market, rather than scientific knowledge about a product or production process. This is a different class of knowledge, and one that requires different capabilities to obtain it and to utilize it effectively in the company.

In addition to the institutional knowledge, there are some forms of business activity that are favoured in emerging markets and that are less frequent in Triad countries, especially the United States and the United Kingdom. In particular, the operation of *business groups* that cross industry lines is quite common in emerging markets. Knowledge of how to manage such a diversified organization is a strength of many leading emerging market firms, and the knowledge can be applied to additional countries and businesses – different from the typically more focused business strategies of US or UK firms.

Key emerging markets in the early 21st century

China

The Chinese economy was second largest in the world in 2013, with a GDP estimated at $US 9.2 trillion (just over half of US GDP). China's per capita income ranked only 84th in the world, far behind the Triad countries, but gaining ground rapidly. China's economic growth rate remained far above the Triad countries, as it has for the past two decades, at 7.7 per cent per year in 2013.[5]

China is clearly the largest challenger to the United States for global economic hegemony in the 21st century. Whether we see this as a natural progression to the 'normal' state of the world over many centuries (see, for example, Morris, 2010), or a potential threat to the current hegemon, in which a new leader may take the lead and then ultimately be unseated (eg, Shenkar, 2006); in either case it is indisputable that China will become the largest economy in the world within this decade. What does this imply for companies from the United States and other Triad countries? Certainly, on the one hand there are threats to large US companies that dominate existing industries (such as cars, banking, telecommunications equipment, hotels, and many more sectors). In addition to French, German and Japanese rivals, these firms are now (or soon will be) facing Chinese rivals as well. From Shanghai Automotive (SAIC) to Industrial and Commercial Bank of China (ICBC), Huawei in telecoms and Shangri-La hotels, these competitors are becoming world-level behemoths.

Cost conditions for production remain attractively low in China, despite inflation and slight currency appreciation in the early 2000s.[6] As a target for offshore assembly of products later sold in international markets, China remains very attractive. Indeed much continues to be made of the value of US goods that are partially produced in China, from Apple iPhones to Nike sneakers.

On the demand side, beyond the threat of new competitors in existing markets, the growth and development of China implies new markets for

FIGURE 2.1   Map of China (showing key manufacturing/assembly sites and natural resource deposits)

Triad country companies. In 2012 the largest market for sales of General Motors (GM) vehicles was China, ahead of the United States. Similarly, Yum Brands (Kentucky Fried Chicken and Taco Bell) had 51 per cent of its global sales in China in 2012; Advanced Micro Devices had 58 per cent of its global sales in China; and 41 per cent of Android sales were in China in 2012. These situations portend further emphasis of Triad companies on the Chinese market, and thus a growing need to understand that market and to operate successfully within it. This development of the Chinese market itself poses a challenge to these traditional MNEs, since their growing dependence on China presents for them a risk of slowdown if the Chinese economy does not continue its breakneck pace – which is assured as it becomes the largest market in the world, and thus less able to produce growth rates that depend on increasing exports to other markets.[7]

Interest in China began with economic opening in the late 1980s, and at that time it was focused more on China as a base for low-cost production of manufactured goods such as clothing and electronics rather than as a market. All of the world's largest clothing companies have owned or contracted facilities in China, to keep their production costs down (eg, Levis, Benetton, Gap, Ralph Lauren, H&M and Zara). Likewise, all of the major consumer electronics and telecommunications equipment companies have manufacturing in China, owned or contracted, and this also enables them to keep costs and prices down.

Probably the most notable characteristic of the Chinese market relative to those of Triad countries is the degree of government regulation and participation in the market. Foreign companies are restricted to a maximum of 50 per cent ownership in cars; they are not permitted in media; they are restricted by having to compete with state-owned enterprises that are favoured/subsidized by the government in natural resources; and many more major constraints exist.

Despite these constraints, the possibilities for Triad-based companies to incorporate China into their value-added chains are numerous and often very large. Beyond the companies that have a large percentage of their global revenues coming from China today, there are even greater numbers that are manufacturing there or contracting manufacturing there to lower their costs. The transfer of back-office business activity has not occurred in a major way in China, because of the language barrier; whereas this activity has moved massively into India, where English is widely spoken.

The possibilities for Chinese companies to expand into international business are plentiful for manufacturers that assemble clothing and electronics for foreign multinationals wanting to lower their production costs. As discussed earlier, Hon Hai (actually based in Taiwan) does an enormous business in assembling mobile phones in China for the major brands such as Apple and Nokia. And Guangzhou Hui-He Clothing & Textile Manufacturing Co. Ltd (**jeans-china.com**), among other major manufacturers, assembles clothing for a wide range of clothes brands such as Levi Strauss and Forever 21.

Chinese companies are increasingly expanding overseas and building their own value chains globally. Huawei today is the world's largest producer of telecom switching equipment, and is linked to most of the major telephone operating companies around the world as a key equipment provider. Baosteel is the world's second largest steel producer, with marketing affiliates in the United States and the European Union, but still retaining almost all production in China. Baosteel is less tied to overseas customers than Huawei, though even so Baosteel is a major supplier to GM, Volkswagen (VW) and the other car manufacturers in their Chinese plants. Electric appliance and air conditioner manufacturer Midea has sales operations worldwide and manufacturing in several Asian countries along with joint-venture plants in Latin America and Africa with Carrier Corporation.

Chinese participation in global business networks is largely located on the coast, around Shanghai and Beijing, as well as Hong Kong (as shown in Figure 2.1). In this case of the world's most populated country, there are another dozen cities where global supply chains operate, typically with low-cost assembly of apparel or electronics. The bold rings show regions where manufacturing and offshore assembly for global markets are concentrated. Natural resource deposits, particularly coal and bauxite, are located in a dozen or more places around the country, so they are not marked on the map here.

Brazil

The Brazilian economy was seventh largest in the world in 2013, with a GDP estimated at $US 2.2 trillion. Brazil's per capita income ranked only 65th in the world, far behind the Triad countries, but moving up fairly consistently in the 2000s. Brazil's economic growth rate was only just above the Triad countries in 2013, at 2.5 per cent per year, but estimates are for growth to resume at about twice the US rate in the years ahead.[8]

Different from most of the other emerging markets discussed here, Brazil has never been a target for offshore assembly to take advantage of low-cost labour. The country's location far from the Triad probably accounts for much of this, since Brazilian wages have been low relative to those in the other countries. Even so, cost-based competition has not characterized Brazilian manufactures or Brazil-based MNEs. In fact, Brazil-based MNEs tend to be in natural resource industries (such as mining giant Vale, paper producer Aracruz Celulosa and oil major Petrobras), or in closely related downstream industries such as steel (Gerdau, Usiminas and CSN). In these cases competitiveness comes more from access to the raw materials, or preferential treatment by the government, rather than low costs.

On the market side, Brazil constitutes a very attractive target for Triad multinationals, since its population of about 200 million people is becoming wealthier and more consumption oriented. Especially US-based multinationals have found Brazil to be a desirable target market in the Latin American

FIGURE 2.2 Map of Brazil (showing key manufacturing/ assembly sites and natural resource deposits)

Key
—— Manufacturing centres
---- Natural resources

region, since it is viewed as being part of their own back yard. The distance to Brazil from Triad production bases and distribution channels is fairly extreme, so that this country has not been as desirable as Mexico within the Latin American region. Nevertheless, as transport costs fall, and as Brazilian consumers become more globalized, this country is growing quickly into a preferred market for US and also European suppliers.

A striking feature of Brazil in comparison with China is that Brazil ranks very low in research and development. The Asian emerging markets (along with Japan and Korea) tend to be much more adept at carrying out R&D and developing new (and sometimes copied[9]) products. Brazil spends less than 1 per cent of GDP on research and development, in comparison with Triad countries that almost all spend at least 2–3 per cent of GDP on this activity. In Latin America Brazil is the leader, but in comparison with China (2.0 per cent), and other Asian leaders such as Taiwan (2.3 per cent) and Singapore (2.2 per cent), it lags far behind. Interestingly Russia (1.0 per cent) and India (0.9 per cent), also trail the Chinese region substantially (**http://en.wikipedia.org/wiki/List_of_countries_by_research_and_development_spending**). This may indicate a fundamental weakness of Brazil as a future source of globally competitive firms, but up to now the impact of low R&D has not been noteworthy.

Brazil is definitely not a challenger to the United States in terms of economic leadership in the 21st century, but at the same time it is the source of some very attractive opportunities for US firms in terms of both markets and supply sources. Perhaps the most notable sector presenting enormous opportunity is oil, given the discovery in 2006 of vast oil reserves offshore from Santos along the southern coast of the country all the way past Rio de Janeiro. This 'Lula' oil field is estimated to hold up to 8 billion barrels of oil.[10]

Because Brazil constitutes about one-third of Latin America's total economy, the country for some time has attracted the interest of MNEs, particularly from the United States. Especially in the car and telecommunications equipment sectors, Brazil has attracted foreign direct investment for local production and sales of these manufactured goods since the 1980s. Interestingly, Brazilian production locations, often in the São Paolo region, fit tightly into global supply chains for Triad multinationals, and usually the Brazilian operations are subsidiaries of the MNEs, rather than locally owned businesses.

Government participation in the Brazilian economy is not large in comparison with other emerging markets or Triad countries. While the state-owned oil company, Petrobras, dominates that sector, most others are led by private-sector firms, with domestic or foreign roots. Regulation of foreign firms has varied over time, with the recent Lula and Rousseff governments offering generally an unrestrictive policy profile. Looking at the largest companies in Brazil, many foreign multinationals top the list; they include Telefónica from Spain, InBev from Belgium, Banco Santander (Spain), and Casino Guichard Perrachon from France. In addition, GM and Volkswagen do Brasil are near the top, along with Nokia and Samsung. In sum, the Brazilian market is quite attractive to foreign multinationals, and it has not presented as severe constraints as those for companies wanting to operate in China or India.

As shown in Figure 2.2, centres of global manufacturing activity in Brazil surround the two major cities of São Paulo and Rio de Janeiro, along with other metropolitan centres in Rio Grande do Sul and Porto Alegre, plus Belo Horizonte in the State of Minas Gerais. Major iron ore and other mining deposits parallel the coast from Rio de Janeiro northward, and huge oil reserves have been discovered in the ocean offshore from Santos up to almost Vitoria.

India

The Indian economy was tenth largest in the world in 2013, with a GDP estimated at $US 1.9 trillion. India's per capita income ranked only 148th in the world, but it has been gaining ground steadily for two decades. India's economic growth rate remained far above the Triad countries, as it has for the past 20 years, at 5.0 per cent per year in 2013.

As a production-cost-reducing centre, India has long stood out in information technology. Beginning with low-tech call centres, operated 24 hours a day and 7 days a week, India established a reputation for having phone operators able to offer expert advice in English at a fraction of the US or UK cost. Thus, numerous companies established call centres there, particularly in Bangalore, including IBM, Tesco, Dell, DEC, Siemens, ABB, Ericsson, Ernst & Young, GE, H-P, PwC, Swiss Re and Accenture, among many others.

Subsequently, India's companies have built additional strengths in software development, particularly in the cases of Tata Consulting Services, Wipro and Infosys. These companies have gone far beyond call centres, offering not only software development but also back-office support for accounting services, logistics management and other business services. In this way, Indian firms are closely tied into multinational value-added chains through back-office service provision to multinational firms in a wide range of industries.

Production of manufactured goods to take advantage of low-cost labour has not been a major business activity in India, perhaps due to the permission issue that burdens companies that want to move quickly and take advantage of labour cost advantages. Even so, there are some examples of offshore manufacturing in India, such as Harley Davidson's motorcycle assembly plant in Gurgaon, Haryana, for sales in Asia, and Victoria's Secret apparel production facilities near Chennai.

On the market side, India is famous for demanding permissions for all manner of business activities, and for allowing government bureaucrats (the 'licence Raj') to delay the process of gaining those permissions, to the great detriment of business development by local as well as foreign firms. Despite this

FIGURE 2.3   Map of India (showing key manufacturing/
assembly sites and natural resource deposits)

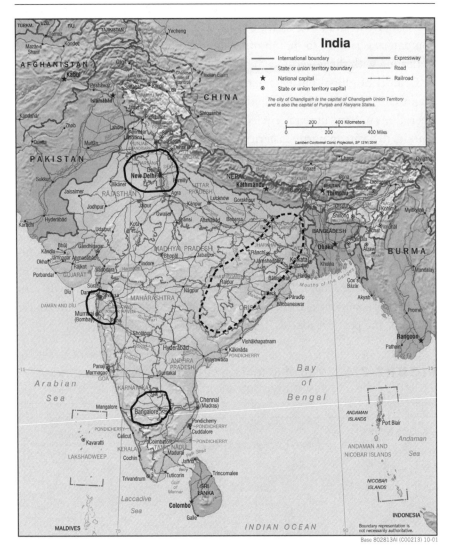

regulatory or bureaucratic burden, the 1.2 billion people in India constitute a very attractive target market. And with their per capita incomes rising fairly rapidly, these consumers are increasingly attractive to Triad MNEs. Also, the licensing system was partially dismantled starting in 2005, as India's government sought to put the economy on a more competitive footing.[11]

Because of weak infrastructure and long distances between population centres in India, markets tend to be isolated from each other and somewhat difficult to serve together. These are real challenges to the foreign multi-nationals looking to serve this increasingly attractive country.

The government as an owner of companies has not been especially problematic in India for foreign firms. The number of government-owned companies is similar to that in other large countries, and the real challenge of dealing with the government comes more from the regulation side.

Centres of global business activity in India include the regions around major cities such as Mumbai and Delhi, as well as the software/call centre operations in Bangalore (as circled in bold in Figure 2.3). Coal, iron ore and bauxite deposits in north-eastern India make the country a major producer of these minerals.

Indonesia

The Indonesian economy was 16th largest in the world in 2013, with a GDP estimated at $US 868 billion. Indonesia's per capita income ranked only 100th in the world, far behind the Triad countries and the other emerging markets discussed here, but improving with a high income growth rate. Indonesia's economic growth rate remained far above the Triad countries, as it has for the past decade, at 5.8 per cent per year in 2013.

FIGURE 2.4   Map of Indonesia (showing key manufacturing/
assembly sites and natural resource deposits)

Indonesia is the least-discussed country in our group of emerging markets, though it is significantly larger economically than South Africa. And with a population of over 240 million people, it is the third largest country here, after China and India. With its growth rate today exceeding those of Brazil and Russia, it certainly has the potential to move up in the economic rankings fairly rapidly. Yet Indonesia consistently fails to spark international interest as far as its market and its ability to produce manufactured goods at low cost are concerned. This may be due to comparisons with its South Asian neighbour, India, and its East Asian neighbour, China, both of which have proven more dynamic and more attractive to international companies. Regardless, Indonesia represents a huge potential market and equally a possible production/assembly base for international manufacturing business.

The main drivers of Indonesia's international competitiveness have been mining and oil and gas exports, commodities whose prices and quantities have increased strongly in the period of China's rapid growth and demand for such inputs. Indonesia is the world's largest exporter of palm oil, second largest exporter of coal and eighth largest exporter of natural gas. In addition, Indonesia is a major exporter of oil, copper, gold, rubber, and wood products. All of these commodity exports have helped keep Indonesia's economic growth at above 5 per cent per year since the 1990s. And they place Indonesia and Indonesian companies in global value-added chains as suppliers of basic commodity inputs, but not further downstream in manufacturing or services.

As far as cost conditions are concerned, Indonesia is one of the Asian countries that offer low-cost labour used in the assembly of clothing, electronics and other products. In Indonesia's case there has been relatively little offshore assembly activity, except in athletic shoes and some clothing. All of the major brands (Nike, Reebok, Adidas, Puma) assemble shoes in Indonesia, most since the 1990s. This activity has thus far not spread nearly as extensively to other industries such as clothing or consumer electronics, although some assembly for export does occur in these sectors as well. In fact, Indonesia overall ranks eighth among apparel-exporting countries, just ahead of Mexico. Still, this activity is far less important than the commodities production and footwear assembly. It appears that Indonesia is poised for possible large-scale expansion into these other offshore assembly activities.

The market in Indonesia is relatively small in terms of purchasing power – that is, per capita income is quite low. At the same time the huge population makes Indonesia more attractive for international suppliers than a smaller country; and again with the rapid growth rate of the economy, it should become more attractive all the time. Regardless of these possibilities, Indonesia as a target market remains a fairly low priority for most international firms.

Government participation in the economy is extensive, from ownership of the national oil company to quite restrictive regulation of ownership and operations in natural resource industries in general. On the other hand, in manufacturing and service provision, foreign MNEs face a much more open environment, and so Indonesia is certainly poised to become a major growth market in the next decade.

Indonesia's participation in global value-added chains is based largely on clothing assembly around large cities such as Jakarta (circled in bold in Figure 2.4) and oil and coal production in the countryside, principally on the island of Sumatra (within the dotted line).

Mexico

The Mexican economy was 15th largest in the world in 2013, with a GDP estimated at $US 1.3 trillion. Mexico's per capita income ranked only 69th in the world, and has not improved very much in the 2000s. Mexico's economic growth rate dropped to 1.1 per cent per year in 2013, after remaining at about double the US rate during most of the 2000s.

As far as natural resources are concerned, Mexico has been a major producer of oil and gas, though keeping complete control over the industry

FIGURE 2.5   Map of Mexico (showing key manufacturing/ assembly sites and natural resource deposits)

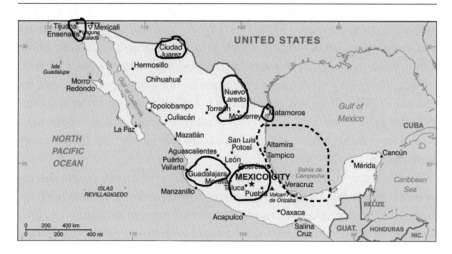

through the state-owned national oil company, Pemex. Other major mineral and metal exports include copper, silver, bismuth and iron ore molybdenum. Mexico also has been a major agricultural product exporter, particularly to the United States, of fruits and vegetables ranging from bananas, oranges, papaya, mango and pineapple, to corn, tomatoes, avocados and coffee. And along with the plants, cattle and chickens are major export items for Mexico. In sum, Mexican international competitiveness in natural resources is not different from that of the other emerging markets in this group.

At the same time Mexico has long been a target for offshore assembly (maquila) of clothing, electronics and cars for MNEs serving the US market. From Ford, GM and Chrysler assembling cars in Mexico, to Gap, Benetton and Levis assembling clothes, Mexico has been a favoured offshore production location for decades. Since the 1990s, more than 1 million Mexicans have been working in the offshore assembly factories around the country, making this Mexico's second largest industry after oil, if we were to combine all of the different products that are assembled in Mexico.

As a market for MNE goods and services Mexico also has long been seen as attractive, with its 120 million people as well as its free-trade relation to the United States through NAFTA since 1994. Given its border with the United States, Mexico is often a market targeted by US firms for their international expansion. Retail stores such as JC Penney and Sears appear in malls (and Walmarts nearby[12]) around the country, and US branded products dominate many segments of the Mexican market, from cars to chemicals to clothing.

Mexican companies have long been integrated into international supply chains, as suppliers of both raw materials and agricultural products as well as manufactured goods such as car parts to US multinational companies, and as assemblers of textiles, cars and electronics. Mexico's banks are almost all owned by foreign commercial banks, and thus form parts of the global networks of Citibank, Banco Santander, BBVA, Hong Kong & Shanghai Banking Corporation (HSBC) and others. Mexico's second largest beer company became part of Heineken's network in 2011, and its former owner (FEMSA) is the largest Coca-Cola bottling company in the world. In sum, Mexican companies are heavily involved in global supply chains, from providing inputs, to carrying out manufacturing, to providing distribution and other services.

Government regulation is generally not overly burdensome in Mexico, to some extent due to the requirements of transparent regulation under the NAFTA agreement with the United States and Canada since 1993. The oil and gas sector is reserved for the national oil company, Pemex, but most other sectors are open to domestic and foreign private-sector investors. The oil and gas production region, onshore and offshore, is circled in red in Figure 2.5.

Mexico fits into global value-added chains through offshore assembly of many products, including apparel, cars and electronics, generally close to the US border and in Guadalajara. Also, many local and foreign multi-nationals have production in the Mexico City region, generally for local consumption or for regional sales in Latin America. (These locations are circled within solid lines on Figure 2.5.) Mexico's major oil deposits are largely in the Gulf of Mexico, as shown inside the dotted line on the map.

Russia

The Russian economy was ninth largest in the world in 2013, with a GDP estimated at $US 2.1 trillion. Russia's per capita income ranked only 51st in the world, far behind the Triad countries, but improving steadily, and much higher than any of the other emerging markets in our group. Russia's

FIGURE 2.6   Map of Russia (showing key manufacturing/
assembly sites and natural resource deposits)

economic growth rate remained somewhat above the Triad countries, as it has for the past two decades, at 3.6 per cent per year in 2012, though it dropped to 1.3 per cent in 2013 as economic sanctions slowed growth down.

Russia historically has been a source of both natural resources and technological advances, with a highly developed educational system and many technology successes. The natural resources include most of the key sources of energy (oil, natural gas, coal, uranium and so on) as well as agricultural and ocean resources in the world's largest country by geography. For some reason Russia has also been blessed with an abundance of technological development for several centuries.[13] Perhaps it began with decisions of Tsar Peter the Great in the early 1700s to establish the Russian Academy of Sciences and St Petersburg State University.[14] Many famous Russian scientists and inventors were émigrés, like Igor Sikorsky, credited with invention of the first helicopters, and Vladimir Zworykin, often called the father of TV, economists Simon Kuznets (1971 Nobel Prize) and Wassily Leontief (1973 Nobel Prize), and physicist Georgiy Gamov (an author of the Big Bang theory). Even so, far more Russian scientists – from natural scientist Mikhail Lomonosov (for whom Moscow State University was named), to chemist Dimitri Mendeleev, zoologist Alexandre Middendorf and physiologist Ivan Pavlov – living in Russia have won Nobel Prizes and made scientific discoveries that have greatly advanced human understanding of the universe.

Despite these comments about technological sophistication, the main driver of Russia's international competitiveness in recent years has been similar to that of the other emerging markets here – natural resources. In Russia's case these resources are mainly oil and natural gas, although major additional commodity exports include wood, metals and chemicals.

As far as cost-based production is concerned, Russia has not been a source of such activity, since wages and other costs there have exceeded those in many other emerging markets. The offshore assembly that does take place in Central and Eastern Europe today tends to be in other countries such as Poland, Hungary and the Czech Republic, and then the products are imported into Russia. This is particularly true for business process outsourcing, where these three countries all have developed numerous operations (**http://www.ft.com/intl/cms/s/0/66e94cbe-8667-11e2-ad73-00144feabdc0. html#axzz2c3DhFTix**).

Russia's 150 million people with per capita income of about $US 14,000 per year in 2013 present a very attractive target market for international companies in most sectors. Although income inequality is extremely high, the consumer base in Russia is already large for Triad companies, and the challenges have been to deal with the bureaucratic barriers to entry and then to break into the local distribution system in many cases. In fact, government regulation and participation in the market is especially challenging to both foreign and domestic private-sector firms, going back to the legacy of the communist regime that ended in 1991.

Russia fits into global value-added chains principally as a source of raw materials in locations away from major cities (as circled within dotted lines in Figure 2.6). Oil fields are largely concentrated in the southwestern area around Volgograd, while natural gas resources are based largely in Siberia, onshore south of the Kara Sea. Although Russia has tried to promote the development of high-tech manufacturing, especially in the Skolkovo Innovation Center outside Moscow, there are few Russian companies that are globally competitive in this activity today. Russian manufacturing is concentrated largely around Moscow and St Petersburg, the two largest cities (circled in solid lines on Figure 2.6).

South Africa

The South African economy ranked 34th in the world in 2013, with a GDP estimated at $US 351 billion. South Africa's per capita income ranked only 89th in the world, far behind the Triad countries, but gaining ground steadily. South Africa's economic growth rate fell to the level of the Triad countries, at 1.9 per cent per year in 2013; and it was far lower than growth in the other emerging markets discussed here.

South Africa, like the other six countries discussed here, has been internationally competitive primarily because of raw materials/commodity exports. South Africa is the world's leading producer of platinum and diamonds, and until just a few years ago, the leading producer of gold as well. In addition, it is a leading producer and exporter of other precious metals and minerals, including palladium, chromium, manganese and vanadium. It is also the third largest exporter of coal, adding to the overall focus on raw materials. While South Africa also exports agricultural products, particularly within Africa, and some manufactures, those products constitute a far lower percentage of overall exports than mining. The companies operating in all of these sectors are private sector based, and many of them are subsidiaries of foreign multinational companies. Interestingly, the amount of employment in South Africa in the mining sector is only about 3 per cent of total employment, with the job distribution looking more like a Triad country than an emerging market (ie two-thirds of employment is in services and 13 per cent in manufacturing).

FIGURE 2.7   Map of South Africa (showing key manufacturing/ assembly sites and natural resource deposits)

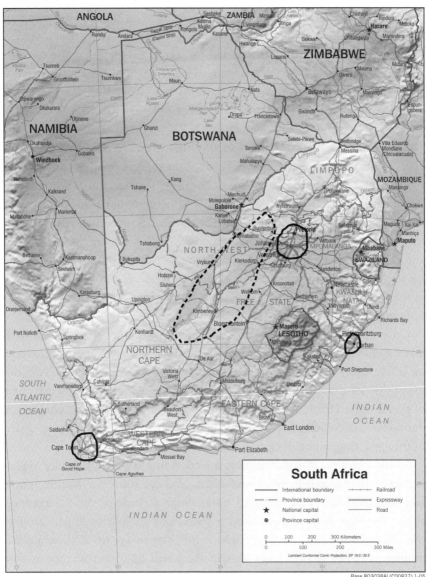

As far as cost-based business activity is concerned, South Africa probably has the potential to carry out offshore assembly of various kinds, but the distance to key Triad markets is extreme. As with Argentina and Brazil, South Africa is so far from regular trade routes in the northern hemisphere that it has not attracted any significant amount of assembly activity.

When we look at the fit of South African companies into international supply chains, the natural resource companies such as Anglo-American mining and De Beers diamonds are quite visible at the commodity end of the spectrum. At the same time, large manufacturing firms such as South African Breweries (SABMiller) and Tiger Brands are global competitors. And a number of services firms have joined the ranks of major multinationals, including Standard Bank, Naspers media group, Old Mutual insurance and MTN telephone company. These firms tend to be global or regional, top-to-bottom competitors, rather than niche players involved in only one or two stages of the value-added chain.

The market in South Africa is smaller than those of the other countries here, but it constitutes about 40 per cent of the market of all of sub-Saharan Africa. The economic development of South Africa is so much greater than that of other countries in the region, it is certain that this country will remain the principal engine of growth in the near-term future, with a threat from much larger Nigeria as that country builds a greater industrial base and relies less on oil exports. The educational level of South Africa is by far the highest in the region, and several of its universities rank among the best in the world, so this skill advantage may enable the country to maintain its economic leadership.

Government regulation and participation in the market are both relatively low for emerging markets, except in the mining industry, where the government frequently sets policies to push companies towards higher local employment, greater downstream production of the mined ores, greater payment of taxes, and so forth. After the exodus of foreign multinational companies during the later years of the Apartheid period that ended in 1994, the presence of foreign companies still lags in comparison with that in the BRICs.

South Africa fits into global value-added chains as both a provider of raw materials, particularly minerals and metals, and as a source of manufacturing and service-sector multinationals that compete through the value-added chain. The manufacturing and service operations are located largely around the three main cities (circled within solid lines in Figure 2.7), while the mining activities span a large area in the north and west of the country (marked with a dotted line).

Conclusion

The emerging markets described above have a number of common features. They are all major commodity exporters. They all have relatively large populations which are younger and less wealthy than in the Triad countries. Their infrastructure generally is poorly developed relative to the Triad countries, but even so, the main emerging market cities are modern metropolitan centres with advanced technology, and infrastructure sometimes better than in older Triad cities.

At the same time there is quite a variety of conditions in these countries as far as government policies, numbers of globally competitive companies, economic growth rates and other key features are concerned. Mexico and South Africa are highly open to foreign business, while China, Russia and India present numerous barriers to foreign companies in general and to many industries in particular. Brazil and Indonesia fall somewhere in the middle, with many open industries at the same time as more extensive government intervention than in the two more open economies.

As far as their overall fit into value-added chains is concerned, Mexico, China and India operate much more offshore assembly than the other countries, depending on cheap labour and on the ability to produce large volumes of products and services. Russia and Indonesia are more dependent on the oil and gas sector, while Brazil and South Africa are somewhat more diversified. None of these countries is a one-industry economy, even though natural resources are leading sectors in all of them. Only China is established in recent years as a technological leader worldwide, but this condition may very well change, as discussed in Chapter 8.

Notes

1 See, for example, 'Mapping China's middle class', *McKinsey Quarterly* (June 2013). http://www.mckinsey.com/insights/consumer_and_retail/ mapping_chinas_middle_class

2 See, for example, 'Special report: Outsourcing and offshoring', *The Economist*, 29 January 2013. http://www.economist.com/news/special-report/21569572- after-decades-sending-work-across-world-companies-are-rethinking-their- offshoring

3 This is not to ignore the Triad countries' very important leadership in creation and commercialization of new technology. This activity may be the single most important one for international competitiveness in the 21st century, as discussed in Chapter 8.

4 This is not necessarily a major challenge or 'liability of foreignness', since foreign firms often may be able to obtain the knowledge by hiring a small number of local people who possess the knowledge, or to acquire a local company that possesses it.

5 These data come from the World Bank's database, available online at: http://data.worldbank.org/indicator/NY.GDP.MKTP.KD.ZG

6 There has been some debate about China's cost competitiveness in the early 2000s. Some analysts see other Asian countries such as Vietnam taking low-cost production from China, as Chinese wages rise and as the renminbi also appreciates. See, for example: http://www.bloomberg.com/news/2013-04-09/china-surging-wages-threaten-economy-s-competitiveness-adb-says.html; and http://www.cnbc.com/id/100651692

7 This phenomenon is described along with the situation for other major emerging markets in *The Economist*, 'When giants slow down', 27 July 2013. http://www.economist.com/news/briefing/21582257-most-dramatic-and-disruptive-period-emerging-market-growth-world-has-ever-seen

8 Data from the World Bank database, available online at: http://databank.worldbank.org/data/home.aspx

9 The problem of illegal copying of patented, trademarked, or copyrighted materials by Chinese companies is well known. See, for example, http://www.forbes.com/sites/michaelzakkour/2014/04/30/copycat-china-still-a-problem-for-brands-chinas-future-just-ask-apple-hyatt-starbucks/ and http://www.foreignaffairs.com/articles/139452/kal-raustiala-and-christopher-sprigman/fake-it-till-you-make-it

10 In 2008 another huge hydrocarbon field was discovered near the Lula basin. The Jupiter natural gas field is estimated to be similar in size to Lula. See, for example, http://www.economist.com/node/13348824

11 See, for example, Aghion *et al* (2008).

12 While Walmart stores generally are not physically under the same roof as a mall in Mexico, they are co-located in most instances, rather than appearing as independent 'big-box' stores on their own separate plots of land.

13 See, for example, http://www.tristarmedia.com/bestofrussia/scientists.html and http://www.famousbirthdays.com/profession/from/scientist-russia.html

14 The great mathematician, Mikhail Lomonosov, was the founder of Moscow State University, and a contributor to its focus on scientific endeavour.

References

Aghion, P, Burgess, R, Redding, S J and Zilibotti, F (2008) The unequal effects of liberalization: evidence from dismantling the License Raj in India, *American Economic Review*, 98(4), 1397–412

Central Intelligence Agency (nd) *The World Factbook*, CIA, Washington, DC [Online database] https://www.cia.gov/library/publications/the-world-factbook/

International Monetary Fund (2014) *World economic outlook database* (October) [Online] http://www.imf.org/external/pubs/ft/weo/2014/02/weodata/weoselco.aspx?g=2001&sg=All+countries

Morris, I (2010) *Why the West rules – for now: The patterns of history, and what they reveal about the future*, Farrar, Straus and Giroux, New York

PricewaterhouseCoopers (2013) *The world in 2050*, PwC, London [Online] http://www.pwc.com/en_GX/gx/world-2050/assets/pwc-world-in-2050-report-january-2013.pdf

Shenkar, O (2006) *The Chinese century: The rising Chinese economy and its impact on the global economy, the balance of power, and your job*, FT Press, London

The time horizon

03

What to expect in Chapter 3

When we talk about emerging markets, the relevant countries depend on the time frame. If we consider the past 300 years, then the United States definitely was an emerging market in the early part of that time. If we talk about the past 50 years, then South Korea was definitely an emerging market in the 1960s, but certainly not in the 2000s, when it is clearly part of the advanced post-industrial economy. If we look at per capita incomes, then most of Central and Eastern Europe is much closer to the United States, European Union and Japan than it is to China and India. This chapter looks at both individual (per capita) incomes and also country size (GDP) over a long history – the past 2,000 years.

During the first thousand years of the modern era, India was the largest economy in the world. After that, for most of the past one thousand years, China has been the largest country economy in the world. After the Industrial Revolution the United States overtook China – but not until the 20th century in fact. And now in the early 21st century it appears certain that China will once again become the single largest economy in the world for the foreseeable future. In individual incomes the leading countries have been those who developed technological leadership over their contemporaries, from Egypt 2,000 years ago to the United Kingdom in the 1800s to the United States since that time.

Among emerging markets the Eastern European countries look most likely to challenge the United States and northern European countries for leadership in individual incomes during the 21st century, while India and Indonesia may follow China into world-leading economic size (GDP) in the second half of the century. The reasons for these shifts in global economic power have largely to do with population size in these countries, along with technological catching-up that occurs as they develop further. China and Eastern European countries such as Slovenia and the Czech Republic are investing heavily in technology development, and their per capita incomes are already rivalling those in many Triad countries.

While it seems that emerging markets have been growing rapidly for a generation, it really depends on your perspective. There is no doubt that quite a few of the non-Triad countries have grown rapidly relative to the United States, European Union and Japan during the past 25 years. If we focus on the two largest countries, China and India, they appear to be absolutely booming relative to the Triad during this period of time. While these facts are incontrovertible, there are many other aspects of emerging markets that are not so clear. There are many emerging markets whose growth rates are not impressive. Haiti for the past 25 years has had negative GDP growth, as has North Korea. Other countries that are not such extreme examples – including Ukraine, Iraq, the former Yugoslavia, Jamaica and Liberia – have hardly grown at all.

Something that is also interesting to consider is the definition of an emerging market: does Haiti or Zimbabwe qualify, or is it only Asian countries? We won't revisit the definition that was resolved in Chapter 1: emerging markets for our purposes are all countries that are not in the OECD group with relatively high per capita incomes. Also, how long is our time frame? If we consider the past 200 years, then the United States was an emerging market at the beginning of that period, and clearly it has emerged. If we look to the future, how long should this relative boom of today's emerging markets be expected to last? And are we interested in market sizes of these countries, or just in per capita incomes? These are just a few of the elements that need to be established for us to really understand where the action is.

Let's start by looking at the past 25 years. Most people are aware that China and India have been growing faster than the Triad countries, and we looked at this phenomenon in Chapter 1 (Table 1.2) and Chapter 2 (Table 2.1) to some extent. If we expand our horizons to include the largest three countries in each of the emerging market regions of Latin America, Africa, Middle East, Asia and Eastern Europe, plus the largest Triad countries, we can see in Table 3.1 that these emerging markets of today are indeed generally growing much faster than the Triad during the past quarter-century.

Russia is a main exception to this rule, with compound annual growth since the end of the Soviet Union of less than 1 per cent. The Czech Republic also has shown slow, Triad-like growth in the past 25 years, as have other countries in Central/Eastern Europe. The other emerging markets listed here are growing at much higher rates, with China and India topping the list. It should be noted that there are plenty of slow-growing emerging markets in the world, if we include all of the more than 200 countries that are not in the Triad or OECD groups of countries.

TABLE 3.1 Growth rates of selected countries, 1990–2014

GDP-Growth	1991	1992	1993	1994	1995	1996	1997	1998	1999	2000	2001
France	1.04%	1.60%	−0.01%	0.02%	2.09%	1.39%	2.34%	3.56%	3.41%	3.88%	1.95%
Germany	5.11%	1.92%	−0.96%	2.45%	1.70%	0.78%	1.82%	1.97%	1.99%	2.98%	1.70%
United Kingdom	−1.24%	0.45%	2.65%	4.02%	2.53%	2.67%	2.55%	3.51%	3.15%	3.77%	2.66%
United States	−0.07%	3.56%	2.75%	4.04%	2.72%	3.80%	4.49%	4.45%	4.69%	4.09%	0.98%
Japan	3.32%	0.82%	0.17%	0.86%	1.94%	2.61%	1.60%	−2.00%	−0.20%	2.26%	0.36%
Czech Republic	−11.61%	−0.51%	0.06%	2.91%	6.22%	4.28%	−0.67%	−0.32%	1.44%	4.29%	3.05%
Poland	−7.02%	2.51%	3.74%	5.29%	6.95%	6.24%	7.09%	4.98%	4.52%	4.26%	1.21%
Russian	−5.05%	−14.53%	−8.67%	−12.57%	−4.14%	−3.60%	1.40%	−5.30%	6.40%	10.00%	5.09%
Argentina	12.67%	11.94%	5.91%	5.84%	−2.85%	5.53%	8.11%	3.85%	−3.39%	−0.79%	−4.41%
Brazil	1.51%	−0.47%	4.67%	5.33%	4.42%	2.19%	3.39%	0.35%	0.49%	4.38%	1.28%
Mexico	4.22%	3.63%	4.06%	4.73%	−5.76%	5.87%	6.96%	4.70%	2.67%	5.30%	−0.61%
China	9.27%	14.28%	13.94%	13.08%	10.99%	9.92%	9.23%	7.85%	7.62%	8.43%	8.30%
India	1.06%	5.48%	4.75%	6.66%	7.57%	7.55%	4.05%	6.18%	8.85%	3.84%	4.82%
Indonesia	8.93%	7.22%	7.25%	7.54%	8.40%	7.64%	4.70%	−13.13%	0.79%	4.92%	3.64%
Iran	12.59%	4.25%	−1.58%	−0.35%	2.65%	7.10%	3.38%	2.74%	1.93%	5.14%	3.67%
Saudi Arabia	9.10%	4.63%	0.03%	0.67%	0.20%	3.38%	2.59%	2.83%	−0.75%	4.86%	0.55%
Turkey	0.72%	5.04%	7.65%	−4.67%	7.88%	7.38%	7.58%	2.31%	−3.37%	6.77%	−5.70%
Egypt, Arab Rep.	1.08%	4.43%	2.90%	3.97%	4.64%	4.99%	5.49%	4.04%	6.11%	5.37%	3.54%
Nigeria	−0.62%	0.43%	2.09%	0.91%	−0.31%	4.99%	2.80%	2.72%	0.47%	5.32%	4.41%
South Africa	−1.02%	−2.14%	1.23%	3.20%	3.10%	4.30%	2.60%	0.50%	2.40%	4.20%	2.70%
World	1.39%	1.92%	1.63%	3.13%	2.92%	3.29%	3.68%	2.55%	3.36%	4.26%	1.82%

SOURCE: http://data.worldbank.org/indicator/NY.GDP.MKTP.KD.ZG

2002	2003	2004	2005	2006	2007	2008	2009	2010	2011	2012	2013	2014	Average
1.12%	0.82%	2.79%	1.61%	2.37%	2.36%	0.20%	-2.94%	1.97%	2.08%	0.18%	0.66%	0.18%	1.44%
0.01%	-0.72%	1.18%	0.71%	3.71%	3.27%	1.05%	-5.64%	4.09%	3.59%	0.38%	0.11%	1.60%	1.45%
2.45%	4.30%	2.45%	2.81%	3.04%	2.56%	-0.33%	-4.31%	1.91%	1.65%	0.66%	1.66%	2.55%	2.01%
1.79%	2.81%	3.79%	3.35%	2.67%	1.78%	-0.29%	-2.78%	2.53%	1.60%	2.32%	2.22%	2.39%	2.48%
0.29%	1.69%	2.36%	1.30%	1.69%	2.19%	-1.04%	-5.53%	4.65%	-0.45%	1.75%	1.61%	-0.10%	0.92%
1.65%	3.60%	4.95%	6.44%	6.88%	5.53%	2.71%	-4.84%	2.30%	1.96%	-0.81%	-0.70%	1.99%	1.70%
1.44%	3.56%	5.14%	3.55%	6.20%	7.16%	3.87%	2.62%	3.71%	4.77%	1.82%	1.71%	3.37%	3.70%
4.74%	7.30%	7.18%	6.38%	8.15%	8.54%	5.25%	-7.82%	4.50%	4.26%	3.41%	1.34%	0.64%	0.95%
-10.89%	8.84%	9.03%	9.20%	8.40%	7.97%	3.07%	0.05%	9.45%	8.39%	0.80%	2.89%	0.47%	4.17%
3.07%	1.22%	5.66%	3.15%	4.00%	6.01%	5.02%	-0.24%	7.57%	3.92%	1.76%	2.74%	0.14%	2.98%
0.13%	1.42%	4.30%	3.03%	5.00%	3.15%	1.40%	-4.70%	5.11%	4.04%	4.01%	1.39%	2.12%	2.76%
9.09%	10.02%	10.08%	11.35%	12.69%	14.19%	9.62%	9.23%	10.63%	9.48%	7.75%	7.68%	7.35%	10.09%
3.80%	7.86%	7.92%	9.28%	9.26%	9.80%	3.89%	8.48%	10.26%	6.64%	5.08%	6.90%	7.42%	6.56%
4.50%	4.78%	5.03%	5.69%	5.50%	6.35%	6.01%	4.63%	6.22%	6.17%	6.03%	5.58%	5.02%	4.98%
7.52%	7.11%	5.08%	4.62%	5.89%	6.37%	1.52%	2.28%	6.63%	3.95%	-6.56%	-1.92%	1.46%	3.56%
0.13%	7.66%	9.25%	7.26%	5.58%	5.99%	8.43%	1.83%	4.76%	9.96%	5.38%	2.67%	3.47%	4.19%
6.16%	5.27%	9.36%	8.40%	6.89%	4.67%	0.66%	-4.83%	9.16%	8.77%	2.13%	4.19%	2.87%	3.97%
2.37%	3.19%	4.09%	4.47%	6.84%	7.09%	7.15%	4.69%	5.14%	1.82%	2.19%	2.11%	2.20%	4.16%
3.78%	10.35%	33.74%	3.44%	8.21%	6.83%	6.27%	6.93%	7.84%	4.89%	4.28%	5.39%	6.31%	5.48%
3.70%	2.95%	4.55%	5.28%	5.59%	5.36%	3.19%	-1.54%	3.04%	3.21%	2.22%	2.21%	1.52%	2.60%
2.07%	2.80%	4.15%	3.59%	4.12%	3.94%	1.48%	-2.07%	4.08%	2.84%	2.23%	2.35%	2.47%	2.67%

Many of the former Soviet republics are floundering, some with negative growth since 1990. In the Americas, Jamaica and Haiti are laggards behind solid growth in most other countries of that region. In Africa, Sierra Leone, Zimbabwe and Zaire/Congo have had negative growth over the past quarter-century. In Asia most countries have done extremely well during this time, with the notable exception of North Korea, which has experienced negative growth. In the Middle East growth has been quite good, with the exceptions of Iraq and the Palestinian territories.

We should also consider individual or per capita incomes during this period, since they also contribute to an understanding of economic leadership in the world. Table 3.2 shows the same group of countries over the same time horizon, this time looking at individual incomes.

In this comparison of economic development, we see that the Triad countries lead for the entire period, though some emerging markets, particularly in Eastern/Central Europe, are not too far behind. Argentina as well stacks up favourably in per capita income during the past quarter-century. Per capita income growth shows China and India improving at three times or more the rate of the Triad countries. East Asian countries, with the exceptions of North Korea and Mongolia, also have leapt forward relative to the rest of the world, with per capita income growth on average about twice the rate of the Triad during the past 25 years. The countries closest to entering into Triad-level per capita incomes are in Central/Eastern Europe – and these countries have remained almost exactly as far behind (ie 50 per cent) as they were 25 years ago.

The future

What does this growth imply for the future? For one thing, it shows that China and India are poised to become the largest (not the wealthiest) economies in the world in the near future: China before 2020, and India probably before 2050. The implications here are for both economic power and economic opportunity. Both countries have much lower per capita incomes than the Triad countries, and will not pass them until long after 2050, if at all during this century. So, in that sense of individual incomes, economic power will not shift dramatically. However, the more than one billion people in both countries mean that their governments will have economic power to allow or constrain foreign companies wishing to do business there, and capacity to subsidize their domestic companies in international competition.

TABLE 3.2 Per capita incomes in selected countries, 1990–2013

Per capita GDP	(1990 International Geary–Khamis dollars)							
	1990	1995	2000	2005	2008	2009	2010	2013
France	17,647	18,349	20,422	21,536	22,223	20,297	19,539	19,480
Germany	15,929	17,299	18,944	19,417	20,801	18,836	18,674	19,784
United Kingdom	16,430	17,561	20,353	22,518	23,742	19,209	19,578	20,001
United States	23,201	24,603	28,467	30,481	31,178	30,040	30,539	31,866
Czechoslovakia	8,513	7,956	8,833	10,771	12,925	11,156	11,063	10,455
Poland	5,113	5,623	7,309	8,527	10,160	8,201	8,826	9,149
Russian Federation	7,779	4,813	5,277	7,303	9,111	6,658	8,177	10,593
Argentina	6,433	8,013	8,581	9,019	10,995	10,083	12,074	14,765
Brazil	4,920	5,296	5,532	5,878	6,429	6,196	8,026	7,780
Mexico	6,085	6,001	7,275	7,511	7,979	6,370	7,300	8,009
China	1,871	2,863	3,421	5,575	6,725	7,328	8,564	12,486
India	1,309	1,553	1,892	2,423	2,975	3,250	3,967	3,984
Indonesia	2,514	3,369	3,276	3,870	4,428	4,583	5,873	6,577
Japan	18,789	19,979	20,738	21,976	22,816	23,537	25,403	21,532
Iran	3,526	4,162	4,838	6,045	6,944	6,936	7,886	6,285
Saudi Arabia	8,993	8,091	7,650	8,079	8,435	6,799	8,108	10,298
Turkey	5,399	5,775	6,446	7,449	8,066	6,652	7,723	7,919
Algeria	2,947	2,658	2,863	3,374	3,520	2,752	3,136	3,670
Egypt	2,523	2,496	2,936	3,200	3,725	4,219	4,748	5,329
Nigeria	1,112	1,113	1,161	1,346	1,524	1,199	2,491	3,104
South Africa	3,834	3,646	3,890	4,316	4,793	4,883	6,119	5,358
World average	5,150	5,446	6,038	6,960	7,614	7,073	7,572	8,061

SOURCES: data from Maddison database: http://www.ggdc.net/maddison/oriindex.htm and World Bank database: http://data.worldbank.org/indicator/NY.GDP.PCAP.CD

In addition, the products and services sold in these two countries will continue to blossom in the next decade or more, providing opportunities for domestic and foreign companies to generate major sales and income increases.

One could also speculate about the sustainability of the growth paths of China and India. A number of authors (eg Khanna, 2011 and *The Economist*, 2010) assert that the Indian institutional conditions (particularly its constitutional democracy and relatively market-based economy) are more favourable to continued growth than the Chinese ones, with the high degree of government control over the economy there. This point of course is debatable, since the 'Licence Raj'[1] still has not disappeared in India, and the economic system is probably more bureaucratic in India than in China. Still, the Chinese system with limited political freedom could face upheaval in the next half-century, so a linear growth path is not likely in either case.

A fascinating related question is: where will India be going relative to China in the next few decades? With China's large lead in per capita income and overall economic size, it seems like a stretch to think that India will surpass China in either measure before 2050. Even so, there are some indicators that suggest things may change. Perhaps the most important one is population. China in 2013 had 1.35 billion inhabitants, while India had 1.24 billion. With its one-child-per-family policy in place since 1979, China has effectively cut its population despite the relatively young average age there. Projections are that India will have over 1.5 billion people by 2030, while China's population will decline slightly to 1.34 billion and continue downward after that. Just as we saw in earlier historic episodes, the larger-population countries tend to dominate the world economy, even when their per capita incomes may diverge significantly. Even so, with total Chinese GDP almost triple that of India in 2013, and per capita income more than double, it will take India a long time to potentially catch up, unless underlying factors such as political stability or the rate of innovation change dramatically in the next three decades.

A lot is made of China's government-controlled economy, with many state-owned companies and relatively few home-grown MNEs from the private sector. India on the other hand has had an elected, democratic government and relatively free private sector even during the period of intense inward-looking industrialization under Jawaharlal Nehru from 1947 to 1964. This underlying institutional structure could hinder Chinese growth once the state-owned enterprises (SOEs) become less important in the economy – or hinder it as well if the generally slower-moving SOEs continue to lead in many sectors. Either way, if we look at the past 25 years, many more Chinese companies have moved into the Fortune Global 500 (95 companies in 2014) than Indian firms (8 companies in 2014). Perhaps the Indian firms are more innovative; it remains to be seen if innovation really does grow faster in India in the years ahead.[2]

In the very long run

Let's back up to take a broader historical perspective and think about emerging markets in a longer-term context. How do we define emerging markets in this context? If they are challengers to the established leading economies, then emerging markets are of course different countries at different times. At the time of the Roman Empire, emerging economies would have been those in neighbouring regions such as Europe, Africa and the Near East beyond the empire. Looking at the time of the Roman Empire, it may be surprising to see that the leading countries/empires based on economic size were China and India – both much larger than the Roman Empire itself. Table 3.3 shows this relationship, along with economic size measures of several key leading countries over time.

So at the time of the Roman Empire from, say, AD 1–500, the leading 'country' or empire was arguably either Rome or India. As you can see in the table, India's economy was much larger. In fact, even at the earliest time that countries or kingdoms could be identified economically, the two Asian giants, India and China, had the largest economies. This should not be too surprising, given that per capita incomes were fairly similar around the world, at somewhat above subsistence level, and the populations of India and China were much larger than those in the European areas even then.

While the Roman and Holy Roman Empires dominate the history of 1–1600 taught in the West, it remains true that both India and China had larger economies than any Western country or kingdom up until the Industrial Revolution.

During the 1200s Genghis Khan and his grandson Kublai Khan (plus several intervening family members in the middle part of the century) built an empire that was the largest ever known, covering at its peak in about 1275 the countries of China, Mongolia, Turkey, Persia, most of Russia and Eastern Europe and Central Asia and extending to other countries on the periphery. The Mongol Empire survived only a few decades, and it is not widely discussed in economic terms, but it clearly contained the major part of the world economy during the half-century from about 1240 to 1290. Figure 3.1 shows the approximate geographic size of the empire in AD 1279.

TABLE 3.3 Country economic size comparisons in the long run (GDP in constant $US 1990 MM)

Note: Dark shaded cells show the largest economy that year.

Country/Year	1	1000	1250	1500	1600	1700	1820	1870	1913	1950	2003
United States	272	520		800	600	527	12,548	98,374	517,383	1,455,916	8,430,762
Roman / Holy Roman Empire*	13,193	10,421		43,551	64,627	80,107	n.r.*	n.r.	n.r.	n.r.	n.r.
Mongolian Empire√			90,000								
China	26,820	26,550		61,800	96,000	82,800	228,600	189,740	241,431	244,985	6,187,984
India	33,750	33,750		60,500	74,250	90,750	111,417	134,882	204,242	222,222	2,267,136
United Kingdom†	320	800		2,815	6,007	10,709	26,232	100,180	224,618	347,850	1,280,625

*The Roman Empire ended around AD 500. The Holy Roman Empire largely replaced it in about AD 800, with Charlemagne's coronation, and then ceased to exist, arguably, in 1806. The countries formerly in the Empire had combined GDP of about $130,000 in 1820, still ranking far behind China.

√The Mongolian empire only lasted from about AD 1210 to 1294. During that time, nevertheless, the empire encompassed most of China, northern India, Mongolia, Turkey, Persia, most of Russia, Eastern Europe and Central Asia. If we add up the GDPs of these various pieces, the Mongolian Empire was by far the largest economy in the world during the 13th century.

† The UK is shown without its colonies. So if, for example, colonial India were included until independence in 1947, the UK would have been the largest economy during most of 1612–1913.

SOURCE: Angus Maddison database, Statistics on World Population, GDP and Per Capita GDP, AD 1–2008 http://www.ggdc.net/maddison/oriindex.htm

While one can criticize the Mongol Empire for being more of a bloody set of conquests than a coherent civilization of its own, nevertheless the empire stretched from the Mediterranean to the Pacific Ocean and it was ruled by the Khans or their designated local rulers. And while neither Genghis Khan nor his descendants were able to create a single culture within the empire, he did establish rules for governing that kept conquered tribes and kingdoms under control – by leaving most governance to local leaders in cases of 'loyal' tribes or societies, and by putting his own lieutenants in charge of less compliant areas. Genghis Khan encouraged his assigned lieutenants to marry into local families of conquered societies and thus to become part of the local social structure. And he set rules of civil society, such as penalties for stealing and the establishment of a legal representative in each area to ensure adherence to the laws. Even with these elements of common governance, the Mongol Empire never achieved any degree of homogeneity among the many cultures of the realm, from China to Russia to India.

Because the Mongols were hunters rather than farmers, they did not have an established structure of towns and cities. The Mongols moved from one area to another in pursuit of game for food, and they became skilled horsemen as a result of this lifestyle. It served them well in the military context, when they fought other tribes or kingdoms for control of resources. This society without a geographic base did not serve well in developing settled communities and production, so it required adjustment to the conquered people's lifestyles in order to maintain infrastructure. And Genghis Khan was very successful in either coopting local leaders to join his kingdom, or in defeating them militarily and inserting his own leaders over the conquered areas. In sum, although their own society was nomadic, the Mongols were able to build bases in other contexts through the combination of force and willing subordination of local leaders.

Measures of the economic size of the Mongol Empire are necessarily sketchy, since the empire was so diffuse and diverse. One could make a broad generalization that it summed up to more or less $90 billion in 1279 at its peak, well above the size of India or China in the previous century and also larger than China in the measure presented above for the year 1500. Ultimately, the lack of a cohesive cultural base, and probably also due to the immense geographic spread of the empire, the Mongol Empire disintegrated. This last step was due more to the problem of succession after Kubai Khan than to the general factors of culture and geography, but in any event by 1300 the great empire was gone.

Even separate from the Mongolian invasions, China passed India in economic size somewhere after the Middle Ages and before the Industrial

FIGURE 3.1   Map of Mongol Empire to 1280

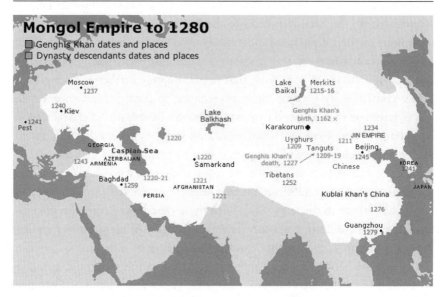

Mongol Empire to 1280
☐ Genghis Khan dates and places
☐ Dynasty descendants dates and places

Moscow
•1237

Lake   Merkits
Baikal   1215-16

1240
• Kiev

Lake
Balkhash

Genghis Khan's
birth, 1162 ×

•1241
Pest

Karakorum ◆

1234
JIN EMPIRE

1220

Uyghurs
1209 Tanguts
1211

Beijing

GEORGIA
Caspian Sea
AZERBAIJAN
1243 ARMENIA

•1220
Samarkand

Genghis Khan's
death, 1227

1209-19
1245

KOREA
1241

Chinese

Baghdad   1220-21
•1259

1221
AFGHANISTAN

Tibetans
1252

JAPAN

PERSIA   1221

Kublai Khan's China

1276

Guangzhou
1279 •

SOURCE: http://www.fsmitha.com/h3/h11mon.htm. Reproduced with permission.

Revolution. By 1700 the Holy Roman Empire had grown to about the same economic size as India and China, with a much smaller population. That is, the per capita income in the European parts of the empire had begun to grow more quickly than in the rest of the world, such that by the mid-1800s and led by the United Kingdom, family income far exceeded that in India or China. Although China's GDP still exceeded that of the United States in 1870, it was far less than the combined GDPs of the Western European countries – construed as either former members of the Holy Roman Empire or future members of the European Union.

The United States was the emerging market of the late 1700s and early 1800s. By the late 1800s, however, the United States had already passed the United Kingdom, and by the beginning of the First World War the United States was far and away the largest economy in the world, double the size of China. Within the span of just one century the United States went from being a newly formed country and emerging market to being the industrial powerhouse of the world and by far the largest economy. This condition held, with the lead growing before the Second World War and then declining over time, until China once again (most likely will) reclaim the title of largest economy in 2017 or so.

There is a big difference between overall economic *size* and economic *standard of living*. If we look now at per capita income as a measure of standard of living, the comparison across countries and time changes notably. Maddison estimated that in AD 1 the population of India was about 75 million, in China it was about 60 million, in the Middle East and North Africa it was about 27 million, and in all of Eastern and Western Europe combined it was about 30 million. The Roman Empire, with parts in both Europe and Middle East/North Africa, had an estimated population of 44 million.[3] This implies that per capita income in AD 1 in India was about $450 per year, while in the Roman Empire it was overall about $380 per year.[4]

Even here one could debate the 'leading country' label for India. If the Roman Empire is subdivided, and just the part of the empire that was on the Italian peninsula is considered, then Rome's per capita income at about $530 per year actually exceeded that in India by quite a margin. However, if we also subdivided India into a core, leading area and only counted that for per capita income, the number would again be much higher, and India could once again be labelled the lead country. Suffice it to say that Rome and India vied for economic leadership during the first few centuries of the modern era.

Now consider per capita incomes over the same long run that we examined for country size, as shown in Table 3.4.

It is very clear that the Roman Empire, followed by Egypt, had the highest per capita income/standard of living in the year AD 1; Iran and Turkey (the Middle East) had the highest in 1000, and then European countries dominated the personal income table from 1500 until the rise of the United States in the mid-1800s. The Triad countries have dominated in per capita income/standard of living since the Second World War, and they show no signs of losing their leadership in the 21st century. In principle, if the Chinese and Indian growth rates were to continue at double the rate of the Triad ones, then China would enter the Triad group towards the end of this century, and India sometime after that.

Without going into too detailed a discussion of economic history, it is still very striking to note that the 'normal' scheme of things economically put China and India at the top of the pile in terms of economic size for most of history since the time of Greek city-states, Athens and Sparta, before the Roman Empire. And leadership with respect to individual incomes has shifted from the Roman Empire to Iran/Turkey by AD 1000, to Europe in 1500, and more broadly to the Triad since then. Will India's and China's individual incomes ever exceed the rest?[5]

TABLE 3.4   Per capita incomes AD 1–2013

Note: Dark shaded cells show the highest per capita income that year

Per capita GDP	(1990 International Geary–Khamis dollars)												
	1	1000	1500	1600	1700	1820	1870	1913	1950	1973	2003	2008	2013
Western Europe													
France	473	425	727	841	910	1,135	1,876	3,485	5,186	12,824	20,891	22,223	19,480
Germany	408	410	688	791	910	1,077	1,839	3,648	3,881	11,966	19,088	20,801	19,784
United Kingdom	400	400	714	974	1,250	1,706	3,190	4,921	6,939	12,025	21,461	23,742	20,001
United States	400	400	400	400	527	1,257	2,445	5,301	9,561	16,689	29,074	31,178	31,866
Czechoslovakia (Czech Republic for 2013)						849	1,164	2,096	3,501	7,041	9,664	12,925	10,455
Poland							946	1,739	2,447	5,340	7,804	10,160	9,149
Russian Federation										6,582	6,335	9,111	10,593
Argentina							1,311	3,797	4,987	7,962	7,744	10,995	14,765
Brazil			400	428	459	646	713	811	1,672	3,880	5,536	6,429	7,780
Mexico		400	425	454	568	759	674	1,732	2,365	4,853	7,159	7,979	8,009
China	450	466	600	600	600	600	530	552	448	838	4,803	6,725	12,486

TABLE 3.4 *continued*

Per capita GDP	(1990 International Geary–Khamis dollars)												
	1	1000	1500	1600	1700	1820	1870	1913	1950	1973	2003	2008	2013
India	450	450	550	550	550	533	533	673	619	853	2,134	2,975	3,984
Indonesia (including Timor until 1999)			565		580	612	578	874	803	1,490	3,582	4,428	6,577
Japan	400	425	500	520	570	669	737	1,387	1,921	11,434	21,092	22,816	21,532
Saudi Arabia									2,231	11,040	7,629	8,435	10,298
Turkey	550	600	600	600	600	643	825	1,213	1,623	3,477	6,499	8,066	7,919
Algeria		450				430	715	1,163	1,365	2,357	3,130	3,520	3,670
Egypt	600	500	475	475	475	475	649	902	910	1,294	3,052	3,725	5,329
Nigeria									753	1,262	1,258	1,524	3,104
South Africa						415	858	1,602	2,535	4,175	4,130	4,793	5,358
World average	**467**	**453**	**566**	**596**	**615**	**666**	**870**	**1,524**	**2,111**	**4,083**	**6,469**	**7,614**	**8,061**

SOURCES: data from Maddison database http://www.ggdc.net/maddison/oriindex.htm and World Bank database http://data.worldbank.org/indicator/NY.GDP.PCAP.CD

Expected leading (emerged) countries for later in the 21st century

As an exercise in speculation, think about the countries in the world today, and try to identify which emerging markets are likely to be the leaders in the next 50 years or so. Of course, China and India will lead in economic size (GDP). It will be interesting to see if Indonesia can take advantage of its very large population and join the top 10 countries in economic size, as Brazil and Russia have already done.

Where will per capita income be highest, and perhaps challenge incomes in the Triad countries? If we look at the recent historical record in Table 3.3, it appears that the Central/Eastern European countries are the most likely candidates to join this group, just as a number of them have joined the (Western) European Union. In Central/Eastern Europe per capita incomes are about half of the average for the European Union, which is well above any other region of emerging markets. However, the growth rates in Central/Eastern Europe are quite similar to those in Western Europe, so the convergence does not look rapid based on the experience of the past 25 years. By contrast, emerging markets such as Argentina and Turkey have achieved per capita income levels like those in Central/Eastern Europe and at the same time have much higher growth rates than this group of countries. This leads to the expectation that, surprisingly, it may be one of these two countries that performs the next 'economic miracle', to join Japan, Korea and the East Asian Tigers (Singapore, Hong Kong, Taiwan, plus South Korea) along with the traditional Western powers in the Triad group.

If we argue that innovation and technological development are key elements to competitiveness today, as discussed in Chapter 8, then only China ranks among the Triad countries in R&D spending (ahead of France and the United Kingdom) and other indicators of innovation. Eastern European countries such as the Czech Republic and Slovenia also rank highly in this comparison. A slew of additional Eastern European countries along with India and Brazil rank reasonably competitively, with R&D spending of just under 1 per cent of GDP, which is approximately half the global average. These facts would tend to imply that China and Eastern Europe should grow faster than other emerging markets, but the record is pretty clear that the Eastern European countries have not outpaced their Western European rivals in recent decades. India has grown relatively rapidly, but the measures of technology intensity and innovation do not show a special emphasis or strength for that country.

Some heretical thinking on emerging market leaders in the future

First of all, let me be clear that among emerging markets China and India, in that order, will dominate economic growth and development of successful international companies in the next several decades. The question is: which additional emerging markets will also be the brightest stars in growth rates, per capita incomes and company competitiveness? I am convinced that Mexico, Indonesia and the Czech Republic are the most likely emerging markets to demonstrate rapid growth and to spawn globally competitive MNEs in the next quarter-century. Where does this thinking come from?

First of all, economic size is important. So it is not likely that a small country will have sufficient market size and innovative skills to become a global leader. This statement may be challenged by looking at Luxembourg and Norway, very small countries that have among the world's highest per capita incomes, but with virtually no globally competitive multinational firms based there (except for two natural resource companies in Norway, and the India-based, Mittal-controlled ArcelorMittal steel company legally established in Luxembourg). So, given that economic size is important, larger countries are more likely to become global leaders – and the three countries identified here all fit that criterion.

In the case of *Mexico*, the logic is two-part. Mexico's oil and gas reserves are sufficient to keep that country as a net exporter of fossil fuels for the rest of the century. This resource advantage underpins Mexico's ability to operate a successful macroeconomy well into the future. And Mexico's size and proximity to the United States will continue to make it attractive for US (and rest of the world) firms to carry out local assembly (maquila) and manufacturing in general, to take advantage of Mexico's lower costs than in the United States as well as access to the domestic market and to the US market.

Mexico's main weakness is the low level of innovative activity, seen in its low commitment to R&D (about 0.4 per cent of GDP, compared to a world average of about 2.1 per cent[6]). Even so, there are several Mexican companies that have become globally competitive, from Cemex to Bimbo – or at least regionally competitive, from FEMSA to Carlos Slim's Grupo Carso – all discussed elsewhere in this book. There are seven Mexican firms in the Fortune Global 500 in 2014.

In the case of *Indonesia* major reserves of oil and gas will provide the basis for growth throughout the 21st century. In addition, Indonesia's reserves of tin, copper, coal, and other minerals and metals will provide sources of growth for many years to come. Beyond this primary sector, the economy is also developing some pockets of excellence, in low-cost manufacture of clothing and potentially some IT outsourcing. The fundamental reason that Indonesia will continue to grow rapidly is its abundance of exportable natural resources and its low-cost labour, which continues to attract offshore assembly of clothing and other textile products. As China's wages increase more rapidly, Indonesia becomes more attractive for assembly activities of leading Japanese and Western MNEs, for sales particularly in Asia. And with 250 million people, Indonesia will become an increasingly attractive market for international companies as more Indonesians enter the middle class.

As far as world-leading companies are concerned, Indonesia boasts fairly few. The national oil company, Pertamina, leads the list. In addition, the national electric power company, state-owned PNL, is in the Fortune Global 500. Pertamina certainly has the possibility of becoming a significant international competitor, since it owns natural resources and has the capability to expand downstream into international distribution and perhaps other oil-related activities. The electric power company is probably limited to the protected domestic market, though with its size, PNL could potentially develop competitive strengths that would enable it to expand overseas. This short list of large Indonesian companies does not translate easily into areas of competitive advantage where new entrants could challenge existing global firms, but perhaps the textile sector may produce a national champion or two, and certainly other natural resources such as tin or copper could lead to domestic companies entering international competition.

Indonesia faces one major weakness relative to these other leading emerging markets in the fact that its educational system is very underdeveloped, and education levels are quite low compared not only to Mexico and the Czech Republic, but also relative to China, Russia and Brazil. On a key World Bank measure of educational quality, Indonesia falls far down in the country rankings according to percentage of GDP spent on education (2.8 per cent in 2011 relative to a Triad average of about 5.6 per cent and an average for the emerging markets discussed in this chapter of about 5.0 per cent). This weakness implies that Indonesia will have a more difficult time in developing the human capital needed to manage and lead its organizations and to create successful, globally competitive companies.

Finally, the *Czech Republic* is a very different case, with no oil reserves and a heavy dependence on manufacturing. This medium-sized country has a history of industrial dynamism over the past two centuries. It has been a centre for car manufacturing, producing over one million cars in 2010 and subsequently, with most exported to the European Union. The Czech Republic joined the European Union in 2004, so it is already arguably an emerged rather than emerging market. Its per capita GDP is more than twice that of China and several times those of India and Brazil.

The Fortune Global 500 shows no Czech companies in the list, although car manufacturer Skoda (as a major part of VW) is included in the sense of being part of that corporate group.[7] State-owned electric power company Cez is a huge company, although not quite to the level of sales needed to join the Fortune list. Just as with the Indonesian electricity supplier, there is no evidence that Cez has world-leading technology or management, and thus it is not likely to compete internationally unless by acquisition of a more innovation-intensive company elsewhere.

The Czech Republic differs from the previous two cases because its per capita income already rivals those in the Triad countries. With per capita income of $US 27,000 in 2013, and a growth rate of about 4 per cent/year during the past decade, the Czech Republic shows every sign of equalling countries such as France and the Netherlands among the European leaders in the next couple of decades.[8] This is most likely due to the ability of Czech companies to innovate and to produce high-quality manufactured goods. With R&D spending at 1.8 per cent of GDP, the Czech Republic is in the top third of countries globally and second only to China among the emerging markets. With a population of only 11 million people, the Czech Republic will not become a major market itself in the near future – although as an EU member, it has tariff-free access to all 300+ million consumers in the region.

So while more Chinese and Indian companies will continue to move into the group of the world's largest enterprises, we still can expect to see more emerging market members of this group from countries such as Mexico, Indonesia and the Czech Republic. In these first two instances, Mexico and Indonesia are major oil producers and exporters as well as large countries in terms of population and GDP. It is natural that some of their companies would join the group of the world's largest, though not necessarily to lead the list for their industries. In the case of the Czech Republic, the country has a reputation for innovation and a long history of producing internationally competitive manufactures, from autos to chemicals. So the Czech companies that are likely to join the Global 500 are more likely to be in manufacturing industries, particularly related to cars and chemicals.

One may wonder why Russia and Brazil are not listed here as probable leaders among emerging markets in the decades ahead. In the case of Russia this is due to the complicated political situation that has produced near-zero growth during the 2000s, despite enormous oil and other natural resource wealth. There is no question that Russia has the potential to rival the two leading BRICs, although it has not done so thus far. Russia certainly has the technological capability, having produced dozens of Nobel prize-winning scientists in mathematics, chemistry and physics over the years. However, translating knowledge into business application simply has not worked well.

The transition from Soviet rule to elected regimes had produced by 2014 a regime led by Vladimir Putin that was re-concentrating power in the hands of a few powerful leaders and not leading to a strong market-based economy. The political forays of this regime, forcibly taking the Crimea from Ukraine and then attempting to re-absorb the Ukraine, have led to widespread opposition from other countries worried about this military-backed empire building. Since European countries depend so heavily on Russian oil and gas (about 25–30 per cent of total supply to Europe), economic dependence may enable the Russian imperialism to succeed in Ukraine and other former Soviet states.

Moving away from the political/military theme back to business, a number of large companies have been created through privatization of former SOEs. Almost none of these firms have demonstrated international competitiveness except for those possessing natural resources. Russia has nine companies in the Fortune Global 500, of which seven are natural resource companies and two are banks.

And finally, Russia faces the same constraint that is operating today in Western Europe – a trend to declining population. Russia's 140 million people in 2012 are forecast to decline to 110 million by 2050. This trend alone accounts for a significant portion of the expected slowdown in Russian growth in the next several decades.

As for Brazil, it is more a case of slower expected growth than in Mexico and definitely in comparison with Asian emerging markets. Brazil does not have the nearby US market as in Mexico's situation, and it does not have the Asian focus on R&D, spending proportionately half as much as the leading Asian countries. Even so, with the oil discovered offshore in Brazil in 2006, there appear to be proved reserves sufficient for Brazil to serve domestic needs and to be an oil exporter for the rest of the 21st century. Production in these fields is expected to go online in 2014, so oil wealth should begin to have an impact on Brazilian wealth and GDP in short order.

Despite this natural resource wealth, Brazil has demonstrated a historical difficulty in breaking out from slow growth and structural limits on the economy's development. From strong unions to anti-foreign politics, Brazil has repeatedly run into barriers that impede faster growth of the economy.

The country is far from the backward society that rejected foreign-owned computer companies in the 1970s and 1980s,[9] but that kind of view recurs to block opportunities for growth on frequent occasions.

Brazil's education system ranks well down the list based on indicators such as the percentage of GDP spent on education or the rate of graduation from secondary school.[10] This factor contributes to the problem of the low level of innovation demonstrated by Brazilian companies and individuals.

Brazil's economic growth and success of companies competing internationally both depend on a greater commitment to innovation and probably greater links to the rest of the world's major economies. Brazil is fairly isolated geographically, with no major economic centres nearby, other than Buenos Aires. Brazil is not attractive for offshore assembly of manufactured goods, because the distance is so far from major markets. This may be less of a barrier in the 21st century, but the geographic isolation does seem to hold Brazil back from greater integration into the global economy.

Conclusions

The goal of this chapter has been to demonstrate which countries/empires have led the world economy over the past two millennia, and which ones have been the 'richest' in terms of per capita incomes over time. The underlying issue is to try to understand *why* these countries have been leaders over the years, and thus what may lead to new leaders in the future. The number one feature of the largest economies (highest GDP) is population. Even with great disparities in per capita incomes, China is already a larger economy than Japan, Germany or the United Kingdom, and India will follow suit in a few years. With any reasonable continuation of growth faster than in the United States, China will overtake the United States in economic size before 2020.

Per capita incomes were at one time fairly similar across countries/empires, before the Industrial Revolution. Once machines had been harnessed to serve mankind, the leading countries in innovation took the lead in per capita income – namely the United Kingdom and other European countries, and then the United States. From differences of about 50 per cent between richest and poorest countries in the first millennium AD, per capita incomes diverged such that the richest countries have been enjoying incomes three or four times as high as the poorest countries after 1800. The challenge is to see whether the major growth poles in emerging markets, particularly China and India, can keep up their disproportionately rapid growth and move past the United States and European Union in economic size, as well as continue to catch up in individual incomes.

In the very long run of centuries in history, China and India have been the largest economies for most of the past 2,000 years. Within the next couple of decades it appears that this world order will be re-established. Just as in earlier centuries, however, other countries have often led the world in standard of living, and this certainly will be true for the rest of the 21st century. Since the big jump in per capita incomes happened with the Industrial Revolution, there is reason to believe that innovation may be the driver of such success in the future as well. If this is an accurate interpretation, then one may expect countries such as the United States, Scandinavia and Israel (see Chapter 8) to be among the leaders in personal incomes.

A very important question is how China and India will use their economic might as the largest economies during the second half of this century. Will they be protectionist or relatively open to international business? Will they continue to demand that foreign companies play limited roles in most sectors of the economy? Will either one become a technology leader the way Japan did in the late 20th century and Korea and Taiwan have done more recently?

Notes

1 The 'Licence Raj' in India was/is the person in the government who must authorize a business activity, typically with a long delay and a non-trivial cost to getting that authorization. India was widely known as excessively bureaucratic in this context for most of the post-Second World War period, until in the mid-1990s some degree of economic opening was begun. See for example: 'The License Raj Is Dead. Long Live the License Raj' http://www.wsj.com/articles/SB123451653488482115; and 'Modi tackles India's "License Raj" with a thousand cuts' http://www.ft.com/intl/cms/s/0/5badad82-3ff6-11e4-a381-00144feabdc0.html#axzz3SGWjXhoP

2 R&D spending in 2011 was 1.97 per cent of GDP in China, while it was 0.9 per cent in India. The number of patent filings in the US Patent and Trademark Office in 2012 included 13,273 from China and 5,663 from India. This does not indicate to me that India is more innovative than China, at least based on these traditional criteria.

3 See Maddison database, population tab. Also see Maddison, *Contours of the World Economy*, Table 1.2, p 50.

4 See Maddison database, per capita GDP tab. Also see Maddison, *Contours of the World Economy*, Table 1.10, p 65. Maddison estimates that per capita income around Rome in the Italian peninsula was actually about $530 per year at that time, and significantly less in other parts of the empire.

5 If historical precedent is a guide, then the answer is no. If current trends continue, then yes. The author expects that historical precedent will be followed, and that some country(ies) other than India or China will be the leader in per capita income in the future.

6 Global R&D spending is shown in the World Bank's data tables: http://wdi.worldbank.org/table/5.13

7 Just as Ambev from Brazil is a major part of Fortune Global 500 company AB Inbev, Banamex in Mexico is a major part of Citibank, and South African Breweries is a huge part of Fortune Global 500 company SABMiller.

8 The Czech Republic was very hard hit by the global financial crisis of 2008–09, and its GDP growth has stalled in the five years since then.

9 A government agency called CAPRE in 1974 (succeeded by another agency, SEI, in 1979) laid out rules for approving computer imports into Brazil, effectively handing the market to domestic companies unless a particular type of computer (eg, mainframe) were not able to be produced locally. This policy stimulated (low-quality, expensive) local production of PCs and minicomputers for more than a decade, until it was discontinued in the late 1980s. See, for example, Armijo, Kearney and Manzetti (2008). Also see Luzio (1996).

10 See World Bank, World Development Indicators. http://data.worldbank.org/data-catalog/world-development-indicators

References

Armijo, L E, Kearney, C and Manzetti, L (2008) Does democratization alter the policy process? Trade policymaking in Brazil, *Democratization*, **15**(5), pp 991–1017 [Online] http://citation.allacademic.com/meta/p_mla_apa_research_citation/1/8/0/0/8/pages180082/p180082-29.php

Jones, G (2005) *Multinationals and global capitalism: From the 19th to the 21st century*, Oxford University Press, Oxford

Jones, G and Khanna, T (2006) Bringing history (back) into international business, *Journal of International Business Studies*, **37**, pp 453–68

Khanna, T (2011) *Billions of Entrepreneurs: How China and India are Reshaping Their Futures – and Yours*, Harvard Business School Press, Boston, MA

Luzio, E (1996) *The microcomputer industry in Brazil*, Praeger, Westport, CT [Online] https://books.google.ae/books?id=sm9rkwv-Of8C&pg=PA5&lpg=PA5&dq=capre+brazil&source=bl&ots=VNogIRO3XK&sig=Xxp06Nwqh3F_gjH2k7txn89QVJQ&hl=en&sa=X&ei=i2AWVbbRKsLcaP2OgqgB&ved=0CDYQ6AEwAw#v=onepage&q=capre%20brazil&f=false

The Economist (2010) India's surprising economic miracle, *The Economist*, 10 September [Online] http://www.economist.com/node/17147648#sthash.qjhDZSMj.dpbs

Appendix: Emerging market characteristics

TABLE A3.1   Emerging market R&D expenditure by all sources, 2014

Rank	Country	R&D as % of GDP @ PPP	Expenditures on R&D, billions of $US at PPP	Global rank based on total R&D spending
1	China	2.00%	284.0	2
2	India	0.90%	44.0	8
3	Russia	1.50%	40.0	9
4	Brazil	1.30%	33.0	10
5	Turkey	0.90%	11.0	20
6	Iran	0.80%	9.0	24
7	Mexico	0.50%	8.0	25
8	Poland	0.87%	7.0	27
9	South Africa	1.00%	6.0	29
10	Qatar	2.70%	6.0	30
11	Czech Republic	1.80%	5.0	31
12	Argentina	0.60%	5.0	32
13	Malaysia	0.80%	5.0	34
14	Pakistan	0.70%	4.0	35
15	Saudi Arabia	0.30%	3.0	38
17	Indonesia	0.20%	3.0	40

SOURCE: Battelle Institute, http://www.battelle.org/docs/tpp/2014_global_rd_funding_forecast.pdf?sfvrsn=4

TABLE A3.2   Emerging markets ranked by GDP and by services/GDP

Country/GDP	GDP ($US bill)	GDP/capita ($US)	Services as % of GDP
Argentina	611.7	14,760	65%
Brazil	2,245.7	11,208	69%
China	9,240.3	6,807	46%
Czech Republic	198.4	18,861	60%
India	1,876.8	1,499	57%
Indonesia	868.3	3,475	40%
Iran	368.9	4,763	n.a.
Malaysia	312.4	10,514	50%
Mexico	1,260.9	10,307	62%
Pakistan	236.6	1,299	53%
Poland	517.5	13,432	65%
Qatar	202.5	93,352	n.a.
Russia	2,096.8	14,612	60%
Saudi Arabia	745.3	25,852	37%
South Africa	350.6	6,618	70%
Turkey	820.2	10,946	64%

SOURCES: World Bank, 2013 data http://data.worldbank.org/indicator/NY.GDP.PCAP.CD and
http://data.worldbank.org/indicator/NV.SRV.TETC.ZS

TABLE A3.3   Annual GDP growth rates of selected countries, AD 1–2014

Note: Fastest-growing countries for each year are highlighted. For the entire two millenia, the US, UK and Netherlands had the fastest growth.

Annual growth of GDP (PPP) %/year					
Country	Austria	Germany	Italy	Netherlands	UK
1	–	–	–	–	–
1000	+0.034	+0.016	–0.106	+0.041	+0.092
1500	+0.312	+0.351	+0.328	+0.347	+0.252
1600	+0.393	+0.428	+0.221	+1.058	+0.761
1700	+0.171	+0.076	+0.015	+0.672	+0.580
1820	+0.420	+0.564	+0.361	+0.048	+1.021
1870	+1.447	+1.999	+1.244	+1.698	+2.055
1913	+2.411	+2.808	+1.939	+2.161	+1.895
1950	+0.248	+0.302	+1.489	+2.429	+1.189
1973	+5.350	+5.676	+5.640	+4.736	+2.931
2003	+2.394	+1.723	+2.173	+2.307	+2.153
mean AGR 1–2003	+0.335	+0.358	+0.257	+0.416	+0.415

SOURCE: Angus Maddison, *Contours of the World Economy*, p 379, Table A.4

Portugal	Spain	USA	Japan	China	India	World
–	–	–	–	–	–	–
+0.035	−0.004	+0.065	+0.098	−0.001	+0.000	+0.013
+0.173	+0.183	+0.086	+0.177	+0.169	+0.117	+0.145
+0.296	+0.448	−0.287	+0.223	+0.441	+0.205	+0.289
+0.702	+0.062	−0.130	+0.471	−0.148	+0.201	+0.114
+0.517	+0.415	+2.677	+0.249	+0.850	+0.171	+0.523
+0.656	+0.932	+4.204	+0.406	−0.372	+0.383	+0.944
+1.337	+1.774	+3.936	+2.442	+0.562	+0.970	+2.116
+2.347	+1.056	+2.836	+2.212	+0.040	+0.228	+1.822
+5.726	+6.595	+3.934	+9.294	+4.920	+3.542	+4.900
+2.789	+3.189	+2.938	+2.619	+7.338	+5.204	+3.174
+0.335	+0.295	+0.518	+0.386	+0.272	+0.210	+0.298

What is the challenge from emerging markets?

04

What to expect in Chapter 4

The challenge from emerging markets is that companies originating in those countries are becoming the global leaders of today and the future, taking market share and sales away from the existing leaders. They will enter local markets outside their home countries and take business away from local competitors there as well. Even this threat is not the complete picture. As the emerging markets themselves become the most attractive places to build sales in the future, these emerging market companies are already established there, and are likely to prove to be formidable competitors.

Half a dozen companies are discussed here: PetroChina, Embraer, Hon Hai, Tata, SABMiller and Bimbo. Each of these companies is a world leader in at least one industry, while the Tata Group competes strongly in multiple different industries. PetroChina is the most vertically integrated company in the list, with activities very similar to the range at Exxon or Shell, and additionally it is the only state-owned enterprise in our list. Tata Group is the most diversified company in the list, and it has demonstrated the 'classic' emerging market strategy of entering additional businesses when opportunities arise, and leaving businesses when the returns no longer justify the investment.

Embraer began as a state-owned enterprise, moved into private ownership, and has become the largest manufacturer of regional jet aeroplanes (competing principally with Bombardier). Embraer purchases the vast majority of its components from other companies, and focuses on assembling aeroplanes and marketing them. Hon Hai likewise is very focused in the value-added chain, carrying out assembly of cell phones and other consumer electronics products for the original equipment manufacturers.

Bimbo and SABMiller aim at the consumer market, selling bread and drinks in several regions of the world. Bimbo is more focused on South and North America plus Spain. SABMiller is more focused on Africa, China and the United States. Both companies have designs on worldwide competition, while their strengths are clearly in limited regions. They both buy food inputs from other companies, produce bread and beer in their own factories, and then sell to grocery stores and other retail stores.

The chapter shows how these six companies fit into global value-added chains, and it identifies opportunities for them to expand both vertically and horizontally into new markets and stages of production.

Introduction

What is the real challenge of emerging markets? Certainly the increase of competitor companies originating there is a concern for major multinationals such as telecom equipment makers, with the rise of Huawei and ZTE in China, and for software developers given the global success of Tata Consulting Services and Wipro from India. This challenge is really much broader, as national champions arise in country after country in the emerging world, first succeeding locally and then expanding into international markets.

The other side of the coin is just as important, and perhaps even more so. Emerging markets are markets, with consumers and companies that are potential clients for companies from the Triad countries, as well as competitors that include local companies and those from other emerging markets. It cannot be overstated that global growth since 1990 has been dominated by growth in emerging markets, led by China, but also including a wide range of large and small countries, and that the growth of sales and earnings at international companies, from General Motors to General Electric to General Mills, and from Toyota to BASF to Shell, are coming from emerging markets. This growth path will continue into the indefinite future, as those countries catch up in per capita income with the rich countries of today. So, companies that want to continue to grow outside their local markets must look to national and international targets, whose growth will be led by these emerging markets into the future.

The growth rates and market sizes of key emerging markets are summarized in Table 4.1. These markets were the focus of Chapter 2, so we will not dig into this subject in detail here.

TABLE 4.1 GDP (market size) and GDP growth rate, selected countries and years (in current $US billions and in annual percentage rates)

Country / Year		Brazil	China	India	Indonesia	Mexico	Russia	South Africa	United States	Germany	Japan
2000	GDP	644.7	1,198.5	476.6	165.0	683.6	259.7	132.9	10,289.7	1,886.4	4,731.2
	Growth rate	4.3	7.6	3.8	4.9	5.3	10.0	4.2	4.1	3.1	2.3
2005	GDP	882.2	2,256.9	834.2	285.9	866.3	764.0	247.1	13,095.4	2,766.3	4,571.9
	Growth rate	3.2	11.3	9.3	5.7	3.0	6.4	5.3	3.4	0.7	1.3
2010	GDP	2,143.1	5,930.5	1,708.5	709.2	1,051.6	1,524.9	365.2	14,958.3	3,304.4	5,495.4
	Growth rate	7.5	10.4	10.3	6.2	5.1	4.5	3.1	2.5	4.0	4.7
2012	GDP	2,248.8	8,229.5	1,858.7	876.7	1,186.5	2,017.5	382.3	16,244.6	3,426.0	5,937.8
	Growth rate	1.0	7.7	4.7	6.3	4.0	3.4	2.5	2.8	0.7	1.4
2013	GDP	2,245.7	9,240.3	1,876.8	868.3	1,260.9	2,096.8	350.6	16,800.0	3,634.8	4,901.5
	Growth rate	2.5	7.7	5.0	5.8	1.1	1.3	1.9	1.9	0.4	1.5

SOURCE: World Bank, World Development Indicators, http://data.worldbank.org/indicator/NY.GDP.MKTP.CD

These numbers show at once the somewhat small sizes of current big emerging market economies (other than China), in terms of their national incomes compared to key Triad countries. And they also show how rapidly those markets are growing, before and after the global financial crisis of 2008–09, in comparison with the Triad countries.

While this discussion focuses on markets, don't forget that the emerging markets are the largest sources of commodity production as well. Another facet of the picture is that emerging markets will increasingly lead commodity industries, as both the sources of production (as discussed in Chapter 2) and as the sources of companies that become world leaders in these commodity sectors. Of course, these companies will move downstream, from oil to petrochemicals; from iron ore to machinery; from cotton to clothes; from wheat and corn to processed foods.

In addition to the commodity producers from emerging markets, there also is a wide range of companies that produce products and services, from highly commoditized clothing to high-tech machinery and software. Let's look at some of them, which are already joining the ranks of the Fortune Global 500. The focus of this chapter is thus on the challenge to existing Triad companies from new competitors arising in emerging markets.

Emerging market competitors

A look at some of the major international firms based in emerging markets gives us an idea of the wave of competition that is growing and that will sweep world markets in the future. The six firms selected here range from raw materials producers to service providers, and from SOEs to family-owned business groups. They are meant to illustrate the wide range of bases from which emerging market competitors are entering into international competition.

PetroChina (China)

This oil company is the public face of the China National Petroleum Corporation (CNPC), a state-owned enterprise.[1] PetroChina was created in 1999, as the publicly traded arm of CNPC. Today PetroChina is one of the ten largest oil companies in the world by most measures (eg reserves; revenues; production), and its shares are traded on the Shanghai Stock Exchange and the Hong Kong Stock Exchange, with American Depositary Receipts (ADRs) traded on the New York Stock Exchange. Controlling ownership remains in the hands of the China National Petroleum Corporation.

PetroChina began as part of a reorganization of the Chinese government-owned petroleum sector, aiming to operate as a global oil company with shares traded on stock exchanges and activity ranging from oil exploration to production of petrochemicals. As with Exxon and Shell, the company is heavily involved in natural gas exploration, production and marketing as well. With proven reserves of over 11 billion barrels of oil, PetroChina ranks ahead of all of the private oil companies in the world by that measure – though well behind the national oil companies of Iran, Iraq, Saudi Arabia and several other OPEC countries.

PetroChina has taken an active role in acquiring foreign oil properties, with purchases of refining businesses from Eneos in Europe, Singapore Petroleum Company in Singapore and Nippon Oil in Japan. In Australia, the company purchased part of BHP's natural gas business in 2012, and previously purchased natural gas fields from Conoco-Philips there as well. In 2012 PetroChina's chairman stated that the firm's medium-term goal is to have half of its production outside of China.[2]

Through both acquisitions of other companies and training of its own people, PetroChina has developed highly competitive capabilities in explo-ration and production of oil, as well as in refining and other downstream activities. The company has begun a program of building petrochemicals production in China and overseas in several other Asian countries.

Key competitive advantages of PetroChina include: oil and gas reserves in China; government support as a state-owned company; large financial resources; and knowledge of operating in (especially Asian) emerging markets. As PetroChina moves to position itself as a major competitor in global oil and gas markets, the company definitely has a strong base with its proven reserves, relative to all of the private-sector oil majors. While the company's financial resources are not necessarily larger than several of these com-petitors, they do give PetroChina the ability to expand globally through acquisitions of oil and gas businesses in other countries. PetroChina does have valuable knowledge of how to operate successfully in China and some other Asian countries, which can be a powerful tool when competing with Shell or Exxon in that region. Also, the company's petroleum-related R&D, while not known widely outside China, is carried out through the Research Institute in Petroleum Exploration and Development and has led to numerous patents and ongoing investigation of upstream petroleum industry challenges.[3]

In principle, PetroChina has the ability to obtain the government's support when it needs bargaining help with a foreign government, or additional financial resources, or even protection against foreign oil companies that want to operate in China. This is 'in principle', because the government also could decide to take financial resources from PetroChina for other uses, and it could support another company (such as Sinopec or CNOOC, the other major Chinese state-owned oil companies) in competition with PetroChina. Thus, government backing is a two-edged sword, but it could certainly provide PetroChina with a competitive advantage against Exxon or Shell in international competition for resources and/or for markets.

How does PetroChina fit into global value-added chains? It is quite similar to Exxon and Shell in running the gamut of activities in the oil and gas sector (Figure 4.1). As a highly vertically integrated oil major, PetroChina partici- pates in each stage of petroleum and natural gas exploration, production and downstream activity. At the same time, the company contracts out to other firms in the sector for provision of transportation, final sale of petrol under other brand names, R&D in petrochemicals, and many other activities that it carries out partly in-house and partly through contracting. And in addition, PetroChina has joint-venture agreements with other oil-producing companies for sharing risks and costs of those upstream activities. This is particularly true in natural gas ventures, where PetroChina operates joint

FIGURE 4.1   PetroChina's value-added chain

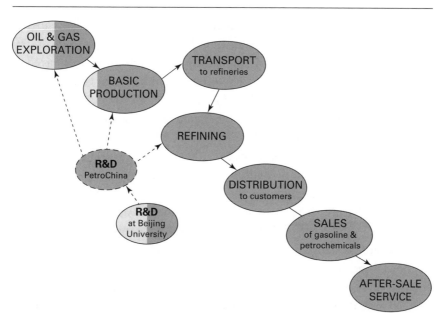

Key: light shading refers to Triad countries; dark shading refers to emerging markets

ventures to produce natural gas in Australia with Shell; in Canada with Encana, and separately another project with Shell, Korea Gas and Mitsubishi; and in Russia with Gazprom.

Historically, PetroChina has been far more domestically oriented that Shell and Exxon today, although those companies also started from strong bases in their domestic markets. With the goal of obtaining half of its oil and gas supplies from sources outside of China by 2017, PetroChina is clearly on a globalization track.[4]

Embraer (Brazil)

Empresa Brasileira de Aeronautica (Embraer) was created by the Brazilian government in 1969 to manufacture aeroplanes mainly for the military, but also with the intent to serve potential civilian users. The company continued a Brazilian tradition of designing and producing aeroplanes going back to the time of the Wright Brothers when Brazilian Alberto Santos-Dumont built and flew a fixed-wing aeroplane in Paris in 1906. Other Brazilian inventors and pilots flew aircraft during the subsequent years, providing transportation among Brazil's far-flung cities and agricultural regions when adequate roads were not available. This history of aviation was much more extensive than in other emerging markets, and so it was not unreasonable to expect Brazil to eventually become the source of a competitive aeroplane manufacturer.

When Embraer was set up, the government's goal was to take a logical next step based on the development of a technical training centre and aircraft design centre in San Jose dos Campos near São Paulo, which occurred in 1950. By the mid-1960s the Brazilian government had been convinced that the technical expertise was in place to build domestically made aeroplanes for the military. A prototype plane, the Bandeirante, had been built and test flown by 1968, and Brazilian President Costa e Silva approved the idea of creating a company that would produce the plane and become a symbol of Brazil's technical capability.[5] Indeed, the new company's first plane was the turboprop Bandeirante, developed for the Brazilian air force and launched officially in 1971. The new company, named Empresa Brasileira de Aeronautica (Embraer), made various adaptations to this first plane, and its third version was a passenger turboprop plane that gave Embraer its start in the commercial aviation market in 1973. From the beginning Embraer focused on regional air service and on smaller planes than the major commercial aircraft manufacturers, Boeing, Lockheed and McDonnell Douglas. By 2012 the firm had global sales of $US 6.2 billion.

In the early 1990s state-owned Embraer encountered a cyclical downturn that produced lower sales and major financial problems. The Brazilian government was not willing to put more money into SOEs, and Embraer was no exception. After a near-death experience for Embraer in 1993–94 because of unprecedented losses, the government agreed to privatize the company, and it was sold in December 1994 to key investors Bozano Simonsen (an investment bank) and Sistel and Previ (pension funds) along with public sale of shares on the São Paulo stock exchange. This move did not produce immediate positive results, but over the following three years the company launched its first jet aircraft, the ERJ-145, and by the end of the decade, Embraer had become solidly profitable.[6] According to the leaders of Embraer at the time, the recovery was due to the company's new flexibility and its switch from being an engineering-focused firm to a customer-focused firm.

In the 2000s Embraer has expanded its market from its original focus on the Americas and a couple of projects in Italy and France to include China and the European Union. With production in China, Portugal and France, Embraer has 'insider' status in those markets, which of course is very important when selling to state-owned airlines such as Air China and China Southern Airlines, as well as Air France and TAP in Portugal.

Embraer, as in the case of its rival Bombardier, and the two main large commercial aircraft manufacturers Boeing and Airbus, is heavily involved in strategic alliances with suppliers of parts, from engines (with GE and Pratt & Whitney) to avionics (with BAE Systems and Rockwell Collins) to furnishings within the aeroplanes. These alliances often come as a result of negotiations with state-owned airlines, which are pressured by their governments to obtain as much as possible of their purchases from domestic suppliers.

The competitive advantages of Embraer, in comparison with its main rival Bombardier, are: its support within Brazil by the national government; perhaps its knowledge of emerging markets; and traditional capabilities such as technology for producing aircraft and an established distribution network of planes and components. While Embraer is no longer a state-owned enterprise, it is still a national champion that has received financing support and other means of protection from the Brazilian government.

In comparison with Bombardier from Canada, Embraer potentially has an advantage in dealing in emerging markets. Although this is not necessarily the case, since Bombardier has been in business longer than Embraer, and has established strong business positions and links with local governments, suppliers and so on in many emerging markets, especially in Asia, Embraer still remains much stronger in Latin America. Technologically, Embraer is on par with Bombardier, in the same way that Boeing and Airbus trade places as leader and follower in the introduction of new aircraft and new adaptations of existing aircraft over time. This is to say that Embraer is a global leader in aircraft technology, despite its emerging market origin, and it does not suffer from a weakness in this arena relative to key competitors.

Embraer fits into a global value-added chain in much the same way that Boeing, Airbus and Bombardier do. Embraer assembles aircraft, purchasing components from a wide range of suppliers, often in the country where the aircraft purchaser is located, and selling relatively standardized aircraft, which are subsequently fitted out with some personalized colours, amenities and other details by the airlines who purchase the planes. Figure 4.2 shows Embraer in this value chain, demonstrating the possibilities for expansion vertically, though more likely horizontally into additional markets.

In the early 21st century, Embraer competes on par with Triad-based Bombardier and increasingly in some product segments with Boeing and Airbus.

FIGURE 4.2   Embraer in the global aircraft manufacturing value-added chain

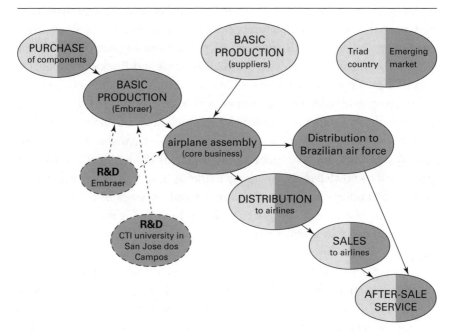

Hon Hai (Taiwan)

Hon Hai is the world's largest contract manufacturer of consumer electronics products, based in Taiwan. Hon Hai also operates under the brand name Foxconn. The company is the main assembler of iPhones for Apple and also smart phones for Motorola, Nokia and Huawei, as well as game consoles for Sony and Nintendo, and PCs for Hewlett-Packard and Dell. The company rose to number 30 in the Fortune Global 500 in 2013 with its contract manufacturing business, and today is looking for extensions of this business to maintain growth in spite of the slowdown in sales of Apple iPhones.

Hon Hai's main manufacturing facilities are in Taiwan, along with mainland China sites in Shenzhen and Huizhou. In addition to these very large facilities, Hon Hai manufactures in a dozen other countries, from Japan to Brazil, the Czech Republic to Mexico, and elsewhere. As it attempts to move into production of peripheral equipment for the PCs, smartphones, TVs and so on that it assembles, Hon Hai is aiming to build up its profit margins, which are relatively low in the pure assembly business. In addition, Hon Hai has stated the intention to move into provision of content for the devices that it assembles. This means the development of software for applications (apps) on smart phones, its own TV network, and cloud computing technology for all devices, among other projects.

What underlying strengths enable Hon Hai to compete against rivals from Triad countries? Hon Hai's competitive advantages in electronics assembly, versus rivals Flextronics and Jabil Circuit, both based in the United States, are: lower-cost production capability; existing relationships with key clients such as Apple and Huawei; and greater knowledge of the markets in Asia. Each of these advantages could be competed away by a strong competitor that lines up alternative suppliers in low-cost locations and hires people with detailed knowledge of Asian markets. Even so, the long-term relationships with key clients such as Apple are not easy to break, and Hon Hai has the opportunity to build even greater links to these clients and to make it even more difficult for them to consider alternative assembly companies.

Hon Hai dominates the market for contract manufacture of electronics products worldwide, and thus fits tightly into the value-added chain for smartphones (as shown in Chapter 1), and for TVs and videogame players. It is clear from an examination of any of these supply chains that Hon Hai could look to extend its core business to downstream and upstream activities in these industries. The television display value-added chain is particularly instructive, as shown in Figure 4.3.

FIGURE 4.3   Hon Hai TV display value-added chain

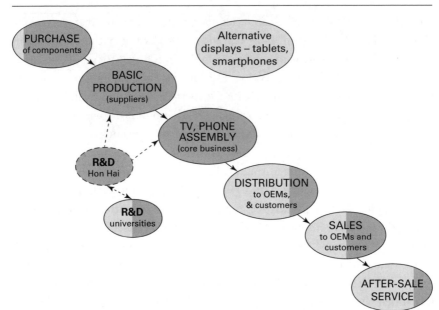

As shown in this figure, the television value-added chain is quite unsettled, as new providers offer TV service, and new instruments (such as tablet PCs and even smartphones) offer display capabilities. Our interest is in the display part of the business, since that is where Hon Hai is starting from. The instrument itself is in question, as the new forms of receiving television programming are evolving.

Hon Hai's potential for expanding its presence in the value-added chain goes in multiple directions. First, the company can try to move upstream into the production of some of its inputs, such as applications for the instruments it produces. Second, Hon Hai can try to move downstream directly to the ultimate TV customers, aiming to connect programming from content providers to TV watchers. And third, Hon Hai can try to move into alternative means of providing TV services, through media such as smart TVs when they are launched, or into an 'iStore' kind of venture to obtain and resell content.[7]

Tata Group (India)

Tata Group is the largest conglomerate based in India. With activities in seven major sectors, Tata Group had revenues of just over $US 100 billion in 2012, which would rank the group 66th in the Fortune Global 500 for 2012. Tata had 475,000 employees worldwide in 2012. While 32 divisions of the group are listed on stock exchanges – for example, Tata Steel, Tata Motors, Tata Chemical and Tata Consultancy Services – the overall group remains in the hands of the Tata family through a holding company arrangement. The group's historic focus has been on manufacturing, especially in cars, steel and chemicals. More recently, Tata has expanded into engineering and consulting services.

Tata's production costs are generally lower than those of its main global competitors in steel, cars and chemicals. For commodity products, this advantage is very significant, while in more differentiated products such as cars, Tata's strength is in the small, economy cars where costs dominate considerations. With its $US 2,500 Nano car, Tata certainly does have an advantage over GM, VW, Toyota and others in international competition in that segment of the market. Overall in manufacturing, Tata tends to have a cost advantage over Triad-based rivals, even those that carry out some manufacturing or assembly in China and other low-cost Asian locations.

Tata currently has more than half of its global sales outside India, and is expanding rapidly, especially in other emerging markets. Different from several of the other examples here, Tata tends to focus on emerging markets and to stay clear of the United States and European Union in general.

To consider Tata's competitive advantages, it is most manageable to compare the group with competitors in specific industries. Let us choose just one of them for a brief comparison: the chemicals business. Tata's competitive advantages relative to rivals BASF, Dow and Monsanto in chemicals are clearly its lower-cost production capability, plus its knowledge of and relationships with customers in emerging markets from India to Latin America to Asia. Tata's division in this industry is significantly smaller than those of the major chemical companies, even after major acquisitions of British Salt in 2010 and soda ash producers Brunner Mond (2006) and General Chemicals (2008) in the United States. So Tata Chemicals has a competitive disadvantage in size and the benefits that size brings relative to the major global competitors.

A final competitive advantage that indirectly helps the chemicals division is the diversification across sectors that gives Tata the ability to weather storms in any particular segment of its overall business in comparison with those more focused rivals. This diversification helps the Tata Group overall to deal with the ups and downs of different product areas, including the flexibility to leave some businesses and to enter new ones. Tata Chemical's fit into global value-added chains is sketched in Figure 4.4.

FIGURE 4.4   Tata's fit into the global chemicals value-added chain

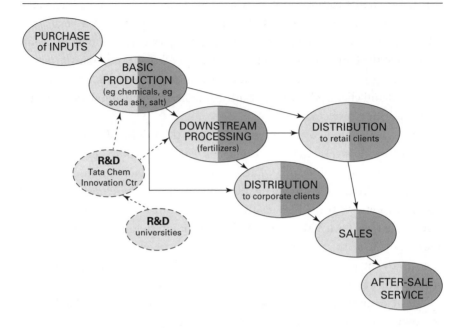

Tata Chemical historically has fit into global value chains as a producer of commodity chemicals such as salt and soda ash – and Tata Group overall has also followed this initial path. In recent years several of the divisions in the group, including chemicals, have entered into more sophisticated product lines and more R&D-based competition. In chemicals, this refers particularly to development of fertilizers; in steel it refers to design and production of automotive and construction applications. With the growth of Tata Automotive, the firm has taken a step further into differentiated manufactures – though even here Tata is best known for its inexpensive, no-frills Nano vehicle. And even Tata Consultancy Services in the services sector has traditionally been known for back-office, business process out-sourcing – TCS is now engaged as well in new IT software development.

SABMiller (South Africa)

SABMiller is the world's second largest beer brewer after Anheuser-Busch InBev, producing about 10 per cent of total world consumption of beer. The company began as Castle Breweries, and subsequently South African Breweries (SAB) in 1895, and then took on the current name with the acquisition of Miller Brewing in the United States in 2002.[8] The company's primary stock listing is on the London Stock Exchange, with a secondary listing on the Johannesburg Stock Exchange.

SABMiller developed a dominant position in the South African market during the Apartheid era (1948–94), when many countries established boycotts against the country and its companies. With very little possibility to expand overseas, SAB was allowed to acquire other beer brands in South Africa, and by acquiring Ohlssons and Chandlers Union it became an almost monopolistic supplier of beer in the domestic market. Additionally, SAB acquired glass production facilities in the upstream direction of the industry and even pubs for selling beer in the downstream direction. This dominant position enabled SAB to generate high profits and a cash base that ultimately positioned the company to expand overseas when the opportunity arose.

SABMiller certainly has low production costs in the many emerging markets where the firm operates, but relative to competitors in those markets, SABMiller does not necessarily have a cost advantage. Through careful attention to the details of production and distribution of beer, SABMiller has established a low-cost capability that gives the company a cost advantage even over other beer producers in the domestic markets where they compete. Economies of scale in producing beer are not the source of the cost advantage, but rather a superior ability to operate the overall supply chain has proven to exist for SABMiller.

As the world beer market has been consolidating over the past two decades, brewers such as Heineken, Anheuser-Busch InBev and SABMiller have been pushing brands internationally. Previously, most beer sold around the world was local brands. Today, SABMiller sells a significant portion of its brands, Miller, Castle, Grolsch and Carling Black Label in particular, across national borders. Even so, most of its brands are local in the various countries/regions where SABMiller operates. The leaders of the company emphasize SABMiller's strategic orientation to provide local brands in the many markets where they operate, rather than to focus on global brands.

As far as markets are concerned, SABMiller is present in most of the world's main beer markets, with leadership positions in China, Africa and some Latin American countries (not Mexico or Brazil), and large market shares in the United States, European Union and India. Through its joint venture with China Resources Enterprises in China, SABMiller has the leading market share in that country, and the world's leading beer brand, Snow.

Competitive advantages for SABMiller relative to Anheuser-Busch InBev and Heineken include existing customer links and distribution channels in Africa, lower operational costs than the two large rivals globally (though

FIGURE 4.5 SABMiller in global beer value-added chain

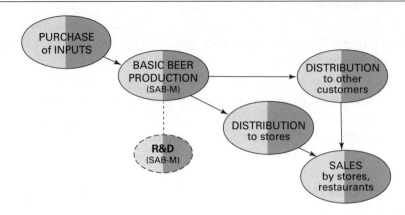

not relative to some local competitors in individual countries), and leadership in the enormous and rapidly growing China market through its joint venture there.

SABMiller fits into a global value-added chain for beer production and distribution as shown in Figure 4.5.

The company's leaders emphasize that beer is a very 'operational' business, with cost structure as a major driver of performance. SABMiller's ability to achieve very low costs in production and distribution of beer in its various markets is seen as a key competitive advantage.

As with a number of other beer companies around the world, SABMiller is also involved with distributing cola beverages, in this case Coca-Cola, in several African countries. In this value-added chain for colas, SABMiller fits purely as a distributor, with bottling, warehousing, trucks and other facilities that take the Coca-Cola from syrup to bottled beverage, and ships it to stores in the countries where SABMiller has the distribution contract.[9]

Grupo Bimbo (Mexico)

Grupo Bimbo was the world's largest baking company in 2013, with 2012 annual global sales of over $US 13 billion and more than 100,000 employees, mostly outside the company's home country, Mexico. With Bimbo's acquisitions of Westin Foods' bakeries in 2008 and Sara Lee's bakery division in 2010, Bimbo became the global leader.

Costs are extremely important in this low-tech business, so Bimbo has had to develop world-leading cost controls in its production and distribution of bread and other bakery products. Operations in low-cost emerging markets help with Bimbo's operational cost control, but with half of the company's total business in the United States, the real advantage comes from superior management of production and distribution. From bread ovens to trucks that carry baked goods to stores, Bimbo has achieved a leading position.

On the revenue side, Bimbo has been very successful in the large US market, with about half of its global sales there. This means that, while future expansion may focus on emerging markets, the expansion that brought Bimbo to world leadership in baked goods was primarily into the United States. Very notably, the distribution system in the United States is predominantly to large supermarkets, rather than to small mom & pop grocery stores as in Mexico. So Bimbo has had to develop strengths in two very different distribution chains, though in both cases using its fleet of dedicated trucks to deliver the bread to clients, and aiming to minimize production costs in its bakeries.

Bimbo's competitive advantages in Mexico relative to local rivals as well as global competitors such as Kraft Foods and Continental Baking/Hostess include a highly vertically integrated value-added chain, in which Bimbo owns suppliers of agricultural inputs (flour and sugar), as well as machinery manufacturing for baking equipment and plastic manufacture for wrapping bread and other baked products.[10] The firm also has a fleet of delivery trucks that dwarfs the distribution capabilities of competitors in Mexico. With this value-added chain, Bimbo has been able to survive the various economic crises in Mexico over the past 50 years, when price controls sometimes were imposed on bread sales, access to flour was limited due to government regulations and competitors' strategies, and external financing became very expensive or even unavailable during financial crises. Bimbo has been able to profit from non-bread businesses when bread faces difficulties, from access to raw materials through its owned suppliers, and through access to funding from internal sources in its diversified group.

Bimbo's competitive advantages relative to Kraft Foods and Yamazaki from Japan internationally arise largely from the company's successes in acquiring market-leading bread companies overseas (such as Orowheat, Wonder Bread and Sara Lee Baking in the United States), and then from managing human resources as well as bread production relatively more effectively than these international rivals.

Bimbo fits into a global value-added chain as the purchaser of enormous quantities of wheat flour and other baking inputs, as the producer of the baked goods, and then as supplier to grocery stores and supermarkets which then sell to ultimate consumers. Bimbo does not own farms that produce the wheat and other grains that go into its baked goods, nor does it own grocery stores that sell its bread, pastries and so on to the final consumers. The firm

FIGURE 4.6 Bimbo's value-added chain

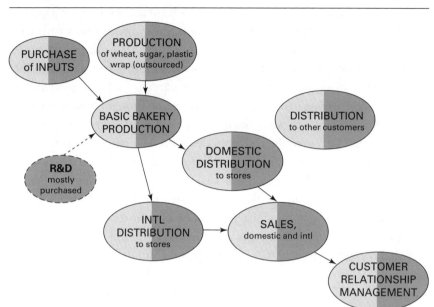

concentrates on basic bakery production and on distribution of baked goods to stores, though historically it has been involved in wheat and sugar farming.

Bimbo's value-added chain for bakery goods is shown in Figure 4.6.

The key competitive strengths of Bimbo are not obvious from the figure, since the company is largely gaining advantage from superior management of production and distribution of bread, rather than by achieving larger-scale economies or technological advantages over rivals.

Conclusions

All of these examples of successful international companies based in emerging markets demonstrate the key element of their links into global value-added chains. In most instances these companies also demonstrate a different entry into those value-added chains in contrast to US and European multinationals, since their strengths tend to come from domestic market domination and the ability to deal successfully with the distribution process in each industry. These emerging market multinationals all demonstrate an ability to adapt rapidly to changing circumstances, whether it be a financial crisis, a major new competitor or a declining business activity. These firms have shown great agility in responding to conditions that affect them in domestic as well as international markets, and this agility may enable them to build sustainable global positions into the future.

These companies will challenge global competitors for leadership in their industries into the 21st century, as more and more importance is attached to a company's ability to move rapidly into new technologies and value chain configurations. Agile firms may just as well come from emerging markets as from the Triad countries, and the emerging market firms may have an advantage of needing to be flexible to survive in their home countries even before competing internationally.

Notes

1 CNPC is the sole sponsor and controlling shareholder of PetroChina. It is a large petroleum and petrochemical corporate group, established in July 1998, in accordance with Plan for the Organizations Structure Reform of the State Council. CNPC is a large state-owned enterprise managed by the investment organs authorized by the state and State-owned Assets Supervision and Administration Commission. (http://www.petrochina.com.cn/Ptr/About_ PetroChina/Company_Profile/)

2 See Chairman Jiang's statement in: http://www.businessweek.com/news/ 2012-03-29/petrochina-annual-profit-misses-estimates-after-refining-losses

3 PetroChina participates in RIPED along with parent company CNPC. The research centre has over 2,000 scientists and engineers working on a wide range of scientific issues and collaborating with Peking University in academic research. See http://riped.cnpc.com.cn/ripeden/index.shtml

4 For more insight into PetroChina, see the company webpage, http:// www.petrochina.com.cn/ptr/. Also see http://www.chinese-champions.com/ petrochina/

5 It should be noted that Embraer benefited greatly from foreign technology, brought in by engineers hired from US and European universities and companies. It also gained manufacturing experience by producing under licence an Italian aeroplane, the Aermacchi, in 1970 and for several subsequent years. And it later manufactured aeroplane parts (wing flaps, wingtip fairing, and other parts) for both Boeing and McDonnell Douglas in the United States. Even so, the goal of Embraer was and remains to build Brazilian-designed and produced aircraft. See Rodengen (2009).

6 The incredibly tortuous process of coming near to bankruptcy and then achieving privatization and finally becoming profitable a couple of years later is described in Rodengen (2009, ch 6).

7 Additional insight into Hon Hai/Foxconn's strategy can be gained from http://www.foxconn.com/GroupProfile_En/GroupProfile.html

8 When SAB purchased Miller, the seller was Philip Morris tobacco company (now Altria). As part of the exchange Altria obtained 36 per cent of the shares of SABMiller (now down to 27 per cent), and it remains by far the largest shareholder in SABMiller today.

9 A useful discussion of SABMiller's growth, performance and strategy appears in Makura (2012, ch 1).

10 This section is based significantly on Moreno-Lázaro (nd) [online] (http://www.economia.unam.mx/cladhe/registro/ponencias/482_abstract.pdf)

References

Chattopadhyay, A, Batra, R and Ozsomer, A (2012) *The new emerging market multinationals*, McGraw-Hill, New York

Chen, M-J, Zimath, A, Maat, A *et al* (2007) *Embraer: Shaking up the aircraft manufacturing market*, University of Virginia case #UV0802

Chittoor, R, Narain, A, Vyas, R and Tolia, C (2013) *Creating a corporate advantage: The case of the Tata Group*, Indian School of Business case #ISB005 (February)

Contractor, F (2013) 'Punching above their weight': The sources of competitive advantage for emerging market multinationals, *International Journal of Emerging Markets*, 8(4), pp 304–28

Dyck, A and Huang, Y (2004) *PetroChina*, Harvard Business School case #9-701-040 (rev. June)

Guillén, M and García-Canal, E (2012) *Emerging markets rule: Growth strategies of the new global giants*, McGraw-Hill, New York

Makura, M (2012) *Going global: Insights from South Africa's top companies*, MME Media, Johannesburg

Moreno-Lázaro, J (nd) Spanish emigration and the setting-up of a great company in Mexico: Bimbo 1903–2008 [Online] http://www.economia.unam.mx/cladhe/registro/ponencias/482_abstract.pdf

Ramamurti, R (2012) What is really different about emerging market multinationals? *Global Strategy Journal*, **2**, pp 41–47

Rodengen, J (2009) *The history of Embraer*, Write Stuff Enterprises, Fort Lauderdale, FL

Sauvant, K (2008) *The rise of transnational corporations from emerging markets*, Edward Elgar, Cheltenham

Siegel, J (2009) *Grupo Bimbo*, Harvard Business School case #9-707-521 (August)

Xu, M (2010) *The truth behind Foxconn*, Zhejiang University Press, Hangzhou, China

Competing in emerging markets

05

What to expect in Chapter 5

There are many challenges facing Triad companies that seek to operate in emerging markets, not the least of which is the entrenched position of a local rival company. Local leaders in many business sectors have well-established distribution channels and relations with key clients, as well as explicit or implicit support from the government. These may be high hurdles for Triad multinationals that seek to enter these markets.

Certainly one logical way to reduce the barriers to entry in an emerging market is for the foreign multinational to buy an existing local company (or form a joint venture with one), so that local relationships are obtained immediately. Several of the companies discussed here have done precisely this: Telefónica buying Motorola's mobile phone business in Mexico; ICBC buying a significant part of Standard Bank in South Africa; Repsol buying YPF in Argentina; and Walmart trying to build a base in India through a joint venture with Bharti.

High-tech firms often use wholly owned subsidiaries to build their business in an emerging market, as in the cases of Novartis in Russia and Google in China (though this strategy has not worked out for Google thus far).

The stories of all of these multinationals in large emerging markets are really rollercoaster rides through competition with local companies and government regulation that appears and sometimes disappears in ways that are very difficult to anticipate.

The challenges of operating in emerging markets

For companies originating in the United States, Europe or Japan, competing in emerging markets has long been viewed as a challenge. This is due to weaker infrastructure conditions, greater government involvement in the economy, and local monopolies or limited competition due to historically protected companies having a well-entrenched advantage – not to speak of the lower per capita incomes that characterize these countries. While this view is not completely incorrect, it is becoming less accurate every day. Countries such as those in most of Central/Eastern Europe are now recognized as advanced industrial markets, with rules and competitors increasingly similar or identical to those in Western Europe. Some of them, such as the Czech Republic and Slovenia, have joined the European Union and are clearly recognized as 'emerged' markets. While a country such as South Africa may retain aspects and areas with less developed characteristics, its three major cities are clearly part of the advanced industrial world economy.

In fact, the main criterion that may be identified today which still differentiates emerging markets from Triad countries is the greater likelihood of changes in rules and changes in government's role in the economy in the emerging markets. This parallels the fact that emerging market companies tend to be capable of more rapid adaptation to change than their Triad counterparts. In fact, adaptability is often a core competency of emerging markets firms, which tend to be more diversified as well as more flexible than their counterparts elsewhere.

One indicator of a company's willingness to adapt to changing circumstances is its accumulated decisions to enter new businesses. A greater number of businesses in which a company operates implies a greater openness to enter into activities outside the firm's original or central activity. A clothing manufacturer may expand into operating retail stores, or a petrol station may decide to operate a convenience store. Or a beer company may move into soft drinks, or a transportation company may move into telecommunications service. The diversification may be horizontal (to new locations) as well as vertical (upstream or downstream in the value-added chain), and it may be into related activities or unrelated ones. Table 5.1 shows a simple comparison of the degree of product/sector diversification of the largest 25 companies in key emerging markets and Triad countries.

TABLE 5.1 Degree of diversification of the 25 largest local firms

Country/company*	Brazil	China	India	Russia	South Africa	Mexico	USA	Germany	Japan
1	Petrobras 3	China Petroleum & Chemical 6	IOC 6	Gazprom 5	SASOL 5	América Móvil/ Grupo Carso 11	Wal-Mart Stores 1	Volks wagen Group 3	Toyota Motor 1
2	Banco Bradesco 2	Petro China 4	Reliance Industries Ltd. 6	Lukoil 5	MTN Group 4	Femsa 3	Exxon Mobil 3	EON 5	JX Holdings 9
3	Vale 3	China Mobile 1	BPCL 3	Rosneft 4	The Bidvest Group 5	ALFA 5	Chevron 4	Daimler 2	Nippon Telegraph & Tel 2
4	Odebrecht 11	Industrial & Commercial Bank of China 1	HPCL 4	TNK-BP Holding 4	Eskom 9	Cemex 3	Phillips 66 4	Allianz 2	Hitachi 11
5	JBS Friboi 6	Agricultural Bank of China 2	SBI 1	Sberbank 2	Shoprite Holdings 4	Grupo Bimbo 2	Apple 4	BASF 5	Nissan Motor 1
6	Ultrapar 4	Bank of China 2	Essar Oil 3	Sistema 15	Sanlam 3	Grupo Mexico 3	Berkshire Hathaway 12	Siemens 6	Honda Motor 2
7	Gerdau 1	China Construction Bank 1	ONGC 3	Surgutneftegas 3	Vodacom 2 Group	Soriana 2	General Motors 1	BMW Group 2	Panasonic 4
8	Eletrobras 1	China Life Insurance 1	MRPL 3	Transneft 1	Imperial Holdings 5	GFNorte 3	General Electric 15	Munich Re 4	Sony 5
9	Embraer 1	China Telecom 2	NTPC 5	IDGC Holding 3	Pick'n pay Stores Holdings 9	Industrias Peñoles (part of BAL)	Valero Energy 2	Metro Group 3	Toshiba 3
10	Itausa 9	Baoshan Iron & Steel 8	Larsen 5	Inter Rao 1	Steinhoff Intl Holdings 6	Grupo Modelo (part of AB Inbev)	Ford Motor 1	Deutsche Telekom 4	Toyota Tsusho 3

TABLE 5.1 *continued*

Country/company*	Brazil	China	India	Russia	South Africa	Mexico	USA	Germany	Japan
11	Ipiranga 3	China Communications Construction 4	Tata Group 5	VTB Bank 1	Massmart Holdings 4	Grupo Carso (see Amer Movil)	Fannie Mae 1	Deutsche Post 4	Mitsubishi Corp 13
12	CPFL Energia 1	Lenovo Group 3	BHEL 4	X5 Retail Group 1	Edcon 4	Grupo Televisa 4	AT&T 3	RWE Group 5	Tokyo Electric Power 1
13	Telemar (Oi) 1	China United Telecommunications 1	GAIL 5	Magnit 1	Impala Platinum 2	Grupo Elektra 4 (part of Salinas)	McKesson 2	Deutsche Bank 3	Aeon 1
14	Banco do Brasil 2	CNOOC 2	Bharti Airtel 1	Severstal 5	SAPPI 3	El Puerto de Liverpool 2	CVS Caremark 3	Bayer 3	Mitsui & Co 2
15	BRF Foods 2	Ping An Insurance 2	SAIL 2	Tatneft 3	Barloworld 3	Mexichem 3	Hewlett-Packard 3	ThyssenKrupp Group 5	Mitsubishi UFJ Financial
16	Braskem 1	Foxconn Intl Holdings 1	Chennai Petro 4	Norilsk Nickel 2	De Beers Consolidated Mines 5	Arca Continental 3	Verizon Communications 3	Continental 2	Seven & I Holdings 4
17	Pao de Acucar 1	Minmetals Development 3	PNB 1	Novolipetsk Steel 3	Anglogold Ashanti 2	Grupo Inbursa (part of Carso)	United Health Group 2	Deutsche Lufthansa 5	Dai-ichi Life Insurance 1
18	Votorantim 7	PICC Property & Casualty 1	M&M 11	Mechel 6	Transnet 5	Grupo Comercial Chedraui 2	JP Morgan Chase 2	Talanx 3	Fujitsu 3
19	CSN 4	China Resources 3	ICICI Bank 2	Rus Hydro 1	Spar Group 6	Mabe 2	Cardinal Health 2	Celesio 3	Marubeni 1
20	Cemig 1	China Shenhua Energy 3	Infosys 2	UC Rusal 3	Aveng 7	Grupo BAL 7	IBM 4	Commerzbank 2	Idemitsu Kosan 8

TABLE 5.1 *continued*

Country/company*	Brazil	China	India	Russia	South Africa	Mexico	USA	Germany	Japan
21	Cosan 4	Aluminum Corp. of China 2	JSW Steel 2	Rostelecom 3	Telkom 3	CFE 2	Costco Wholesale 1	Fresenius 4	Itochu 2
22	Marfrig 4	TPV Technology 1	Bank of Baroda 2	MegaFon 1	Naspers 4	Alpek (part of Alfa)	Bank of America 2	EnBW-Energie Baden 4	Nippon Steel & Sumitomo Metal 3
23	Usiminas 3	Angang New Steel 1	Hindalco Industries 2	Magnitogorsk Iron & Steel 2	Murray & Roberts 6	Grupo Salinas 8	Kroger 4	TUI 3	Sumitomo Mitsui Financial 1
24	Sabesp 3	Bank of China Hong Kong Holdings 1	Coal India 1	Novatek 2	Grindrod 6	Grupo Maseca (Gruma) 2	Express Scripts 1	Henkel 3	Mitsubishi Electric 2
25	Porto Seguro 2	China COSCO Holdings 3	Adani Enterprises 3	Aeroflot-Russian Airlines 1	Datatec 3	Grupo Industrial Lala 2	Wells Fargo 3	SAP 1	KDDI 1
26					Woolworths	Infonavit (govt)			
27					Allied Electronics	Coppel 3			
Average	3.20	2.36	3.44	3.12	4.60	3.55	2.68	3.44	3.4

* Company names and the number of sectors in which they do business are shown. Companies are ranked by annual sales in 2012. Sectors are defined as 4-digit ISIC categories.
SOURCE: Compiled by the author using data from Fortune Global 500, annual reports and other sources

This table shows that the large emerging market companies tend to be more diversified than their US counterparts, though the Chinese firms show even greater focus than all others. The implication is that these companies (except the Chinese) are more flexible to adjust their business activities when unexpected shocks such as financial crises or new technologies or political events occur. This flexibility is likewise notable in the changing portfolios of businesses that emerging market companies tend to hold over time. With the exceptions of state-owned, single-industry companies, these emerging market companies often evolve into and out of a variety of business sectors over time. Interestingly, the German and Japanese companies are more similar to the emerging market companies in being more diversified than the US (and UK) and Chinese firms.

Specific barriers to entry

The main constraints faced by Triad companies entering emerging markets, to greatly simplify, are differences in the rules of the game, and entrenched competitors who have raised various barriers to entry. The rules of business operation, as suggested in Table A5.1 in the Appendix, are restrictive in a variety of ways in emerging markets. These restrictions are not necessarily the kinds that MNEs face in the Triad countries, particularly with respect to limits on foreign ownership. In addition, entrenched competitors in Triad countries may have established strong customer relationships and dominance in channels of distribution; what is often different in emerging markets is the degree of monopoly power of local competitors. This market power may stem from the nature of the business – for example, a formerly state-owned enterprise that maintains its monopoly on some utility service such as water or gas provision or electric power service. Or it may come from the local firm building up relationships with local transport companies that are able to keep out a foreign potential entrant. Or it may even come from associations of local companies that lobby the government to keep out foreign competitors.

Probably the number one barrier to entry facing foreign firms in emerging markets is rules favouring domestic firms, or alternatively, rules prohibiting activities of foreign firms. In China, foreign car manufacturers must accept a Chinese partner if they want to manufacture locally, and the Chinese partner must own at least 50 per cent of the venture. In South Africa, foreign firms are not allowed to provide fixed-line telephone service in competition with the national champion, Telkom. In Brazil, after discovery of enormous oil reserves off the coast in the Atlantic Ocean in 2007, new rules are restricting production of oil from those new fields to Petrobras, the national oil company, and excluding foreign (and other domestic) firms from this activity. In India, foreign firms are prohibited from operating in insurance, real estate purchase/ sale, tobacco-related businesses and gambling activities. These are just a handful of the kinds of blanket restriction facing foreign companies that want to operate in emerging markets, and they illustrate the wide range of activities that are affected (with more details shown in the Appendix to this chapter).

An interesting almost counter-example is Mexico. When entering the close-by Mexican market, a US bank or accounting firm will find a range of entrenched local and multinational banks and accountancies already operating there, with strong links to attractive clients and some with access to the government to request help in fending off new competitors (eg through administrative barriers or creation of new rules on operations that would favour existing competitors). Until the 1994–95 Mexican financial crisis, the three local banks (Banamex, Bancomer and Banca Serfin) dominated that sector, and foreign banks were limited to a maximum of six branches and faced many other restrictions as well. Now Citibank owns Banamex, and the Spanish banks BBVA and Banco Santander own Bancomer and Serfin, respectively. These banks operate thousands of branches throughout the country, and they would certainly look for ways to make it difficult for other foreign entrants to chip away at their market positions. Accounting firms in Mexico likewise have joined forces with global leaders, so that the largest public accounting firms in Mexico today are KPMG, PwC, Ernst & Young and Deloitte – just as in the United States and in many other countries.[1] They have raised barriers to entry by other international firms through their long-standing relationships with prime Mexican clients and their regular interactions with the government of Mexico.

Table A5.1 in the Appendix shows some of the key legislative barriers to entry and operation for foreign companies in selected emerging markets. What is most different from Triad countries' rules and regulations is that these emerging markets present far more restrictions on foreign ownership of companies, and often also on those companies' ability to move funds into and out of the country.

An aspect of competing in emerging markets or foreign countries in general is that the home-country firm's leaders and managers do not know the host country conditions, people, relationships and so on as well as local firms' leaders and managers do. This is an easy barrier to overcome for the foreign MNE: you just have to hire local people who possess that knowledge. So, when a company such as General Electric enters a new market or business, the logical way to do so is by acquiring an existing company, along with the knowledge and skills possessed by the people in that company. The acquisition gives GE all of the benefits of being a local firm – except ownership, which is sometimes subject to restrictions as noted above. The key point is that much of the knowledge of local institutions and markets resides in the people who work there, and frequently foreign companies either acquire existing local companies with that knowledge or hire local managers and executives who likewise possess that knowledge.

Next, we turn to some specific examples of foreign companies and their challenges when trying to compete in an emerging market.

Example: competing in China

Companies from many industries have reported a wide range of experiences in their attempts to compete in China, with the most common refrain being that it is very difficult to make money in China. This is partly because the government restricts foreign companies from many activities, partly because government-owned companies dominate a number of important sectors, and partly due to the foreign companies' general lack of knowledge about the informal institutions that make up the Chinese business environment. From GM which is restricted to producing cars for local sale through a 50 per cent owned joint venture with a Chinese-owned partner to Citibank which is limited to providing financial services that make up far less than 1 per cent of the Chinese market, foreign companies are quite constrained.

An interesting example of a different kind of complexity in dealing with the Chinese market is experienced by Google, which entered China in 1999 to offer its search engine – but just as it does in any other country, with its operation actually based at Google headquarters in California. The company was not initially limited in ownership or control of its business, and by 2002 it was estimated that Google was used in approximately 25 per cent of searches in China. Later that year, Google found its search engine knocked offline for two weeks and subsequently the website encountered a bewildering series of difficulties in its operation. The company discovered that the Chinese government had placed physical barriers to access of google.com for users in China, such that the search engine operated slowly and frequently stopped with a 'page not available' screen. It turned out that this was due to Google's failure to censor content that the Chinese government viewed as unacceptable, chiefly political statements contrary to government interests and pornography.

Not unrelated, a Chinese internet search service, Baidu, had been launched in 2002, and its 3 per cent market share at the end of that year trailed Google by a long distance. Over the following three years, Baidu built up a highly successful search operation, taking a 52 per cent market share in China, while Google languished with a share that still remained at about 25 per cent. Despite Google's efforts to improve the Chinese language interface, and to offer additional services to Chinese users, it was clear that the US-based search engine, partially blocked by the Chinese government, was not going to enable Google to establish a leading market position.

By 2005 Google's Chinese users found that the site was down over 10 per cent of the time, Google News was permanently unavailable, and Google Images worked only about half the time. So in 2006 Google launched google.cn, a local website that was censored by Google to try to comply with the Chinese government's bans on various kinds of content. This step caused an uproar in the United States against Google, with its motto of 'do no evil', since Google was in fact now censoring content from its users.[2] Apart from the US backlash, google.cn enabled Google to try to build up its market share in the constrained Chinese market.

In 2010 Google decided to stop offering google.cn service, owing to the continuing Chinese government-imposed censorship of access to information. Google basically abandoned the market to Baidu and others, choosing instead to retreat to a Hong Kong base, and to offer google.com's global service from there at google.com.hk. By 2013 Google had fallen to a market share of search in China of 3 per cent, far behind Baidu's 66 per cent and even 360 Search's 17 per cent.[3]

A key lesson from this experience is that a foreign MNE trying to compete in an emerging market is subject to the sovereign preferences of the host government, as well as to pressure groups there. The question of legitimacy of the company is always fundamental to the ability to compete, and Google's legitimacy was challenged in China by both the government and local competitors. For Google, trying to fit China into its global value-added chain has proven very difficult, and still without a solution in 2015. If you think about the overall Google value chain for its various services, perhaps the company could use China as a supply source for software, and/or equipment used by Google in other countries. And the Chinese market could potentially be entered more successfully through a joint venture with a local search company, operating under Chinese rules and under a Chinese name. The story of this 21st-century business in the most dynamic economy of that century is far from over.

Example: competing in Mexico

Mexico's telephone system was privatized in 1990 with the sale of controlling ownership of Teléfonos de Mexico (Telmex) to a consortium consisting of Carlos Slim's Grupo Carso, Southwestern Bell and France Telecom.[4] This process itself is worthy of much more detailed analysis,[5] but our interest is in more recent times. During 1990–96, Telmex maintained a legal monopoly on fixed-line phone service in Mexico and also launched mobile phone service under the name América Móvil. By the end of the decade, the sector was partially opened up to new competitors, which entered mainly in the segment of mobile phone service.

The Spanish telephone multinational, Telefónica, entered the Mexican market in 2001, long after the privatization of Telmex, as well as after the entry of local Mexican mobile phone service providers Iusacell (in 1989) and Axtel (in 1999).[6] Telefónica stated the intention to build a Latin American network of affiliates, led by Brazil and Mexico. This 'reconquest' of Latin America was similar to strategies of other Spanish multinationals, particularly in utilities such as electric power (Endesa; Iberdrola) and water (Aguas de Barcelona; Acciona Agua), services such as banking (Banco Santander; BBVA), insurance (Mapfre; Prosegur), hotels (Sol Melia; NH Hoteles) and also oil and gas (Repsol; Fenosa).[7] Telefónica had built an approximate mobile phone market share of 12 per cent by 2012, with more than 22 million customers, operating under the brand name Movistar.

The telecom sector, since it is a utility business similar to electric power provision and water service, has long been either owned by the government or highly regulated. In the case of telecoms, Mexico's government established rules at the point of privatizing Telmex that its ownership must remain in majority Mexican (private-sector) hands. For this reason, Carlos Slim's group was permitted to win the auction of Telmex at privatization, and then to continue to hold the majority voting power in Telmex to date. This monopolistic power for Telmex has made it very difficult for other domestic and foreign competitors to build their businesses, since Telmex has been able to create and maintain barriers along the way. For example, even in 2012 Telmex was able to charge very high interconnection fees for the mobile phone operators to connect to Telmex's fixed-line local telephones in Mexico – despite demands by the World Trade Organization for over a decade to open up this business, and legal procedures by mobile phone operators to try to force Telmex to reduce those fees.[8]

This example of Telefónica's challenges to operating in Mexico illustrates the problems encountered by public utility companies, where service is important to the national economy, and where the industry is characterized by the monopolistic reality that there is room really for one or a small number of competitors. Telefónica had by 2013 gained greater access to the mobile phone market in Mexico, but the inherent preference of Mexico's government for domestic providers of this service is a continuing barrier to the foreign company. Even so, domestic providers of mobile phone service such as Axtel and Iusacell find themselves allied with Telefónica in their attempts to break the monopoly power of Carlos Slim's group, so the challenge is really for all phone companies other than Telmex/América Móvil in the Mexican market.

Looking at Mexico in Telefónica's global array of businesses and its value-added chain, it appears that the domestic mobile phone market may be moving towards a regulatory situation in which the company can take a major market share and compete successfully not only with Telmex/América Móvil, but also with the other domestic Mexican mobile phone service providers. At the same time as this battle is fought, it makes sense for Telefónica to be looking at Mexico as a possible site for sourcing equipment and other supplies, since costs there are much lower than in Spain or the European Union more generally. And Telefónica can pursue Mexican corporate clients to provide in-house telecommunications services separate from operating the mobile phone network that is open to all clients.

Example: competing in South Africa

South Africa has long presented a relatively open environment for private-sector business, and foreign business as well. From allowing major companies such as Anglo-American (platinum and diamond mining) and South African Breweries (now SABMiller) to list their shares on the London Stock Exchange and move legal headquarters there, to willingness to allow Barclays to buy the third largest bank (ABSA) and foreign car companies to operate freely, the South African government during and after Apartheid has demonstrated a very British approach to dealing with business. This is not to deny that there are populist pressures in the country; there clearly are, from calls to nationalize mining companies to general opposition to large white- and black-owned businesses ranging from AngloGold Ashanti gold mining to Cyril Ramaphosa's BEE (black economic empowerment) company, Shanduka, which has stakes in Bidvest, MTN, Standard Bank and Mondi, among other major companies.

Recently HSBC, based in London, entered into a process to potentially acquire Nedbank, the fourth of the four major banking groups based in

South Africa. This acquisition would have been the second foreign takeover in the group, after Barclays purchased ABSA in 2005. The Nedbank opportunity arose from the global financial crisis, when Nedbank's majority shareholder, Old Mutual, a London-based financial group (with roots in South Africa), was forced to increase its capital base and thus had to sell some of its assets. The acquisition did not go through, when HSBC discovered in its due diligence process that Nedbank's financial position was not strong enough to justify the proposed £4.38 billion purchase price.

This situation demonstrates the *de facto* openness of South Africa to foreign investment in its major banks, up to and including the largest one, Standard Bank, as described below. The Nedbank saga may end with another foreign bank deciding to buy out the Old Mutual position, but as of 2014 this had not yet happened. It appears that Old Mutual resolved its capital needs to satisfy regulators even without divesting Nedbank, so the bank looks to remain one of Old Mutual's key divisions along with insurance in the future.

A very interesting counter-example is the acquisition in 2007 of 20 per cent of Standard Bank by the Chinese giant, ICBC. In this case the bank (Standard Bank) had no capital inadequacy problems or major financial needs, but it was interested in building business with China and internationally in more general terms. With Standard Bank's footprint throughout Africa (operations in 32 countries of the continent), the idea of having a Chinese key investor/partner means that the bank can offer financial services to Chinese clients of that investor. ICBC, as the largest bank in China and one of the largest in the world, is interested in building its business in other emerging market regions. To avoid the appearance of colonial-type expansion in the African region, it made sense for ICBC to acquire a significant position in a major African bank, and then to leverage that link to provide financial services to its own clients from China. ICBC effectively uses Standard Bank as a vehicle through which Chinese clients can obtain trade financing for their exports to Africa and general financing for their purchases of raw materials in African producing and exporting countries.

In 2007, during a short period of about three months, the deal was announced, South African government approval was given and the shares were sold to ICBC. This transaction turned out to be very helpful to Standard Bank when the financial crisis hit in 2009, since the bank was sitting on more than $US 2 billion of cash from the sale of shares to ICBC. As global investor confidence in financial institutions dropped dramatically and funding dried up, Standard Bank at least was able to mobilize those funds to carry out its investment and lending activities. Even without any US real estate exposure, Standard Bank was hit by the financial crisis, both from the stand-point of investors' lack of confidence in banks and also from South African clients becoming less creditworthy as their sales declined.

In sum the banking sector in South Africa has proven open to inter-national competition up to and including acquisition of the Big Four banks in the country. This is quite different from the rules in some other key emerg-ing markets such as China and India, where foreign banks are limited to peripheral roles in the financial system. It is similar to the experiences of Mexico and Chile, where foreign banks have been allowed to take leader-ship positions there. We shall see in the years ahead whether one or other of these approaches proves to be more successful for the countries' develop-ment and the companies' success.

As far as strategies for foreign MNE banks are concerned, it appears that the South African market is relatively open to foreign entry, including acquisition of large banks. The experience of Barclays showing that a large local bank can be completely acquired by foreign interests makes that point, and the partial acquisition of Standard Bank by ICBC reinforces it. Thus the possible acquisition of Nedbank by HSBC or another MNE banking giant is clearly feasible, and remains to be justified on the relevant financial and strategic criteria by a possible acquirer. The story is much different in electric power provision or telephone service, but financial services are quite open to competitors from any home country.

Example: competing in Argentina

The Spanish multinational oil and gas company, Repsol, entered Argentina in 1998, with the offer to buy just under 15 per cent of outstanding shares of Argentine oil company YPF. The government of Argentina, which at that point owned this amount, wanted to exit the company completely, having sold majority ownership of YPF in an initial public offering in 1993 to investors around the world (through listings in Buenos Aires and New York). This step was a vital part of Argentina's privatization programme, which led off with sales of the state-owned national airline (Aerolineas Argentinas) in 1990, telephone company (ENTEL, divided into Telecom and Telefónica Argentina) in 1990, and electric power company (Segba, divided into Edenor, Edesur, and others) in 1992.

The initial public offering (IPO) of YPF in 1993 was an extraordinary step in a highly politicized industry in a country renowned for populist policies over most of the second half of the 20th century. After the many failures of the statist system during 1970–90, the Menem government during 1990–2000 moved in an opposite direction, with a large measure of public support. The privatization of the 'crown jewel', the national oil company, was viewed as a major success in putting the economy on a competitive footing, eliminating waste and corruption, and generally moving Argentina towards the new century.[9] YPF operated for half a dozen years under Argentine managers and a widely dispersed set of shareholders on two stock exchanges.

After taking the first step to buy 15 per cent of YPF in 1998, Repsol made a tender offer for the remaining shares of YPF that were traded in Buenos Aires and New York, achieving a purchase of 98.23 per cent of total outstanding shares by June of 1999. The total purchase cost Repsol about $US 15 billion. This put a foreign investor in charge of a major national enterprise in Argentina – but no different from the outcomes of privatizing dozens of other companies, including the main utilities in the country during the 1990s.

Strategically, the YPF acquisition was a clear move by Repsol to obtain much greater oil resources. Repsol traditionally had been primarily a downstream oil company, focused on refining and on operation of petrol service stations around Spain. YPF's oil and gas reserves in Latin America (and some in the United States as well) provided Repsol with desired access to the raw materials that drive the industry. As far as risk goes, the acquisition also seemed to be a good step, since Argentina was clearly embarked on an open-market policy towards business.

The situation changed with the election of populist Nestor Kirchner as President of Argentina in 2003. His government moved the country to the left, not as far as Hugo Chavez in Venezuela, but generally anti-business overall. Kirchner's regime raised taxes on companies, renounced some of the foreign debts that had jumped in cost after the 2001 peso maxi-devaluation, and generally followed a populist path. He was succeeded as President in 2007 by his wife, Cristina Fernandez, who subsequently moved to limit farm price increases, to restrict press freedom and ultimately to renationalize YPF in 2013.

The renationalization of YPF was justified by the government on the grounds that YPF had not invested adequately in producing oil and gas from its reserves, and that the company had failed to produce sufficient benefits for Argentina. The reality is that with price controls on petrol, the company could not generate normal profits, and with the government's demand for YPF to pay most after-tax profits as dividends, there was less money available to invest in greater production of oil and gas.[10]

Repsol probably could not have anticipated the turn of events in Argentina during the Menem regime when the company purchased YPF in 1999. Once Nestor Kirchner won the election in 2003, Repsol could probably have seen problems on the horizon. This is a classic emerging markets problem, and one that returns to plague foreign multinationals from China to Argentina and many places in between. The anti-business position of the Kirchner/Fernandez governments would not have enabled Repsol to have avoided the nationalization through an alliance with local companies, since the regime has demonstrated a consistent opposition to private-sector business of domestic or foreign ownership. A possible strategy would have been to link YPF as extensively as possible to overseas sources of technology, markets, alliances and so on, to make the government's decision to renationalize the firm more costly. *Ex post*, this is clear, but even so, the political nature of the nationalization does not seem to have been based on any economic logic, so such a strategy very likely would not have helped.

It is difficult to see how Repsol could have fitted YPF better into its global value-added chain than what was done over the 13 years that Repsol controlled YPF. The best strategy for a foreign oil multinational in an emerging market is probably to assume that at some point populist or nationalist policies are likely to be imposed, and to design mechanisms to minimize the impact on the company's overall global business. This can be done through tying technology to foreign sources, as suggested above, and also through mundane steps such as importing equipment and other supplies, which could be cut off if the business environment deteriorated, and also by taking out political risk insurance. When oil is such a valuable commodity, and is traded so openly on world markets, the possessor of the oil has tremendous bargaining power. And since the sovereign government can change the rules on a foreign MNE, the company's bargaining position is not as strong as in other industries.

Example: competing in India

India has long been known to business for the 'Licence Raj', referring to the bureaucratic government style of requiring permits or licences for all kinds of business activity – and then taking months or longer to give the approval(s) in question. The system of requiring government approvals for many private-sector business activities was initiated by India's first elected Prime Minister, Jawaharlal Nehru, in 1947 at the time of Indian independence from the United Kingdom. The system grew to such an extreme that it virtually paralysed private-sector development in the 1950s and 1960s.[11] Some degree of economic opening was re-established in the 1990s, so that the Licence Raj is less of a hindrance to business today. And with India's growth of 7–10 per cent per year in the past two decades, clearly the stifling problem of bureaucracy has at least been diminished.[12]

Despite this change in broad policy towards business, many limitations do remain, especially with respect to foreign business. The case of Walmart, competing in large-scale retail stores, is particularly noteworthy in this regard. While many people in the United States bemoan the negative impact of Walmart stores on local small retailers,[13] the overall benefits of low prices and the wide range of products available from Walmart do provide net benefits to consumers relative to traditional small retail stores, which may offer more personalized service, but which cannot compete on either prices or product availability. In a consumer-benefit-maximization context, Walmart clearly wins. In the Indian case, the literally millions of small retail stores there have formed a sufficient lobby to push legislators not to offer the licence for Walmart to operate retail stores.

So, Walmart entered India in 2007 by establishing a 50–50 joint venture with the mobile phone giant, Bharti, and together they built 20 'cash-and-carry' wholesale stores across the country. This kind of operation allows the store to sell to retail vendors such as stores, hotels and restaurants, but not directly to final consumers. For six years Walmart pursued this strategy, while trying to work with Bharti to get the Licence Raj in New Delhi to allow them to open retail superstores on the usual Walmart format used in other countries. Ultimately, Walmart believed that a breakthrough had occurred in late 2012, but the permission to open foreign-owned retail stores came with a requirement to purchase at least 30 per cent of products from local small and medium-sized suppliers. This limit does not apply to Indian-owned stores, but it does preclude Walmart or the joint venture from opening to retail clients. In October 2013, Walmart announced the disbanding of its joint venture with Bharti. Bharti took complete control over the company Cedar Support Services, which it had jointly operated with Walmart, and Walmart took over the 20 cash-and-carry stores, still limited to wholesale business only.

Walmart announced that it has no plans for further expansion in India, and appears to be waiting for potential opening of the retail sector in the future, with a reduced local purchasing requirement, at least from small suppliers. This resistance to Walmart's entry might be attributed to the Indian hyper-regulation that has characterized the country since independence, though certainly less so during the past two decades. However, Walmart has faced similar resistance in the United States, when it seeks permission to open stores in new cities or regions and local retailers mount campaigns to oppose the big-box store. Sometimes Walmart has won such permission and sometimes it has lost, so the Indian case should not been seen as exceptional, other than that it affects potential Walmart operations in the whole country rather than in a local jurisdiction.

In the Indian case, Walmart hurt its own cause when the company disclosed to the US Senate in 2012 that it had spent about $US 5 million per year since 2008 in efforts to gain approvals for its overseas expansion in Mexico, China, Brazil and also India. Walmart had been accused of bribing Mexican government officials in its efforts to gain approvals for new store openings in that country; and US legislators pursued the issue with Walmart executives, leading to this disclosure. While it was not found that Walmart had bribed any government official in India, the negative publicity raised opposition to Walmart just at a time when it appeared that government approval of expansion into retail stores would finally be allowed.

Walmart did appear to have overcome any accusation of bribery in India, and the story faded away during 2013. However, Walmart was also accused of making an interest-free loan to Bharti, which would later be converted into equity. This transaction was criticized as a potential violation of foreign investment rules in India. It also led to a conclusion that Walmart had done nothing wrong, but the process cost Walmart more public relations problems and slowed down its effort to pursue the ultimate goal of retail sales in India.

Both India and China are very important countries for retail store chains such as Walmart, Carrefour, Metro and others. The growing incomes in both countries provide increasing numbers of potential customers for these stores' products. The low-cost environments also provide attractive locations to source products and services sold in other countries. There is no doubt that Walmart wants to find a solution to be a significant retail player in the Indian market, and also that it has not yet figured out that solution. Walmart also should be looking to Indian suppliers for goods that it can sell in its stores elsewhere, and thus build up the supply chain in this way.

Example: competing in Russia

Novartis, the Swiss pharmaceuticals and life science company, has found a challenging environment in Russia, where it has been operating for more than 100 years through its corporate predecessors – Ciba-Geigy and Sandoz

– that merged in 1996. Ciba began marketing its chemical products in Russia in 1876, and established a manufacturing facility in Russia in 1915. For a full century, however, the business of these companies was primarily sales of chemicals and pharmaceuticals in Russia, supported by R&D and manufacturing located primarily in its home base of Switzerland. The combined companies today produce a wide range of proprietary and generic pharmaceutical products, plus eye care products, vaccines and diagnostic tests, and animal health products.

After the fall of the Soviet Union and the economic opening in Russia, Novartis found the Russian domestic market sufficiently interesting, with about 140 million potential clients, that the firm considered expanding its activities there. For the first two decades of this period (namely, the 1990s and early 2000s), growth in Russia was provided primarily by increases in the sales team and in finding institutional clients such as hospitals and government agencies that purchase pharmaceuticals and Novartis' other products. Then in 2010 it was announced that Novartis would invest half a billion dollars in a pharmaceuticals manufacturing facility near St Petersburg.

This decision was not as simple as it sounds, because just prior to that time, the Russian government announced Pharma 2020, a project to build domestic Russian R&D and production of pharmaceuticals products and to reduce dependence on imports. The government programme set guidelines for localization of pharmaceuticals production, such that 50 per cent of pharmaceuticals sold in the country must be manufactured domestically by 2020. The explicit intent is to attract R&D activity and the development of new proprietary drugs in Russia.

So the Novartis decision to build a large plant near St Petersburg may appear to be more of a pull from the Russian authorities than a push from the company to expand its facilities there. At the same time, Novartis subsidiary Sandoz had announced in 2008 that it was looking to build a plant in Russia in the subsequent two years, to produce the generic pharmaceuticals that Sandoz sells worldwide.[14] The two intents seem to have converged – with the Russian government additionally looking to Novartis to establish some level of pharmaceutical R&D in the country, and perhaps in the St Petersburg plant in particular.

While the Russian government wants to stimulate domestic pharmaceuticals R&D, it is not insisting on local ownership of the companies. By 2013 the market shares of Russian-created proprietary pharmaceuticals were close to zero (see Table 5.2).

TABLE 5.2   Top-20 drug manufacturers by sales in the DRP segment in accordance with the '7 nosologies' and EDRP programmes

Rating of 2012	Manufacturer	Sales value, mln Rubles 2012	Ranking 2012	Manufacturer	Sales value, mln Rubles 2012
	7 nosologies			**EDRP**	
1	F. Hoffmann-La Roche	9,895.3	1	F. Hoffmann-La Roche	4,954.9
2	Janssen Pharmaceutic	5,110.0	2	Sanofi	3,628.2
3	Novartis	4,241.6	3	Novo Nordisk	2,812.3
4	Laboratory Tuteur	3,123.7	4	Merck	2,567.0
5	Teva Pharmaceutical	3,010.7	5	Astrazeneca	2,511.7
6	Baxter Healthcare	2,873.7	6	Eli Lilly	1,410.9
7	Pharmstandard	1,731.4	7	Boehringer Ingelheim	1,333.6
8	F-Sintez	1,132.7	8	Novartis	1,177.8
9	Genzyme Corporation	1,122.4	9	Janssen Pharmaceutica	1,126.0
10	Talecris Biotherapeutics	1,101.6	10	Servier	924.0
11	Octapharma	925.0	11	Teva Pharmaceutical	891.1
12	Bayer	808.7	12	Fresenius	840.8
13	Astellas Pharma	614.9	13	Krka	726.3
14	Biotest Pharma	588.9	14	Pharmstandard	687.5
15	Biocad	529.6	15	Glaxosmithkline	647.6
16	CSL Behring	454.7	16	F-Sintez	629.4
17	Sinnagen	204.9	17	Farmfirma Sotex	594.3
18	Generium	120.8	18	Abbott	537.4
19	Panacea Biotec	78.3	19	Farm-Sintez (Moscow)	535.9
20	Veropharm	39.6	20	Veropharm	524.6
Total		99.8%	Total		71.6%

EDRP: essential drug reimbursement programme
SOURCE: http://dsm.ru/content/file/annual_report_2012_eng.pdf p 46.

The government policy thus is to first establish some level of local R&D and presumably then to get locally owned companies into both R&D and production of these drugs. For Novartis to comply with the Pharma 2020 policy, it will have to increase its manufacturing presence in Russia – and the factory in St Petersburg is a solid first step in that direction.

Novartis had fitted their post-Soviet Russian operations into the value-added chain principally as a marketing venture, to sell pharmaceuticals created in Switzerland or in other research labs that the company operates in Triad countries. With the pressure from the Russian government, Novartis is now building a factory in St Petersburg to locally manufacture some generic drugs produced by subsidiary Sandoz. Some proprietary drugs will also be manufactured locally. It appears that local R&D activity will also be undertaken, though to maintain bargaining power against possible policy changes by the government, Novartis presumably will aim to keep the most fundamental R&D in Switzerland and other Triad countries.

Conclusions: tying together these experiences

These experiences of large Triad-based multinationals operating in large emerging markets show that there are often not simple or sustainable strategies that can serve over time to compete successfully there. Perhaps the examples shown here are too negative in their lessons, since none of these Fortune Global 500 companies has completely overcome the barriers to operating successfully in the countries, from Mexico to Russia. In contrast, there are plenty of examples of large companies that have gone into emerging markets and have succeeded impressively – for example, many of the multi-national car companies, aeroplane manufacturers and farm equipment companies. Certainly the high-tech electronics producers have maintained their global leadership, including emerging markets, in segments such as telephones, TVs and other consumer electronics products. And finally, there are many service-sector MNEs that have established strong positions in these same emerging markets.

So the conclusions to draw here are not that Triad-based firms cannot compete in emerging markets, but that some key barriers to success are proving difficult to overcome, even for the most experienced companies. Lessons to draw include recognizing that there are government-related barriers to entry and operation that will continue to burden foreign MNEs in many emerging markets. And also that the most attractive markets based on size – China and India – demonstrate a range of barriers to foreign company entry and expansion there. So, perhaps as has been said about China in many instances, you have to have a long-term horizon for success – because many obstacles are likely to pop up and make business difficult in the short run.

Notes

1   The accounting firms generally enter foreign markets by affiliating with local accountants in an existing firm. Then, often over time, the local group of accountants agrees to be part of the global partnership or other organizational structure of one of the Big Four.

2   See, for example, Wilson, Ramos and Harvey (2006).

3   See, for example, http://searchenginewatch.com/article/2280420/
Googles-Search-Market-Share-in-China-Falls-to-Just-3

4   France Telecom sold its ownership in 2000, partly to Carlos Slim's company and partly in a public offering. SBC continued to own 7.5% of Telmex until 2011, when it sold its share to Slim's company as well. (SBC changed its name to AT&T in 2005 when it acquired AT&T).

5   See, for example, Clifton, Diaz Fuentes and Marichal (nd).

6   The irony should not be missed that Telefónica, just like Telmex, was a state-owned monopoly in Spain, before economic opening there led to privatization (in 1997) and subsequent international expansion, especially in Latin America.

7   On Spanish multinationals in Latin America, see Guillén and García-Canal (2010).

8   A slight reduction in these fees occurred in 2012, while the legal battle continues. See, for example, http://www.reuters.com/article/2012/05/03/
us-americamovil-idUSBRE8421H320120503

9   See, for example, Grosse and Yañes (1998).

10   YPF cites two reasons why it has had to pay money out, rather than spend it on drill-heads. The first is that in 2007 the government concocted a scheme in which Enrique Eskenazi, a bank owner who had previously dealt with Kirchner, would buy a 15% stake in YPF (later raised to 25%). Because he put up precious little cash, the company and a group of banks lent him the money. YPF then agreed to dole out 90% of its subsequent profits in dividends so that he could afford to pay it back. http://www.economist.com/node/21553070?zid
=298&ah=0bc99f9da8f185b2964b6cef412227be

11   The Licence Raj system is described in brief in http://news.bbc.co.uk/2/hi/
south_asia/55427.stm

12 The history of India's economy after independence has been told in many articles and books. For example, Kapila (2014).

13 See, for example, Bernstein, Bivens and Dube (2006).

14 The Sandoz statement appears in: http://www.themoscowtimes.com/business/ article/novartis-unit-considers-russian-factory/410734.html

References

Bernstein, J, Bivens, L J and Dube, A (2006) *Wrestling with Walmart: Tradeoffs between profits, prices, and wages*, Economic Policy Institute, Washington, DC, June

Bhattacharya, A K and Michael, D (2008) How local companies keep multinationals at bay, *Harvard Business Review*, March, pp 84–95

Clifton, J, Diaz Fuentes, D and Marichal, M (nd) *Taking control: Transforming telecommunications in Mexico* [Online] http://altea.daea.ua.es/ochorem/ comunicaciones/MESA5COM/CliftonDiazMarichal.pdf

Grosse, R and Yañes, J (1998) Carrying out a successful privatization: The YPF case, *Academy of Management Executive*, **12**, 51–63

Guillén, M F and Esteban García-Canal, E (2010) *The new multinationals: Spanish firms in a global context*, Cambridge University Press, Cambridge

Hansen, M, Larsen, M, Pedersen, T *et al* (2010) *Strategies in emerging markets: A case book on Danish multinational corporations in China and India*, Copenhagen Business School Press, Copenhagen

Kapila, U (2014) *India's economic development since 1947* (3rd edn), Academic Foundation, New Delhi [Online] http://www.academicfoundation.com/ n_detail/ies47-3.asp

Khanna, T and Palepu, K (2010) *Winning in emerging markets*, Harvard Business Press, Boston, MA

Khanna, T, Palepu, K and Sinha, J (2005) Strategies that fit emerging markets, *Harvard Business Review*, **83**(6), 63–76

Wilson, K, Ramos, Y and Harvey, D (2006) *Google in China*, Kenan Institute for Ethics, Duke University [Online] https://web.duke.edu/kenanethics/CaseStudies/ GoogleInChina.pdf

Appendix: Rules on foreign companies in selected emerging markets

TABLE A5.1   Rules on foreign companies in selected emerging markets

Country/ regulation	Foreign ownership prohibited	Foreign ownership limited	Local content requirements
Argentina	The only restricted sectors for foreign-investor participation are in radio broadcasting, fishing, domestic transport, acquisition of real property in border areas, and weapons and ammunition. Offshore companies are prohibited from setting up in Buenos Aires (Resolution 2/2005, February 2005), and all new foreign companies must provide to the government information about their shareholders (Resolution 3/2005, March 2005).	Since 2003 Argentina has limited foreign ownership of 'cultural goods' to 30%, which includes media and internet companies. An exception exists for investors whose countries allow more than 30% foreign ownership of their cultural goods.	For example, 70% of the production content for companies with radio licences must be of national origin and 30% of music must be of national origin (of which 50% must be independent), and 50% of news must be local. Licensed private television operators must transmit a minimum of 60% national content, 30% local news, and 10–30% local independent content, depending on the category.
Brazil	Since August 1995 major amendments to the 1988 constitution have eliminated legal distinctions between majority-foreign-owned and majority-domestic-owned companies in Brazil.	Restrictions on foreign investment affect some sectors, such as aviation and media communications. There is a 20% limit on foreign investment in domestic airlines, and the government	**Import restrictions** In September 2011 Brazil announced a 30% increase in the Industrial Products Tax (IPI) on vehicles containing less than 65% domestically manufactured content

TABLE A5.1 *continued*

Country/ regulation	Foreign ownership prohibited	Foreign ownership limited	Local content requirements
	Legally registered companies – foreign or domestic – enjoy the same rights and privileges, and they compete on an equal footing when bidding on contracts or seeking government financing. Although no rules expressly prohibit foreign takeovers, special authorization is required for deals made via share purchase on the stock market. **Sectors closed to companies with foreign capital**: • Aerospace industries • Domestic flights • Nuclear power • Public health • Postal and telegraph services • Sanitation	administers commercial airport operations. Foreign ownership is limited to 30% in open-broadcast and print media companies and to 49% for cable-television companies (Law 10,610 of 2002). Foreign investors may participate in private Brazilian financial institutions, but must first present a proposal to the central bank, which then submits it to the National Monetary Council (Conselho Monetário Nacional) for approval. The president must then sign a decree officially authorizing the participation. The central bank (Banco Central do Brasil) usually charges foreign capital a special fee to enter the financial sector.	(defined as sourced from a Mercosur country or Mexico). The increase lifted the range of IPI tax on vehicles to 37.55% (from 7.25%). In force until the end of 2012, the tax hike targeted imported cars, which are also subject to a 35% import duty. In July 2012 the government raised the IPI on air conditioners, microwave ovens and motorcycles to 35%, from 20%, 30% and 15–25%, respectively. In June 2013 the government increased the IPI on furniture (from 2.5% to 3%), stoves (from 2% to 3%), refrigerators (from 7.5% to 8.5%) and washers (from 3.5% to 4.5%), and rescinded reductions granted previously on light fixtures (from 7.5% to 10%), wallpaper (from 10% to 15%) and others.

TABLE A5.1 *continued*

Country/ regulation	Foreign ownership prohibited	Foreign ownership limited	Local content requirements
China	**Prohibited foreign investments**, according to the 2011 Catalogue for Guiding Foreign Investment in Industries, include 39 items, in areas such as the following: • projects that endanger state security or harm the public interest; • projects that pollute the environment or endanger human health; • projects that occupy large tracts of farmland or endanger the security or efficient use of military resources; • projects that use manufacturing techniques or technologies that are unique to China; and • other projects prohibited under state laws and administrative regulations.	**Restricted foreign investments**, covering 74 items in the 2011 catalogue, include the following: • projects involving banking and other financial services, except for venture capital, which is encouraged, and financial leasing, which is permitted; • projects already developed in China, where the tech has already been imported and where capacity can meet market demand; • projects that exert an adverse effect on the Chinese environment and on energy conservation; • projects involving exploring for and/or extracting rare or precious mineral resources • projects in industries requiring central planning by the state.	None found

TABLE A5.1   *continued*

Country/ regulation	Foreign ownership prohibited	Foreign ownership limited	Local content requirements
		Telecommunications: 49% max foreign. **Insurance**: 50% max foreign in lifetime JVs. Brokers for insurance of large-scale commercial risks, reinsurance, and international marine, aviation and transport insurance are allowed up to 100% ownership **Wholesale and retail:** 100% max foreign. Directly upon WTO accession in late 2001, China allowed foreign retail participation in JVs in the five special economic zones of Hainan, Shantou, Shenzhen, Xiamen and Zhuhai, as well as the cities of Beijing, Dalian, Guangzhou, Qingdao, Shanghai and Tianjin. China allowed a maximum of four foreign-invested retailing JVs in Beijing and Shanghai, and a maximum of just two in other locations.	

TABLE A5.1 *continued*

Country/ regulation	Foreign ownership prohibited	Foreign ownership limited	Local content requirements
		Banking: The rules require foreign-funded or JV banks to incorporate in China with registered capital of Rmb1bn. They have to allocate a further Rmb100m in operating capital for each branch they open. The WTO agreement also specifies that foreign financial institutions, in order to be allowed to do renminbi business, must have a three-year record of accomplishment for operations in China and must have been profitable for two consecutive years prior to application. **Cars**: 50% maximum foreign ownership.	
India	Postal services, atomic energy and railway transport and only for public sector. Sectors closed to foreigners: • Gambling • Betting	**Defense production**: 26% max foreign. **FM-radio broadcasting**: 26% max foreign. **News channels**: 26% max foreign; Indian management required.	None found

TABLE A5.1   *continued*

Country/ regulation	Foreign ownership prohibited	Foreign ownership limited	Local content requirements
	• Lottery • Cigar manufacturing, cigarettes, and manufactured tobacco substitutes • Construction of farmhouses • Trading	**Telecommunications services**: FDI of 100% has been permitted since 2000 in infrastructure providers of dark fibre, and in e-mail and voice mail. However, the companies must divest 26% of their equity to the Indian public within five years if they are listed elsewhere in the world. FDI of up to 100% (raised from 74% in August 2013) is allowed in internet service providers with and without gateways, radio paging and end-to-end bandwidth. **State-run petroleum refineries:** 49% max foreign. **Multi-brand retailing**: 51% max foreign with 30% of products from micro, small and medium suppliers whose total investment in plant and machinery is <US$2m. **Civil aviation:** cargo airlines, non-scheduled airlines and chartered airlines, and ground handling services 74% max foreign.	

TABLE A5.1 *continued*

Country/ regulation	Foreign ownership prohibited	Foreign ownership limited	Local content requirements
		Insurance and insurance brokerage: 26% max foreign. **Industries reserved for small units** (those with investment of less than Rs10m in plant and machinery): 24% max foreign.	
Indonesia	Under the Negative List and a maritime law passed in 2008 and in force from May 2011, only companies using Indonesian-flagged vessels may transport goods domestically. However, the government said in April 2011 that oil and gas vessels are exempt from this rule, clearing the way for foreign-flagged vessels to transport oil and gas products domestically. **(1) Closed to domestic and foreign investment** Casinos, archaeological sites, museums, cultural-heritage sites, monuments, coral mining, transport terminals, navigational aids, air-traffic control, hazardous chemicals,	Geothermal power: 90% max foreign. Sugar industry: 95% max foreign. Staple-food plantations: 49% max foreign. Film services: 49% max foreign. Construction: 67% max foreign. Direct selling: 95% max foreign. Art galleries: 67% max foreign. Specialist-hospital services: 67% max foreign. Association of South-East Asian Nations (ASEAN) vs non-ASEAN limits: Cargo handling: 60% vs 49% Vessel ownership: 60% vs 49% Recreation businesses: 100% vs 49%.	None found

TABLE A5.1   *continued*

Country/ regulation	Foreign ownership prohibited	Foreign ownership limited	Local content requirements
	chemical weapons, alcoholic beverages (hard alcohol, wine and malt liquor), alkalines containing mercury and communications towers.	Banks (99% limit, but 40% if there is only one foreign investor in a bank – see below); offshore hydrocarbon drilling outside eastern Indonesia, onshore hydrocarbon drilling, oil and gas operators, engineering and procurement contracting services, power (generation, transmission, consulting, installation, maintenance, operation, research, distribution and nuclear), data-communications system services, toll roads, drinking water, and cultivation of food crops and plantation crops in plots greater than 25 ha (95% limit); insurance and insurance services (80% limit); pharmaceutical drugs and ingredients (75% limit); hospital-management services and specialist hospitals (67% limit); internet interconnection and insurance agents (65% limit); construction-consulting services	

TABLE A5.1 *continued*

Country/ regulation	Foreign ownership prohibited	Foreign ownership limited	Local content requirements
		(55% limit); one- and two-star hotels (51% limit); amusement parks (49% limit); fixed-line telecoms networks (cable or radio-based), internet telephony, multimedia services, education, business consultation services, transport of goods, passenger services, domestic airline routes, airport services, cargo handling, provision of port facilities (ports, warehouses, container terminals, ferry terminals), labour-services providers, film and film-processing (49% limit); and eco-tourism in conservation forests (25% limit).	

TABLE A5.1   *continued*

Country/ regulation	Foreign ownership prohibited	Foreign ownership limited	Local content requirements
Mexico	Oil and gas, petroleum and hydrocarbons. Control and management of ports. Electricity, nuclear energy, postal service, airports. Retail petrol (gasoline) sales, non-cable television and radio communication services, credit unions, domestic transport for passengers, freight and tourism purposes.	Production co-operatives: max 10% foreign. Domestic airlines: max 25% foreign. Railways: max 49% foreign. Insurance companies, currency exchange bureau, bonding institutions, general deposit (financial) warehouses, retirement fund administrators, domestic newspapers, port admin, investment-promotion corps: max 49% foreign. 'Foreign investors can sidestep these limits via "neutral" investments, commonly referred to as N-shares.' These have no voting rights, and are not accounted for as 'foreign' shares. Radio and TV broadcasting: max 49% foreign.	Oil and gas tenders offered by Pemex: 40% local content. Export financial incentives (credit) for local content of 30% and above.

TABLE A5.1 *continued*

Country/ regulation	Foreign ownership prohibited	Foreign ownership limited	Local content requirements
Nigeria	None found	None found	Incentives for local production intended for export: A 25% investment-tax credit for local manufacturers of spare parts and machine tools (those who buy these goods are also entitled to a 15% investment-tax credit). From 31 March 2012, a corporate-tax incentive rebate of 12% is given to bakers who attain 40% cassava blending within 18 months, as part of an effort to encourage the substitution of high-quality cassava flour for wheat flour in bread-making. Nigeria has excess capacity to produce cassava, and the government wants to boost its local use and also reduce imports of wheat.

TABLE A5.1   *continued*

Country/ regulation	Foreign ownership prohibited	Foreign ownership limited	Local content requirements
Russia	None found	Federal Law 57.FZ, On Procedures for Making Foreign Investment into Commercial Organizations Having Strategic Significance for Ensuring the Effective Defence of the Country and Security of the State, has been in force since 7 May 2008. The law increased the number of 'strategic sectors' from 16 to 42. Whenever ownership by foreign investors in a commercial organization in one of these sectors reaches 25% or 50%, the law sets special procedures for their approval. Strategic sectors include armaments, aviation and aerospace, natural resources and nuclear energy. In addition, the fishing industry and 'monopoly' fixed-line telecomm companies, along with some other natural monopolies, are classified as strategic. At the upper limit, any foreign investors wishing to control more than 50% of a	**Automotive industry:** Rules were tightened further in 2011, requiring foreign automotive producers to source at least 60% (double the previous level) of the value of the cars they manufacture in Russia locally, to invest at least US$500m into the Russian economy and to produce 300,000 vehicles in Russia in order to qualify for duty-free imports of components and assembled vehicles. Production sharing agreements related to mining and natural resources: they detailed strict Russian-content requirements for equipment used.

TABLE A5.1 *continued*

Country/ regulation	Foreign ownership prohibited	Foreign ownership limited	Local content requirements
		company in the listed areas need to apply to Russian authorities for a special permit. Only a committee headed by the prime minister can grant the permit; in addition, granting of the permit depends on an assessment by the Federal Security Service of the national-security threat of the proposed transaction. For the lower limit, state-owned foreign companies require the committee's approval for the purchase of a stake greater than 25% and may not in any case gain a majority stake. And in cases when a foreign state-owned entity wishes to invest in a Russian company active in a strategically important sector, the committee's approval is needed for stakes greater than 25%. Also, under no circumstances will foreign state-owned companies be allowed to acquire a majority stake in a strategic Russian company.	

TABLE A5.1 *continued*

Country/ regulation	Foreign ownership prohibited	Foreign ownership limited	Local content requirements
S Africa	None found	There are few limitations on incoming FDI, however, and the government has created a one-stop shop for foreign investors with Trade and Investment South Africa, a subdivision of the Department of Trade and Industry. Except in banking and the media, there is no limit on the level of foreign ownership in companies. Equity ownership (foreign or domestic) of banks exceeding 15% requires the authorization of the Registrar of Deposit-Taking Institutions; stakes exceeding 49% require authorization of the Ministry of Finance. Similarly, foreign or domestic ownership in insurance that exceeds 25% requires the authorization of the Registrar. Foreign ownership in the media is limited to 20%.	None found

SOURCES: constructed by the author using information from Economist Intelligence Unit, *Country Commerce* sections for these countries, February 2014. Also, PwC Guides to Doing Business in... (www.pwc.com/countryname) and KPMG (http://www.kpmg.com/countryname)

Competitive strategies of firms in China

MNEs, SOEs and private firms

The largest and most dynamic of the emerging markets today is clearly China. Some more insight can be gained about challenges and opportunities in this country by exploring competition among local and foreign companies in several industries. The discussion focuses on one foreign MNE, one local SOE, and one locally owned private-sector company in three industries: cars, telecom equipment and banking.

In the car industry foreign companies must accept a minimum of 50 per cent Chinese ownership by a local firm in order to operate locally. The two largest carmakers in the world, VW and GM, both operate several joint ventures in China, and both have their main venture operated jointly with Shanghai Automotive (SAIC). Despite Chinese government efforts and incentives for many years, local Chinese companies still in 2015 have not made much headway in either car design or local market share for purely domestic cars. The foreign–local joint ventures dominate the market, accounting for well over three-quarters of total car sales in China. The challenge to GM and VW, as well as other foreign carmakers, is to stay competitive in China without losing market share to either their local partners (producing local cars) or other local competitors.

In the telecom equipment business there are no local ownership restrictions, and foreign competitors Nokia, Ericsson and Samsung have large market shares. However, both Huawei and ZTE – local competitors – have established major positions in this business, and they have overtaken the foreign rivals in global telecom equipment market share. This is surprising in the high-tech telecom sector, but both ZTE and Huawei are investing heavily in R&D and are producing very competitive phones and switching equipment, so they likely will continue to grow their global reach and market shares. In the domestic Chinese market, Nokia and Samsung still lead the mobile phone business in market share, while Huawei and ZTE are also closing in.

In banking, foreign banks are greatly limited in activities and locations, such that all foreign banks such as HSBC and Citibank combined hold less than 2 per cent of Chinese banking assets (loans). Also, local private-sector banks have very limited market share, with the largest one, Minsheng, holding an approximate 1.8 per cent market share. Thus, most banking services in China are provided by local, state-owned banks, led by the Big Four national government banks. Regulation is the clear driver of this market condition. In a future, possibly less-regulated environment the foreign and private banks may develop a more competitive and significant position in the market.

Introduction

It has been over 30 years since China opened its door to the outside world and initiated its market-oriented economic reform. In the past 30 years, and particularly in the 21st century, China has experienced enormous changes. As the economic reform and open-door policy significantly improve people's lives, China has also developed itself as one of the largest and most dynamic markets in the world. At the same time, one also observes an increasingly intensive competition in China. Although the degree of competition varies across industries, China's market differs from the kinds of market where firms compete on equal footing and which top executives from the West are familiar with. The unique feature of competition in China is the co-existence of MNEs, Chinese SOEs and rapidly growing local private firms. These three kinds of competitor compete in major markets, using their different resources and capabilities; and they compete differently and position themselves differently within the Chinese market. Because of their different ownership types, operating objectives, behaviours and market positions, eventually their performances are very different. That shapes the landscape of many key industries in China and will continue to do so.

The purpose of this chapter is to highlight such differences and show how firms are faring in that unique market environment. More specifically, two sets of questions form the basis of the discussion. The first set of questions is related to competition in Chinese industries. What is the competitive landscape in China's major industries? How has competition evolved in recent years? What are the changing roles of MNEs in shaping competition in China? The second set of questions focuses on the strategies of different firms operating in these markets. What kinds of competitive advantage do these firms enjoy? How do they operate in terms of obtaining/creating technology; dealing with the government; collaborating with other firms? And how do they perform in terms of financial and strategic goals?

These two sets of questions face any MNEs operating in China, and likewise any Chinese firms in those same industries. To make the analysis manageable, the discussion focuses on three sectors: the car industry, the telecommunications equipment industry and the banking industry. These three sectors are selected for a number of reasons: first of all, they are critically important in China and have experienced rapid growth. Multinational firms play important roles in each case.[1] Secondly, institutional environments, and regulatory schemes in particular, are designed and implemented differently in these sectors, therefore the kind of hurdles that multinational firms must overcome are also different. The telecommunications equipment industry was the first to open to the outside world, while the banking sector has only opened gradually after China joined the World Trade Organization (WTO) in 2001. Thirdly, the technology used by these three kinds of firm and the learning processes are different. While the telecom industry is characterized as technology intensive, the banking sector is a relationship- and knowledge-intensive business. The car industry falls in between, and it is much more capital intensive than the other two. The technology and the regulatory variations among these three sectors lead to various degrees of penetration of MNEs and influence the formulation of business strategies.

MNEs need to adopt different business strategies in these different contexts. Figure 6.1 depicts the relationships among foreign MNEs, governments and local competitors, using the car industry as an example.

In the car industry, for instance, the joint venture is a required form of market entry for foreign MNEs. As a result, the major automobile firms have all formed joint ventures with local partners. Alliance formation is

FIGURE 6.1 Key competitive interactions

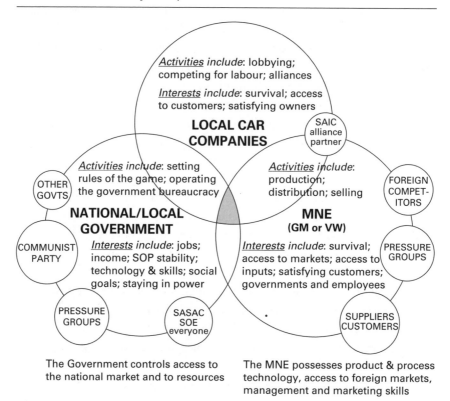

Activities include: lobbying; competing for labour; alliances

Interests include: survival; access to customers; satisfying owners

LOCAL CAR COMPANIES

SAIC alliance partner

OTHER GOVTS

Activities include: setting rules of the game; operating the government bureaucracy

Activities include: production; distribution; selling

FOREIGN COMPET-ITORS

NATIONAL/LOCAL GOVERNMENT

MNE (GM or VW)

COMMUNIST PARTY

Interests include: jobs; income; SOP stability; technology & skills; social goals; staying in power

Interests include: survival; access to markets; access to inputs; satisfying customers; governments and employees

PRESSURE GROUPS

PRESSURE GROUPS

SASAC SOE everyone

SUPPLIERS CUSTOMERS

The Government controls access to the national market and to resources

The MNE possesses product & process technology, access to foreign markets, management and marketing skills

thus a core element of the MNEs' strategy. The telecom equipment sector opened to foreign firms in the 1980s, and it did not require joint ventures with local firms. As a result, over time local competitors emerged, and eventually the market developed into a mixed oligopoly in which the SOEs, multinationals and private firms compete. The banking industry is tightly controlled by the Chinese regulators. Foreign banks are allowed to carry out some functions in China, but with many restrictions, including the inability to take deposits in renminbi[2] and to establish local deposit-taking branches. Therefore this sector is dominated by local banks, while the foreign banks are not only small in numbers of branches, but also in assets/lending.

The Chinese competitive environment

The unique feature of co-existence of MNEs, SOEs and private firms in China's industries can be characterized as a mixed market. Wu and Li (2006) study the decision making of different firms in a mixed market and show empirically that SOEs and MNEs differ in pricing, new product introduction and inventories, and investment decisions. The differences in ownership and decision making lead to different performance of those firms as shown in Xu *et al* (2006).

Market institutions and regulatory regimes in any country play an important role in influencing firms' strategies, and China is no exception. Multinational companies must respond to China's institutional environment. Since China joined the WTO in 2001, legislation and regulations in China have become more transparent and better specified, from procedures to contents. For instance, China enacted its anti-monopoly law in 2008 in an attempt to create a level playing field of competition. Wu and Liu (2012) argue that the barriers to trade and local market protection by administrative authorities are still substantial, and there are a number of clauses that allow some firms to avoid following the laws.

Although multinationals often enjoy technological advantages, some local firms may gain competitive advantages because of their endowments of other resources. Tan and Peng (2003) argue that SOEs in China, often burdened by excessive labour, may turn their seeming redundancy of human resources into competitive advantage in an environment featuring rapid growth. The excessive labour force provides the firms with human resources to respond quickly to unexpected market opportunities.

A focus on three sectors

To address the questions posed above, the discussion focuses on leading companies in three sectors and uses information including industry reports, company annual reports and reports from industrial associations and regulators, as well as discussions with senior executives in the companies. In the automobile industry, GM was the leading MNE in terms of sales in China; Shanghai Automobile Industrial Company (SAIC) is the largest SOE; and Geely Group was selected to represent the local privately owned carmakers. In the telecom equipment industry, Nokia/Siemens is one of the top three MNEs in China; ZTE is the largest SOE; and Huawei Technologies Co. Ltd is the largest local private firm. In the banking industry, HSBC was chosen as a leading foreign bank registered in China, ICBC as the largest state-owned bank and Minsheng Bank as the largest non-state-owned local bank in China.

Based on the value-added chain and competitive advantage perspective presented in this book, we expected the following kinds of outcomes:

- In industries that are technology intensive, companies will be able to operate more independently of government intervention, and should be led by private-sector firms with superior R&D skills.

- In industries that are marketing intensive (ie dependent on advertising or other marketing skills), the leading companies will be private-sector companies with superior marketing skills.

- In industries that are low-tech and low marketing intensive, SOEs will hold the upper hand.

Company strategies, given these conditions, should demonstrate the following characteristics:

- Foreign companies in more high-tech and more marketing-intensive sectors will have greater ability to operate without local partners.

- Domestic privately owned firms will be more successful in sectors that have lower barriers to entry and where the technology can be obtained more readily in the market.

- Domestic government-owned companies will dominate sectors which are low-tech and low marketing intensive.

The analysis here focuses on the period starting in the new century. This is partly because China formally joined the WTO in 2001, and that decision led to a number of important institutional and regulatory changes. Under the WTO agreements, China was required to open a number of important markets, such as financial services, to outsiders. That was expected to create a more level playing field on which the companies could engage in fair competition. The outcome should then depend on the competitive advantages that a company possesses and develops, as well as its bargaining capabilities in relation to the government.

The automobile industry in China

The Chinese car industry has evolved from a monopoly tightly controlled by local government before the 1980s, in which the First Automotive Works (FAW) began producing the Jiefang CA-30 passenger car in Changchun (Jilin Province) in 1956, and subsequently the Nanjing car works produced a truck model beginning in 1958. Other local car manufacturers were set up in Shanghai and Beijing during the period of tightest government control of the economy. At no point were more than 10,000 cars produced per year in China during that period, and clients were almost exclusively government agencies and the state-owned companies such as taxi service providers.

In the mid-1980s, the government decided to allow importation of greater numbers of cars, mainly for use as taxis for the state-owned taxi companies in Beijing and Shanghai. During the second half of that decade, several hundred thousand Japanese cars were imported for this purpose. At that same time, American Motors Company (AMC), later acquired by Chrysler in 1983, agreed with the City of Beijing to assemble Jeeps locally through a joint venture with Beijing Auto Works, the predecessor of Beijing Auto Industrial Company (BAIC). As well, VW in 1984 signed an agreement with the City of Shanghai to produce cars locally in a joint venture, which initially was used primarily to assemble vehicles from imported kits.

VW and AMC, and subsequently other foreign carmakers, were allowed to form joint ventures with the state-owned Chinese partners as long as foreign ownership was limited to 50 per cent of shares in the joint ventures. The government's intent was to develop a car industry rapidly, learning from the foreign companies how to make cars while maintaining control of the car industry. VW came and built the Santana model to serve the envisioned need for taxis. AMC came and built Jeeps, which were expected to be a good fit for China's poor-quality roads and extensive rural population. In fact, the American Motors/Beijing Auto Works was the joint-venture agreement that subsequently formed the basis of China's Joint Venture Law.[3]

When a greater degree of economic opening began in the early 1990s, the national government authorized more foreign car manufacturers to enter China, and more vehicles to be sold. VW was the clear market leader, operating through its joint ventures with SAIC and also with FAW in Changchun, though Chrysler/Jeep held the market lead in Beijing through its joint venture with BAIC.

World car leader GM was noticeably absent from this market in the 1980s and early 1990s. This was not for lack of trying, since GM was repeatedly trying to negotiate joint-venture agreements in Beijing and Shanghai with the local state-owned firms there. However, it was not until 1995 that GM was able to obtain permission from the Shanghai government to launch a joint venture with SAIC, and thus to begin producing the Buick Century and the Buick GL-8 minivan in 1998, and subsequently a range of Buicks, Chevrolets and Cadillacs.[4]

The Chinese car market since the mid-1990s has been divided among three types of firm:

1   Chinese SOEs that form joint ventures with foreign carmakers, such as SAIC, BAIC, FAW among others;

2 foreign MNEs in joint ventures with Chinese SOEs: VW and GM with SAIC and FAW, Hyundai and Chrysler with BAIC, Honda, Nissan and PSA with Dongfeng Auto Works, Toyota with Guangzhou Automobile Corporation, and Ford and PSA with Chang'An Automobile Group.

3 local private manufacturers, including Geely, Great Wall Motors and BYD; and local government-owned manufacturers that are not involved with foreign carmakers in major joint ventures, including Chery and Chengfeng.

These firms compete in a series of relationships and locations in China as depicted in Figure A6.1. We are interested in examining the different strategies and performance results of these three types of car company, to demonstrate the structure of the Chinese market, the opportunities for foreign firms to compete, and to some extent the direction in which the market is headed.

The joint ventures

By the early 2000s, joint ventures involving SAIC in Shanghai, BAIC in Beijing, Dongfeng in Wuhan and FAW in Changchun were the dominant car producers in China (Table 6.1).

Each of the Chinese companies was established by the local (provincial) government to be the main automobile and truck producer in that province. And each was instructed to seek out foreign partners to bring in the technology and management skills needed to produce the vehicles. A clear mandate also existed for each of these state-owned companies to develop its own domestic models alongside their production of the foreign branded models. While the joint ventures continued to dominate car sales in China in 2013, the growth of domestically designed and produced cars, including ones made by SAIC and BAIC, was more rapid than the growth of sales of GM and VW models.[5]

Let us consider one of the main joint-venture local partners – SAIC – as a basis of comparison with the foreign firms and the local non-JV firms.

SAIC is a domestic Chinese car manufacturer as well as a holding company for major joint ventures with VW and GM. SAIC began in the 1950s as a manufacturing company which produced its own model (Phoenix), and focused entirely on the local market. Several other small, local car companies were formed at about that same time. In the early 1980s the Chinese government decided to support the development of several major car manufacturers, linked with leading foreign car firms to obtain technology in return for access to the Chinese market. Under this new policy, SAIC in 1982 signed

TABLE 6.1   Automobile market shares. China – cars: company market share by volume (%)

Market player	2009	2010	2011
SAIC-GM-Wuling Automobile Co, Ltd	9.5	8.3	8.4
Shanghai Volkswagen Co, Ltd	7	7.3	8.1
Shanghai General Motors Co, Ltd	6.9	7.4	8.2
FAW Volkswagen Co, Ltd	6.5	6.3	7.2
Beijing Hyundai Motor Company Corporation	5.5	5.1	5.1
Changan International Corporation	5	4.8	3.8
Dongfeng Nissan Passenger Vehicle Co, Ltd	5	5.2	5.6
Chery Automobile Co, Ltd	4.8	4.9	4.4
BYD Company Limited	4.3	3.7	3.1
Tianjin FAW Toyota Motor Co, Ltd	4	3.8	3.7
Others	41.5	43.2	42.4

SOURCE: China Association of Automobile Manufacturers

an agreement to assemble the VW Santana sedan, which subsequently became the best-selling car in China for more than a decade. In 1998, SAIC began a joint venture with GM, assembling the Buick New Century sedan.

After more than a decade of assembling VW and GM vehicles, SAIC returned to also making its own car, the Roewe 750. SAIC (including partners) was the market leader for car sales in China in 2012, with about 3 million vehicles sold, constituting a market share of more than 20 per cent.

SAIC's strategy is now aimed at becoming a global automotive leader. The company already ranks among the Fortune Global 500 and has made acquisitions in Korea and in Chinese provinces outside of Shanghai. With the launching of its own models largely based on technology from the acquisition of MG Rover in the United Kingdom, SAIC is moving to build the share of its own brands in China and overseas.[6]

Competitive advantages of the SOE joint ventures

In the case of SAIC, as well as for BAIC and FAW, the main advantage possessed by the company is its link to the regional government. In none of these cases has internally developed technology led to new models that have taken large market shares, and most technology continues to come from joint-venture partners. Even so, the same might be said for Toyota or Nissan in the 1960s, when they were largely domestic and internal-market-focused Japanese champions, supported by the government but not known for innovative technology or skills. The reality is that SAIC, BAIC and FAW will continue to receive support from their corresponding local regional governments, and this alone will position them for growth and local success even if they did not progress beyond the joint ventures. Obviously, just as in Japan, the government's intent is to push the firms towards international competitiveness, and with the captive market of hundreds of millions of potential customers in the home region alone, these firms are primed for future success, if they can figure out how to design and market their own models more effectively.

Foreign joint-venture partners

GM is a relative latecomer to the Chinese market, only gaining approval for local production in 1998, in a joint venture with SAIC in Shanghai, long after VW and AMC/Chrysler, as well as Daimler-Benz, but before Toyota and Honda. This is quite an interesting situation, with the two largest foreign car companies (GM and VW) operating through joint ventures in Shanghai with the same local partner.

GM has the advantage of being historically the world's largest car producer, with a wide range of brands and styles, for cars, trucks and other vehicles. GM's Buick brand is said to be the car of the emperors from before the Second World War, and Buicks have sold well in the more recent time since GM set up manufacturing in Shanghai with SAIC. Overall, GM's main competitive advantages in Chinese competition are just like VW's: access to a continuing flow of new models and car production technology, along with management skills for operating a large-scale car business. In the event that SAIC were to seek a world market for its own branded cars, GM would be a likely candidate to work with, since its distribution globally is larger than VW's.[7] And in fact, GM and SAIC have expanded their collaboration through a joint venture in India, and are selling some small cars together in Latin America.[8]

Chinese independent carmakers (Geely)

Geely is the first privately owned carmaker in China, preceding Great Wall and BYD by several years. Geely was established in the 1980s as a refrigerator manufacturing company, and then founder Li Shufu acquired a failing state-owned motorcycle manufacturing business in 1994.[9] Geely began producing automobiles in 1998 in its Hangzhou facilities near Shanghai.

Geely faces the typical emerging market competitor's challenge: how to obtain leading technology and quality control to compete with the existing major firms in the industry. For a decade the strategy was to build low-cost passenger cars using imported technology. Then Geely acquired Volvo of Sweden from Ford in 2011, so that now it has a high-quality brand in the portfolio. The challenge now is: how can Geely take advantage of the Volvo engineering and design skills without diminishing the quality image? The initial direction has been to allow Volvo to function relatively independent of Geely, except for selling Volvo cars imported into China.[10]

Conclusions on the car industry

The car industry in China is clearly booming, and most of the global leaders in the industry are present in China. Foreign brands dominate the market thus far, while Chinese domestic brands are slowly gaining market share. The strategies of the various firms are significantly different, due primarily to the regulatory environment that does not permit the foreign firms to operate independently in China. So GM and VW must collaborate with SAIC, at the same time as they are competing with SAIC's own models – and with each other! It will be interesting to see if Toyota and Honda from Japan can establish a major presence in China, since their geographic location is closer than the Americans or the Europeans, their styling is arguably more similar as well, and they are both allied with Guangdong Automotive. Table 6.1 shows how the competition in China today stacks up among the various kinds of firms operating in China. The critical factor that appears to enable the foreign firms to gain and hold market share is technology – both in manufacturing and in car design.

The telecommunications equipment industry in China

The rapid technological progress in the information and communications technology (ICT) industry calls for a constant supply of equipment with cutting-edge technology. In that process, there is a drastic change in the market structure in the supply of telecommunications equipment in China as well as around the world. This primarily has to do with the move from fixed-line telephone service to mobile phone telephony.

China's telecommunications equipment industry receives a lot of attention from outside China. How a country with a mostly outdated telecommunications system could turn into one of largest markets in equipment and in services in 30 years is remarkable. Some firms with names that were unknown a few years ago now appear in the top five in the global market. And as those firms go overseas to build their businesses, they face scrutiny from host governments. For example, ZTE has *de facto* government ownership and control, and Huawei appears to have links to the Chinese military and the Chinese Communist Party.[11] This statement is not a criticism of either company, but a description of the reason for the opposition that they do and will face in Triad countries where they try to build market share.

China's market for second-generation mobile communications equipment is dominated by European and North American companies, and because of the unique characteristics of mobile communications, most of China's mobile communications equipment demands are filled by imports.[12] The leading international suppliers of network equipment – Alcatel-Lucent, Cisco, Ericsson, Huawei, Nortel, ZTE and Nokia Siemens – as well as the major international suppliers of portable phone sets – Ericsson and Siemens, plus Motorola, Nokia, Samsung and Apple – are well established and well known in China. The quickly rising Chinese manufacturers, however, led by Huawei Technologies and ZTE, are turning to South American, Southeast Asian and African countries for business opportunities and are increasingly raising their market share in China.

In 2009, Huawei Technologies surpassed Nokia Siemens Networks and Alcatel-Lucent to become the second largest manufacturer of telecommunications equipment in the world. Huawei passed Ericsson and became the largest telecoms company in sales in the world in 2012. Although Huawei's total revenue passed Ericsson's, it is still in second place in the telecom equipment segment because its product portfolio is broader than Ericsson's.

A large number of Chinese companies compete now with foreign corporations not only in the Chinese market but also in other countries. Datang is the main TD-SCDMA (Time Division–Synchronous Code Division Multiple Access) manufacturer, and UTStarcom the main PAS/PHS (Personal Handyphone System/Personal Access System) manufacturer. Huawei leads the SMS market, and Great Wall stands out in the broadband sector. Other recognized Chinese equipment suppliers are Shanghai Bell and ZTE.

The SOE – ZTE

As the fifth largest global producer of telecom equipment, ZTE is aiming to increase its domestic market share in China, particularly for wireless telecom equipment and handsets (mobile phones). At the same time the company is pursuing overseas expansion, especially in other emerging markets. About half of ZTE's sales in 2012 were in China, with the rest spread in Asia, Africa and other countries around the world. ZTE's business is split approximately 80–20 between sales to telephone service providers (such as Verizon Wireless and Vodafone) and sales to consumers (mainly mobile phones). ZTE is a listed company on both the Hong Kong and Shenzhen Stock Exchanges, but the Chinese government still owns a controlling interest in the company, so we consider it an SOE.

ZTE is unusual among emerging market multinationals in that the company is heavily involved in R&D in the telecom equipment sector. The company has established 18 state-of-the-art R&D centres in China, France and India and employs over 30,000 research professionals. More than 10 per cent of the company's annual revenue is invested in R&D. This level of activity rivals the industry leaders and is positioning ZTE to move even higher in the global market for telecom equipment.

In 2014, ZTE reorganized its businesses into three divisions: Operator Solutions, in which ZTE offers consulting to telephone operating companies, to provide them with network management as well as hardware and software; Enterprise Business, in which ZTE provides telecom solutions to corporate customers in specific industries such as banking, transportation, utilities and energy; and Mobile Devices, in which ZTE sells smartphones, tablets and other devices to retail clients and looks to add hardware and software innovations.

Foreign multinational firms – Nokia Siemens Networks

Nokia Siemens Networks (NSN) was formed in 2006 as a joint venture between Siemens Communications division and Nokia's network division. Nokia owns a controlling interest in the joint venture, which is based at Nokia's headquarters in Finland. The company bought Motorola's network division in 2011 and declared its intent to refocus all business on the mobile network equipment segment, which has been the fastest-growing part of the business. NSN has manufacturing facilities in three locations in China, where it makes 2G and 3G equipment, as well as 4G TD-LTE (Time-division Long-Term Evolution) equipment, and sells to all major Chinese telephone service providers. The company has also established R&D centres in Beijing, Shanghai, Chengdu and Hangzhou.

The strategy of Nokia Siemens in China is to be the market leader, particularly in the next-generation mobile phone equipment, from handsets to network switching gear. The company trails Huawei at present, and market leadership probably will be difficult to attain, since both Chinese rivals are investing heavily in R&D. There is no clear superiority of NSN products at this point, though the situation certainly could change in the future. Regardless, NSN appears positioned to remain a highly competitive member of the top three suppliers of telecom equipment in China.

Local private firms – Huawei

Privately owned Huawei is the largest Chinese telecom equipment manufacturer and currently the number one producer of switching gear in the world, having overtaken Ericsson in 2011. Huawei began as a private branch exchange (PBX) switching gear importer in 1987, using technology and equipment imported from Hong Kong. It launched its own digital switching gear in China in 1992, and has led the Chinese market ever since. Huawei spends approximately 14 per cent of sales on R&D, operating 20 facilities around the world.

Huawei has been heavily involved in joint ventures with foreign suppliers. In 2013, NSN and Huawei held 51 per cent and 49 per cent shares of TD Tech respectively. In 2006, Huawei established a Shanghai-based joint R&D centre with Motorola to develop Universal Mobile Telecommunications System (UMTS) technologies. Huawei and American security firm Symantec announced in May 2007 the formation of a 51–49 per cent joint-venture company to develop security and storage solutions to market to telecommunications carriers. In sum, Huawei is very active in using joint ventures to obtain technology and to serve specific market segments not supplied by its own product line.

Some conclusions about the telecom equipment sector

Surprisingly in this high-tech sector, it appears that Chinese companies, both public and private, are becoming competitive with the world leaders (Table 6.2). Despite the historical technological leads of Nokia, Siemens, and other Triad-based multinationals such as Alcatel over the Chinese upstarts, both Huawei and ZTE have staked out strong competitive positions domestically and internationally. The two Chinese leaders are investing heavily in R&D, as well as working with foreign high-tech partners, and have already

TABLE 6.2 Market share for wireless telecom infrastructure. Top five suppliers of wireless infrastructure equipment during the first three quarters of 2011 (ranking by revenue in millions of USD)

Q1–Q3 2011 Rank	Company name	2010 Mobile infrastructure revenue	Q1–Q3 2011 Mobile infrastructure revenue	Q1–Q3 2011 Percent of total
1	Huawei	$9,665	$8,938	28.7%
2	Ericsson	$9,710	$8,599	27.7%
3	Nokia Siemens Networks	$10,050	$7,618	24.5%
4	Alcatel-Lucent	$2,190	$2,946	9.5%
5	ZTE	$4,690	$2,000	6.4%
	Others	**$2,676**	**$991**	**3.2%**
	Total	**$38,983**	**$31,092**	**100.0%**

SOURCE: IHS iSuppli Research, October 2012

become market leaders globally. Given the continuing rapid growth of the Chinese domestic market, as well as regional markets in other Asian countries, it appears very likely that these companies will build even stronger competitive positions in the future.

The banking industry in China

Banking competition in China is very different from that in the automobiles or telecommunications equipment markets. The four big government-owned Chinese banks and the government policy banks together hold about two-thirds of banking assets and a similar percentage of banking liabilities in China, as shown in Figure 6.2.

Domestic privately owned banks held a little more than 4.48 per cent of banking assets, and foreign banks had 1.86 per cent of total banking assets, in China in 2012. In sum, the participation of foreign financial institutions in China is minimal, despite efforts of foreign governments in the early 2000s to push the Chinese government to open up the sector as a condition

FIGURE 6.2   China bank loan market share

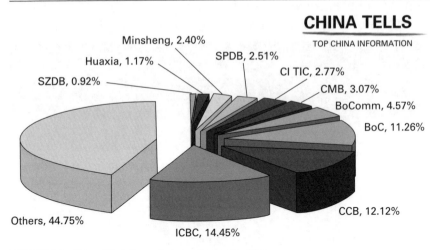

SOURCE: http://blog.chinatells.com/category/corporate-china

for membership of the WTO. And competition for Chinese banking services, therefore, is quite limited to the domestic providers, except in such areas as financing of overseas activities of Chinese firms.

Historically, banking in China was very open to foreign participation, with banks such as HSBC and several other British banks, along with the French Banque de l'Indochine and the German Deutsche Asiatische Bank, operating in the 1800s. HSBC since that time has been the largest and most important foreign bank in China, though its business was greatly curtailed with the Chinese revolution of 1949 and the creation of the People's Republic of China.

The structure of the banking industry in China today thus looks very domestic, with the foreign banks operating at the margin. Our discussion of competition focuses on the largest state-owned national bank (ICBC), the largest private bank, Minsheng, and the largest and oldest foreign bank, HSBC. This approach leaves out of the discussion many important regional banks and the government policy banks such as China Development Bank. And it leaves out the central bank of China, the People's Bank of China (PBOC). Our interest is to examine commercial banking services in which domestic and international banks compete.

The state-owned bank – ICBC

ICBC is currently the fourth largest bank in the world in terms of assets, with 2012 year-end assets of $US 2.78 trillion, more than 427,000 employees, and offices in more than 100 countries. The bank competes across the board in commercial banking services, from loans and deposits to funds transfer, wealth management and credit cards. The bank has more than 280 million retail clients, so it is often seen as a primarily retail bank. Even so, ICBC has over 4 million corporate clients, and offers corporate and investment banking services to them as well.

ICBC's strategy is to continue in its role as the largest provider of financial services to Chinese clients, and to build a global franchise for its services. Competing within China has been easy for ICBC, because the government requires that many state-owned companies use the bank's services. ICBC shifted its lending practices during the most recent five-year plan in favour of key industries and top customers, particularly national government-sponsored major projects under construction or ongoing projects. The first priority was loans for four new markets – advanced manufacturing, strategic emerging industries, modern services and cultural sectors. Loans to local government financing vehicles, real estate developers and companies of 'high energy-consumption, high emission, and over-production' (according to the bank's 2012 annual report) were strictly prohibited. ICBC concentrated on building a balanced loan portfolio covering large and medium-small corporate clients. This strategy is clearly determined by the central government of China, and the bank is complying with its role as the principal source of funding in the market.[13]

Foreign banks operating in China – HSBC

HSBC is the oldest bank in China, founded in 1865. It then developed into a global bank. In response to the return of sovereignty over Hong Kong to China, the bank relocated its headquarters to London and renamed itself simply HSBC. HSBC is one of the first foreign banks to be granted banking licences after China's economic reform. Even before that, HSBC had acquired 20 per cent of equity shares of the Communications Bank of China, the fifth largest state-owned bank in China, to gain exposure in mainland China. HSBC Bank (China) Company Limited incorporated in 2007 and established its headquarters in Shanghai. It has 133 operations on the mainland, including 27 branches and numerous sub-branches.

Private Chinese banks – Minsheng Bank

China Minsheng Banking Corporation (CMBC) is by far the largest privately owned bank in China. Established in 1996 as the first bank owned by non-SOE investors, Minsheng Bank has built a retail banking franchise in Beijing and extending to another dozen major cities in China. Its scale is miniscule compared with ICBC, but it is a sizable bank, nonetheless, with assets of $US 510 billion, about 50,000 employees and about 100 branches in 2012.

Minsheng's strategy is to serve the non-SOE sector of the Chinese economy, as well as to build a retail banking client base. As of 2012, the bank had built a loan portfolio in which 60 per cent of the value outstanding is to non-SOEs, which also constitute over 80 per cent of the bank's borrowers.

Conclusions: a review of the three competitive situations

Table 6.3 gives an overview of the competitive context in China in each of these three sectors.

It is clear that the market shares are dramatically divergent across the three industries. Domestic telecom companies dominate that sector, with major foreign participation, while Chinese (state-owned) banks dominate that sector, with virtually no foreign competition – and the car industry falls in between, with foreign brands commanding greater market share, but in conjunction with local partners who share 50 per cent of the revenues generated by the joint ventures through which GM, VW and the others operate.

We expected that foreign companies would obtain greater market share and performance in general when the sector is characterized by greater technology intensity (and greater marketing intensity, although we were unable to measure this feature) – the traditional strengths of industrial-country

TABLE 6.3 Market shares in the three industries

	SOEs	Foreign MNEs	Local firms
• Autos	50%	40%	10%
• Banking	96%	2%	2%
• Telecom	15%	80%	5%

SOURCE: elaborated by the authors

MNEs. This logic is partially supported by our evidence from three sectors, in which telecoms are characterized by a far higher rate of R&D spending by the competitors than the other two sectors. Even so, the growth of Huawei and ZTE demonstrates that even in this sector, the Chinese firms are likely to dominate within the next decade. While cars cannot be characterized as low-tech, they still are far less R&D intensive than telecom equipment. And in this sector, despite being saddled with required local partners, the foreign car companies (especially GM and VW) continue to dominate.

We also expected that lower-tech industries with less emphasis on marketing capabilities would be led by state-owned firms. And this is precisely what we found in the banking sector, where local banks dominate the sector, and state-owned banks make up most of that group of firms. This outcome is also partially due to the public utility nature of banking, similar to electric power provision, telecommunications service and so on, in which local SOEs dominate.

Overall, we find that the three sectors can be seen as representative of competitive advantages and industry features that are similar for a wide range of industries.

Table 6.4 shows the market shares of companies in several additional industries, noting that the high-tech industries tend to favour foreign MNEs, the capital-intensive industries show mixed results, and public utilities favour

TABLE 6.4   Three industry groups with different foreign market shares

Market shares in major sectors in China					
Capital intensive	Foreign share	High-tech	Foreign share	Utilities	Foreign share
airplane mfre	90+	pharmaceuticals	23	water provision	1
steel	0	computers	35	electric power provision	0
petrochemicals	n.a.	**cell phones**	60	telecom service	0
autos	40	aerospace	n.a.	**banking**	2
oil production	0	biomedicine	23	postal service	0
				airline service	0
				intl express mail	80

SOURCE: elaborated by the author

local SOEs. A key question is whether or not the foreign MNEs that have large market shares will be able to defend or grow those shares as Chinese firms become more competent in developing technology, and the Chinese government continues to support local (SOE) firms.

With respect to the question of how these companies fit into global value chains, it is evident that the Chinese companies in these three sectors are far less global than their foreign counterparts, although the telecom companies have become world leaders in the past few years. Huawei and ZTE are certainly competitive both in China and overseas, and they are among the global leaders in mobile phone (retail) and telephone equipment (corporate) businesses today. These telecom equipment companies do R&D at the same level of intensity as their foreign rivals, and they are vertically integrated in a similar way. They both have clients around the world in Triad countries and in emerging markets. Because of the political/security sensitivity of the telephone system business, ZTE as a government-controlled company and Huawei with its historic ties to the Chinese military may both face major hurdles in building their market share in the United States and the European Union, while at the same time they are not facing similar concerns in the retail, mobile phone business.

In contrast, the Chinese car companies produce cars and other vehicles and distribute them domestically like VW and GM (by force, since the foreign companies operate only through joint ventures with a local Chinese partner). The Chinese companies in this sector do less R&D than the foreign companies, and they depend heavily on imported technology. The Chinese companies have very limited overseas sales networks, although they have been expanding in Asia in particular. While companies such as SAIC and FAW are not any less vertically integrated than VW or GM, they are far less extended into overseas markets and into the R&D of carmaking.

And finally the banks are fairly similar between the Chinese and foreign competitors. The key difference is that regulation precludes the foreign banks from participating in much of Chinese domestic banking services, so that the foreign banks in China are much smaller and more narrowly focused than ICBC or China Construction Bank (CCB). As with the car industry, Chinese banks are trying to expand their activities internationally, but without major impact on markets overseas (such as London or New York). Given the very large size of the major Chinese state-owned banks (the largest half-dozen all have assets worth more than $US 1 trillion), any of them could easily become a major player in the retail or wholesale market in a major foreign financial centre through acquisition of an existing competitor.

Acknowledgements

This chapter was written jointly with Professor Changqi Wu, Guanghua School of Management, Peking University, Beijing, China. Thanks to Xiaonie Zhou and Danxue Gao for their excellent research assistance on this chapter. Prof Wu acknowledges the financial support of the National Science Foundation of China (project no. 71132002).

Notes

1 Although in the banking sector, foreign banks have a miniscule market share; the foreign bank participation is much more important in providing international financial service to Chinese clients, often from abroad.

2 The renminbi is the national currency of China, as with the dollar in the United States. The Chinese currency is often called the 'yuan', which equates to the 'buck' for the dollar.

3 http://factsanddetails.com/china.php?itemid=361

4 See, for example, Dunne (2011).

5 Executives at Chang'An Automotive, currently the fourth largest car manufacturer in China, said that they have set up research and development operations in the United States, Germany and elsewhere outside China; they expect their car quality to equal that of GM and VW within a few years, and for their market share to exceed that of the foreign carmakers after that.

6 Another key competitor is BAIC, or Beiqi. It is a holding company for several automotive firms, including two major joint ventures: Beijing Hyundai and Beijing Mercedes. The company began in 1958, as an assembler of cars using imported technology. Recently, in 2002, the joint venture with Hyundai was established to produce passenger cars. The joint venture with Daimler-Benz was an offshoot of American Motors' original joint venture that produced the Jeep since 1984; BAIC began producing trucks and also two Mercedes Benz car models in 2006.

   BAIC has progressed in the direction originally planned by the Chinese government, though over a time horizon much longer than anticipated. That is, BAIC began by bringing in automobiles to China in the 1950s, looking to learn about making cars and at some point to begin producing its own. This process led to the formation of joint production ventures with American Motors/Chrysler/Daimler-Benz and Hyundai. But it remained until 2013 for BAIC to launch its first solo car model, with the hope of developing further as an independent, and globally competitive, car brand.

7 VW was the first of the current competitors to enter the market, in the 50–50 joint venture with Shanghai Automotive that opened in 1984. VW initially

aimed to serve the local need for taxis with its Passat sedan, and in the 2000s has launched another half-dozen models. In 2002 VW began producing and selling its Skoda brand cars in China, with three models currently in production.

In 1991 VW expanded its geographic scope and its product line through its joint venture with FAW in Changchun. In this case VW accepted a minority ownership position (40%). This JV produces both VW and Audi cars. The competitive advantages of VW in these ventures come down to small-car design and production skills as well as access to a continuing flow of new technology from its operations in Germany and elsewhere.

8 http://online.wsj.com/article/SB100014241278873241623045783043525391 96968.html

9 http://www.economist.com/node/16750095?story_id=16750095&CFID=1522 75665&CFTOKEN=56924159. Geely is described further in Chapter 7 below

10 Chery (Qirui) is a state-owned company founded in 1997 to produce automobiles. It began production in 1999, using a licensed design from VW. Until recently, it had not linked up with a major foreign producer, except for a joint venture with an Israeli company, Qoros. The Chery–Qoros venture is expected to begin production of passenger cars in 2013. In 2012 Chery formed a JV with Jaguar Land Rover to produce those two brands in a factory in Changshu beginning in 2014.

Chery has chosen a strategy of competing in China with passenger vehicles, while at the same time pursuing other emerging markets such as countries in Southeast Asia and North Africa. By 2012 Chery was assembling knocked-down kits of its cars in more than a dozen countries.

11 ZTE and Huawei have been criticized in this regard when they attempted to expand in the US market. See the US Congress report, http://intelligence.house.gov/ sites/intelligence.house.gov/files/documents/Huawei-ZTE%20Investigative%20 Report%20%28FINAL%29.pdf

12 This refers to telecommunications switching gear and other service provision equipment. The mobile phone part of the market is already aggressively competed by Huawei and ZTE against foreign rivals, and the local companies easily could dominate the mobile phone segment within this decade.

13 Another key competitor, CCB, is currently the eleventh largest bank in the world, with 2011 year-end assets of $US 1.97 trillion, more than 330,000 employees, and offices in 13 countries. CCB has a historic emphasis on building infrastructure in China, and holds the largest mortgage loan portfolio in China, as well as the largest portfolio of loans for infrastructure development. CCB was founded in 1954 as the People's Construction Bank, a wholly state-owned bank under the direction of the Ministry of Finance of the PRC to administer and disburse government funds for construction and infrastructure related projects under the state economic plan. CCB became a broader, more general-purpose bank once government policy reforms in the early 1990s allowed it to expand into other activities and to serve additional clients.

Since the global financial crisis, CCB has refocused its attention on the large corporate clients that build infrastructure in China, and also on selected small and medium-sized companies and retail clients. The bank's retail business is led by mortgage lending, a traditional business that was part of its historical role of financing construction throughout China. Since the mid-1990s, CCB has become increasingly similar to ICBC and the other two main state-owned banks in China, offering a full range of financial services to wholesale and retail clients.

References

Chang, S J and Xu, D (2008) Spillovers and competition among foreign and local firms in China, *Strategic Management Journal*, **29**, pp 495–518

Cheng, L and Wu, C (2001) Determinants of performance of foreign invested enterprises in China, *Journal of Comparative Economics*, **29**(2), pp 347–65

Dunne, M (2011) *American wheels, Chinese roads: The story of General Motors in China*, John Wiley & Sons (Asia) Pte Ltd, Singapore

Hu, W-M, Xiao, J and Zhou, X (2014) Collusion or competition? Interfirm relationships in the Chinese auto industry, *Journal of Industrial Economics*, **62**(1), p 8

Ling, Y and Grosse, R (forthcoming 2015) Competing in China: Multinationals, state-owned firms, and alliances, *Journal of Business Research* special issue

Studwell, J (2002) *The China dream*, Atlantic Monthly Press, New York

Tan, J and Peng, M W (2003) Organizational slack and firm performance during economic transitions: two studies from an emerging economy, *Strategic Management Journal*, **24**(13), pp 1249–63

The Economist (2012) *Special report: State capitalism*, *The Economist*, London

The Economist Intelligence Unit (2004) *Coming of age: Multinational companies in China*, *The Economist*, London

The Economist Intelligence Unit (2011) *Multinational companies and China: What future?* The Economist, London

Wu, C and Li, D (2006) Firm behavior in a mixed market, the case of China, in *China's domestic private firms: Multidisciplinary perspectives on management and performance*, ed A Tsui, Y Bian and L Cheng, M.E. Sharpe, Armonk, NY

Wu, C and Liu, Z (2012) A tiger without teeth? Regulation of administrative monopoly under China's Anti-Monopoly Law, *Review of Industrial Organization*, **41**, pp 133–55

Xu, D, Pan, Y, Wu, C *et al* (2006) Performance of domestic and foreign-invested enterprises in China, *Journal of World Business*, **41**, pp 261–74

Appendix: Structure of the Chinese car industry

FIGURE A6.1 Major manufacturers in the Chinese automotive industry

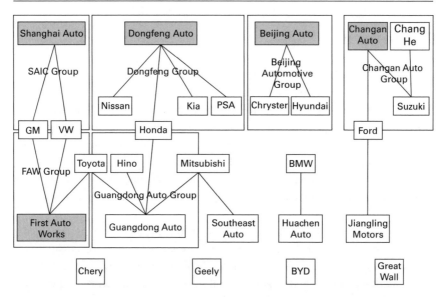

NOTES: Each rectangle with bold border line represents a corporate group, in which are joint ventures between Chinese firms and foreign brands, linked by a line (eg, Dongfeng-Honda is a joint venture in the Dongfeng Group). The foreign brands on the borders of two corporate groups are those that have joint ventures in both groups (eg, Honda has two joint ventures: Dongfeng-Honda and Guangzhou-Honda, belonging to Dongfeng Group and Guangdong Auto Group, respectively). Manufacturers, such as Geely and Chery, are independent from big auto groups.

SOURCE: Hu, Xiao and Zhou (2014). © 2014 The Editorial Board of *The Journal of Industrial Economics* and John Wiley & Sons Ltd

TABLE A6.1 Overall company characteristics

company name/item	indicator	Cars			BANKS			Mobile phones		
		GM	SAIC	Geely	HSBC	ICBC	Minsheng	Nokia-Siemens	Huawei	ZTE
annual sales 2012 (million USD)		152,259	76,848	3,403	82,545	84,082	16,367	17,383	35,363	13,399
sales in China 2012 (million USD)			76,711			81,142	16,367	1,661	11,756	6,293
profits in China 2012 (million USD)	operating profits	1,521	3,347.00	279	6,340	37,887	8,040			
profits/sales (%)	profits after tax/total sales income	4.98%	4.36%	8.18%	18.58%	45.06%	49.12%	−10.81%	6.98%	3.37%
R&D spending 2012 (million USD)			919	17				2,750	4,807.63	1,404
R&D spending/sales (%)		5.41%	1.20%	0.50%				15.82%	4,807	1,404
government ownership (%)			81.08%		0.00%	71%	0%	0%	0%	31.85%
foreign ownership (%)			0.68%			24.6%	20.37%	0%	0%	18.27%
advertising/sales (%)			1.42%						0.57%	0.61%
brand recognition?										
capital intensity (thousands USD)	assets per employee	818	8,246	230,563	9,972	41,048	65,248	231	224	218
qualify of top mgt team	TMT size	10			13	11	11	11	45	20
	percentage of TMT with master degree or above					100%	90.09%		62%	85%
	percentage of TMT with a BA degree					45%	55%			35%
	average years of working experience in the focal industry		26.6		26.6	25.6	20.9	15	17.13	18.75
	CEO years of working experience in the focal industry		32		32	27	27	17	22	23

Emerging market MNEs competing in industrial countries and globally

07

What to expect in Chapter 7

How can emerging market-based companies compete in Triad countries and elsewhere outside their home countries? Since they tend not to have technology-based competitive advantages, what other features or capabilities enable them to compete overseas? This chapter explores the question through a number of case examples, demonstrating how companies from China to Mexico have been able to build successful business activities abroad.

By once again viewing a company's business activities within a global value-added chain, it is possible both to evaluate the strength of that position and to look at ways to expand the business within the value-added chain and across countries. Geely aimed for more than a decade at building an overseas presence, and with the acquisition of Volvo in 2010 it immediately gained that position, which the company now seeks to expand to include its own models as well. A key challenge here is to try to further build the well-respected Volvo brand, without losing the image due to Chinese ownership – and to incorporate Volvo technology in Geely vehicles.

Additional examples include Latin American regional powers FEMSA from Mexico and LAN in Chile, both building their international activities largely inside the region – though by merging its beer business into Heineken, FEMSA arguably is now a global player. Additionally, Itaúsa from Brazil and Grupo Económico Antioqueño (GEA) from Colombia have built very large and diverse businesses in their domestic markets before expanding internationally, mostly within the region.

These examples also include Wipro from India and Aramex from the United Arab Emirates, both of which have made major inroads into global business, serving United States and European clients in business process outsourcing and in package delivery in these two cases. Although production of a lot of their services occurs locally in the home country, still each company is heavily involved in providing those services in the Triad countries.

In every case one of the key competitive advantages of the emerging market company is its flexibility to move into more attractive businesses and to leave less viable ones – an uncommon trait among Triad multinationals. And their overseas activities do tend to focus on other emerging markets, which are smaller than the Triad markets but are growing much faster.

Earlier we looked at emerging market companies and their ability to compete domestically against local rivals and foreign multinationals that enter their turf. Here we want to explore the competitiveness of emerging market companies when they go abroad and compete with traditional multinationals in their home markets and in other countries. This means taking a look at a company such as Geely and its attempts to build sales and market share for cars in Asia, Europe and elsewhere. It's also helpful to look at Wipro as it competes with IBM, Accenture and other Triad-based business process outsourcing companies in the Triad countries, and at companies from smaller emerging markets, such as express delivery company Aramex of the United Arab Emirates, which are also gaining international competitiveness. Let's begin by looking at Geely Automotive competing outside China as a first example, and then come back and consider the key elements of the company's ability to compete successfully away from its often-sheltered home country. That will establish a pattern that can be used to examine other companies and countries.

Zhejiang Geely Holding Group Co., Ltd from China

Geely was founded by Li Shufu in 1986 as a private refrigerator manufacturing company. Mr Li decided to expand into motor vehicles in 1994, when he bought a failed state-owned motorcycle manufacturing company. Four years later the motorcycle business was extended to producing vans, and in

2001 to producing automobiles. Mr Li has persistently built the company to be an internationally known car manufacturer, starting from the third-tier Chinese city of Hangzhou in Zhejiang province near Shanghai. Given constraints on expanding into first-tier cities where governments have been supporting local champions such as Shanghai Automotive and Beijing Automotive, it made sense for Geely to look overseas, as well as at smaller Chinese cities/regions. Starting in 2006 the company began its overseas push, displaying its cars at the Frankfurt Motor Show and at the Detroit Auto Show. Geely also announced a joint venture with British taxicab maker MBH, to fabricate the partner's taxis in Shanghai for sale in the United Kingdom.[1]

Geely took the boldest step among the Chinese carmakers by purchasing Volvo from Ford Motor Company in 2010. This acquisition gave Geely a foothold in the European car market, and even more importantly a knowledge base that includes high-tech automotive design from the Volvo engineers who were acquired along with the brand name and the manufacturing facilities. Geely's stated intent was to leave Volvo relatively independent as far as car design under the Volvo brand name is concerned, but to take advantage of Volvo knowledge and skills to improve the cars sold under the Geely brand name. Additionally, Geely wanted to reduce Volvo production costs by assembling some vehicles in China. By 2013 Volvo had two production facilities operating in China, and Geely had begun to export cars to the United States and Europe as well as to Asian countries.

The Geely strategy has evolved from initially aiming to build the brand name with domestic and export sales, and thus to become competitive in world markets by becoming visible, with showrooms and car sales in foreign markets. In the early years Geely operated with three separate brand names – Emgrand, Gleagle and Englon. Then Li Shufu decided to take a major international step, by acquiring Volvo and instantly establishing a global presence in the industry, albeit under another brand name. In 2014 the company moved to consolidate its branding under the Geely name, along with the separately branded Volvo name.

As with other Chinese domestic car manufacturers, public and private, Geely's domestic sales have been weak, while foreign brands such as VW and GM have built sales significantly. The Chinese market has demonstrated a preference for foreign brands, based largely on perceived quality differences. Again, this situation supports the Geely decision to acquire Volvo and to try to improve its own car quality by learning from the Volvo people.

Internationally, Geely is increasing sales of Volvo cars in the United States and Europe, and lowering production costs of some of them by assembling in China. The Geely-branded cars have still not made a major inroad into overseas sales, but the logic is to sell them through Volvo dealers outside

FIGURE 7.1 Geely in the global automobile value-added chain

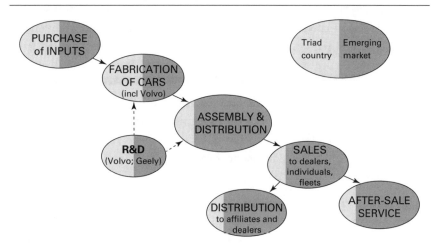

China. The MBH taxis in the United Kingdom may be re-branded as Geely at some point, since the original company is gone and Geely is already making the vehicles in both England and China.

Geely's fit into the global value-added chain for automobile production can be seen in Figure 7.1.

It is clear that Geely is concentrating production of its vehicles in China, while doing much of its research through Volvo in Sweden. Market share is intended to grow in Triad countries and emerging markets alike, and Geely wants to build sales under both brand names worldwide.

MTN from South Africa

MTN was founded in 1994 as M-Cell, a local mobile phone service provider in South Africa, competing with the historic monopoly phone company, Telkom (and Telkom, for its part, competed in the mobile phone segment through a 50–50 joint venture with Vodafone, called Vodacom). MTN, as the underdog in South Africa, has consistently carried out more extensive advertising and alliance efforts than its much larger competitor. Nevertheless, in South Africa MTN remains in second place among mobile phone service providers, with an approximate market share of 35 per cent (relative to Vodacom's 43 per cent and Cell C's 17 per cent).[2]

Early on, MTN looked overseas for expansion opportunities. By the year 2000 MTN was operating in Uganda, Rwanda, Swaziland and Cameroon.

In 2001 the company entered Nigeria, and over the next decade this became the single largest market served. Subsequently, MTN has moved into another half-dozen African countries along with Syria, Iran, Yemen and Afghanistan. By 2013 the company had about 40 per cent of its revenues coming from South Africa, 45 per cent coming from Nigeria, and the rest from the other dozen or so countries.

MTN's stated strategy is to become the leading telecommunications provider in emerging markets. With its expansion into much of Africa and some of the Middle East (which can be seen in Figure 7.2), the company is poised to become a broader-scope telecommunications service provider.

FIGURE 7.2   MTN's geographic spread

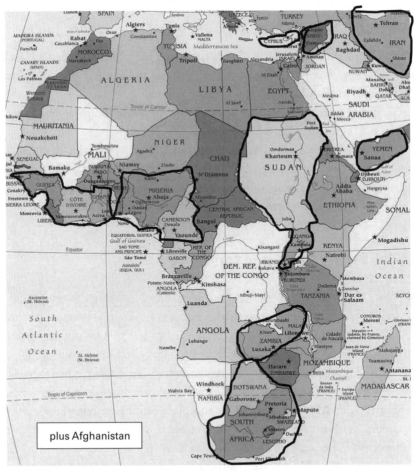

plus Afghanistan

SOURCE: *CIA World Factbook.* Political Africa [Online]
https://www.cia.gov/library/publications/the-world-factbook/docs/refmaps.html

Given that almost no other company has been able to establish multi-region service, other than Vodafone, this idea of expanding into Asia, Latin America and Eastern Europe is probably overstated. Even so, there is a huge potential for expansion in Africa and the Middle East, so MTN does have solid growth prospects.

MTN's fit into a global value-added chain is clearly as a mobile phone service provider, with no manufacturing and offering service only in Africa and the Middle East (connecting, of course, to phone systems literally around the world from those bases). It would be a very natural step to offer fixed-line phone service in some market(s), but MTN has not entered that segment thus far. Given the lower costs involved with mobile phone service, the logical direction for MTN is to expand this service into other emerging markets in its two regions, particularly larger countries such as Egypt, Turkey and Kenya.

FEMSA from Mexico[3]

FEMSA was founded in 1890 as Cerveceria Cuauhtémoc, a brewery based in Monterrey, Mexico. As it grew in the early years, the company founded a bottle-manufacturing company, which became Vitro, and a number of other industrial companies. Along the way, the brewery acquired other brewers, most notably Cerveceria Moctezuma in 1985. The combined Cerveceria Cuauhtémoc Moctezuma (CCM) produces beers including Dos Equis, Tecate, Indio and Carta Blanca among its international brands.

In 1936 the various businesses were grouped under a holding company called Valores Industriales, SA, or VISA. By the 1970s it was one of Mexico's largest companies. In 1973 the group was divided into VISA, which kept the brewery and the country's third largest bank, Serfin, and Grupo Alfa, which held the industrial non-beer activities, including Hylsa, a steel manu-facturer, and Titan, a packaging company. Several decades later the beer part of FEMSA's business was sold to Heineken in 2010, in exchange for 20 per cent ownership of Heineken and two seats on the board of directors. So as far as beer is concerned, FEMSA is a global portfolio investor today, with a major but still minority stake in Heineken.

FEMSA began working with Coca-Cola in 1991, forming a joint venture called Coca-Cola-FEMSA (KOF). This joint venture was initially owned 51 per cent by FEMSA, 30 per cent by Coca-Cola and 19 per cent by share-holders on the Mexican stock exchange. KOF combined the Mexican company's existing local soft drink brands and bottling facilities with the Coca-Cola brand. After initially operating just in Mexico, Coca-Cola FEMSA has acquired bottling companies throughout Latin America. In 2003 KOF transformed itself into a major international player by acquiring Panamco, a Coca-Cola bottler with operations in southern Mexico and in Guatemala, Nicaragua, Costa Rica, and Panama, as well as in Colombia, Venezuela and Brazil. By 2012 KOF had become the largest Coca-Cola franchise bottler in the world. More recently, KOF has acquired additional bottlers in Brazil. Also, the company has broadened its scope to include bottled water and juices in addition to soft drinks.

Along with beer and soft drinks, FEMSA has built a major presence in the convenience store business. OXXO stores were started in 1977, when the company decided to set up its own retail store network to sell its beer. The small stores quickly took on the 7-Eleven or Circle K style of convenience stores, selling not just beer and related snacks but also soft drinks, a more extensive food selection, and other assorted items. By 2014 there were more than 11,000 OXXO stores in Mexico and 34 in Colombia.

In 2014 FEMSA was a two-industry company, with its Coca-Cola bottling and distributing business and the retail OXXO stores. The beer business remains only as a portfolio investment, in that FEMSA owns a large but non-controlling minority share in Heineken. FEMSA's globalization is completely in the Americas (see Figure 7.3), with OXXO trailing KOF in its cross-national footprint by a long way. The company clearly fits into the downstream end of the global value chain for soft drinks and for food and beverage sales, operating retail stores and a distribution network for Coca-Cola. The leaders of the company have demonstrated a flexibility across businesses over the years, always aimed at consumers of beverages (and food).

While geographically FEMSA has remained in the Americas to date, its product portfolio has shifted from the original focus on beer to a broader array of retail food businesses. In recent years the company has also diversified into non-cola beverages such as juices and milk. A logical direction for FEMSA is to expand into the markets in the Americas where they are not already present (including Venezuela, Canada and the Caribbean), to look for further food and beverage offerings to supplement the KOF products, and to sell through the OXXO stores. OXXO itself faces a very positive challenge of trying to expand into Latin American markets beyond Mexico and Colombia, since convenience stores are a common phenomenon throughout the region.

FIGURE 7.3   FEMSA's geographic spread

North and South America

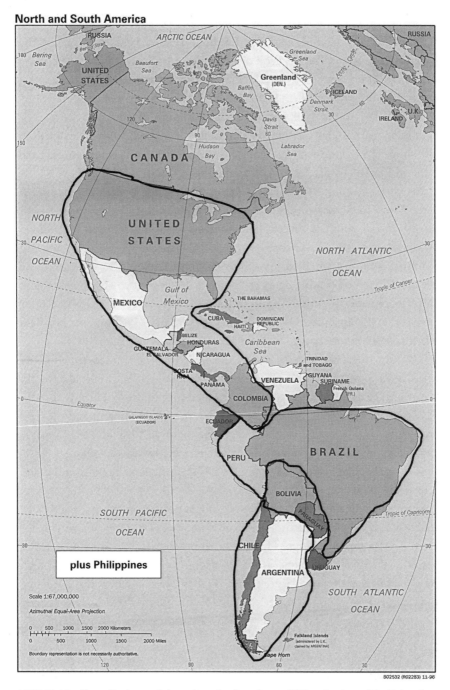

Wipro from India

Wipro was founded in 1945 near Bombay as a vegetable oil manufacturer, Western India Vegetable Products Limited. Twenty years later, when the founder's son (Azim Premji) took over the business, he began slowly shifting the company's focus to new businesses, particularly related to information technology. In 1983 the firm launched Wipro Systems to sell computer software, and two years later entered into marketing of personal computers. Simultaneously, Wipro continued its manufacturing path, with diversification into soap (1982), industrial hydraulic cylinders (1988) and a joint venture with General Electric to produce medical diagnostic equipment (1989).

As with the majority of emerging market major companies discussed here, Wipro pursued a diversified business plan, in this case producing both manufactured goods in several industries and also information technology products and services. Through the 1990s, Wipro invested more in, and put more attention on, information technology activities. By the end of the decade Wipro was producing its own branded PCs (Wipro SuperGenius PC) and had set up a joint venture with Royal Dutch Telecom (KPN) to offer internet service in India. IT outsourcing was launched as a major business line through a joint venture with KPMG Consulting in 2000.

Through the first decade of the 2000s Wipro continued to build its various business lines through acquisitions, alliances and internal growth. It was only in 2012 that the company decided to split the IT businesses from the manufacturing businesses in consumer products. Subsequently Wipro Enterprises holds the consumer soaps and lighting business, the General Electric joint venture for medical devices and the hydraulic cylinders business. The IT outsourcing and manufacturing businesses remain under the Wipro Ltd name.

Since 2012 Wipro Ltd has offered business process outsourcing, internet service, R&D consulting, computer resale, and other IT services. Wipro's global reach is extensive, providing IT services to more than 90 companies in the Fortune Global 500. It is one of the four largest business process outsourcing companies in the world (along with IBM and Indian competitors Infosys and Tata Consultancy Services, TCS). The company divides its revenues into four geographic areas based on the location of the client, as seen in Table 7.1.

Wipro has quite diversified revenues dominated by the United States and Europe, and with major segments in India and the rest of the world as well.

Wipro's fit into a global value-added network for business process outsourcing is shown in Figure 7.4.

TABLE 7.1   Wipro global revenues

Region/revenue	2014	%	2013	%
India	46,226	10.5	48,489	13
United States	200,343	46	172,470	46
Europe	120,868	27.5	99,644	26
Rest of the world	70,182	16	56,323	15
Total	437,619	100	376,926	100

SOURCE: Wipro 2013–14 annual report, p 176 (in millions of crore)

FIGURE 7.4   Wipro's fit into a global value-added network

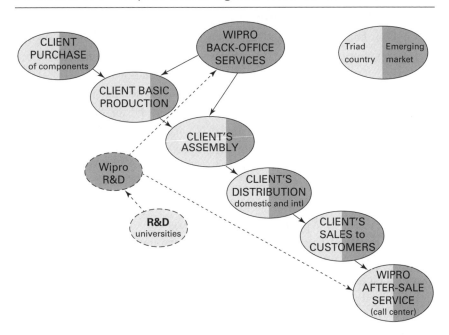

In comparison with IBM, Wipro is able to offer lower-cost business process services, due to its base in India. Relative to TCS and Infosys, Wipro is essentially a head-to-head competitor, with a stock of existing client relationships that enable Wipro to maintain a large volume of sales and thus economies of scale. The most logical extension of Wipro's activities will be to serve more clients from emerging markets such as China, Brazil, Indonesia and other large countries. Wipro also could move further into software design, and thus move up in the value chain of business processes.

LAN (now LATAM) from Chile

LAN Chile was launched in 1929 as a state-owned enterprise by Chilean army air force Commander Arturo Merino Benitez. The stated goal of the company was to provide passenger and mail transportation within Chile, connecting distant cities of Puerto Montt and Antofagasta with the capital, Santiago. It was made the national airline in 1932 and continued as a state-owned company, with generally weak financial and operational results, until privatization in 1989. At that time the airline was sold to Stockholm-based SAS, and then five years later was resold to a group of investors led by the Cueto and Piñera families, owners of Fast Air, a Chilean cargo airline. This background led to a number of interesting developments over time in LAN Chile's subsequent history, as cargo and passengers were transported throughout Latin America and into the United States and Europe as well.

LAN expanded actively in the 1990s and early 2000s, with acquisitions of AeroPeru (LAN Peru), Ecuatoriana (LAN Ecuador) and Aires (LAN Colombia). In addition, LAN joined the One World alliance with American Airlines and British Airways, giving it a global scope for passenger transport. The main obstacles to achieving LAN's vision of being Latin America's main airline were the difficulties in gaining access to Argentina and Brazil. The Argentine government on repeated occasions rejected LAN bids to buy Aerolineas Argentinas, the often-failed national carrier that had been sold to several foreign owners, including Iberia Airlines from Spain. Ultimately, in 2005 LAN set up a *de novo* company in Argentina and began to operate as LAN Argentina. This left Brazil, whose enormous domestic market made it difficult for LAN to enter without buying an extremely expensive national carrier such as Varig (which went bankrupt) or Gol.

LAN finally entered Brazil with a massive acquisition of TAM airlines in 2012. This merger of the much more international LAN with the larger (domestic) airline TAM produced the largest airline in Latin America, now called LATAM. Owing to Brazilian law prohibiting foreign ownership of more than 20 per cent of a domestic airline, the acquisition had to be structured in a complex manner, as shown in Figure 7.5.

So, LAN has a controlling minority ownership of LATAM Group and only a direct 19.5 per cent ownership of TAM. In fact, investors in the stock

FIGURE 7.5   LATAM corporate structure

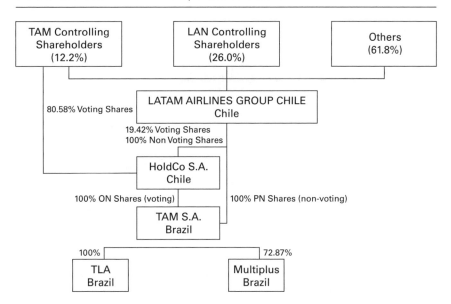

SOURCE: LATAM website, derived from
http://memoria2013.marketinglan.com/LATAM_Annual_Report_2013.pdf

exchanges where LATAM is listed (in Chile, Brazil and the United States) hold a majority of the shares of the combined airline, with LAN holding management control.

In 2013 LATAM was the largest passenger airline in Latin America, transporting 67 million passengers during the year. The airline is global in the sense that it offers passengers the opportunity to fly on code-shared flights with either LATAM or partners such as American Airlines, British Airways, Cathay Pacific and so forth, to destinations literally around the world. Within Latin America LATAM has more flights to more destinations than any other airline, including the three big US-based airlines that have historically dominated international flights in the region (American, United and Delta). LATAM has had the largest cargo network in Latin America among the passenger airlines for more than a decade, although it still trails FedEx, UPS and DHL for cargo shipments in the region. LATAM's range of activities is shown in Figure 7.6, emphasizing the two quite different segments of the air transport market.

LATAM's logical extension of activities internationally would be to include Mexico and Central America in the portfolio of routes and facilities that they operate. This has been complicated not for regulatory but for

FIGURE 7.6 LATAM's value-added chain

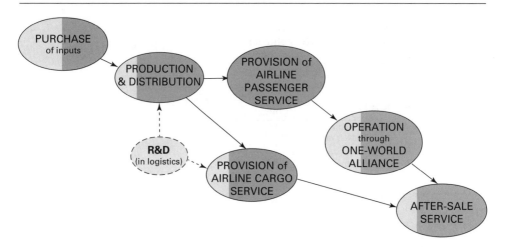

competitive reasons. Both major airlines in Mexico (Aeromexico and Mexicana) have gone bankrupt and been sold and resold several times since the 1980s. The Mexican market is reasonably large, but low-cost budget airlines plus competitors from the United States and Central America (particularly Taca/Avianca and Copa) have put enormous pressure on the two large Mexican carriers. Since LATAM has repeatedly demonstrated an ability to turn around failed domestic airlines in Latin America, this appears to be a very logical next step in the largest remaining market of the region. And, of course, the cargo business in which LAN/LATAM excels could also be extended more deeply into Mexico.

Itaúsa from Brazil

The Itaú group was founded in 1965 as Brazil's first investment bank. The group borrowed in the financial markets to finance loans or investments in Brazilian companies. Over time the bank gained significant positions in the equity of a number of Brazilian companies, such that a decision was made in 1974 to restructure the group's activities. All business was placed under the umbrella of Itaú Investments (Itaúsa), and the banking activities were put into Banco Itaú and later Unibanco, while industrial holdings were concentrated in three companies: Duratec (a manufacturer of wood panels and porcelain and metal bathroom fittings for the construction industry); Itaútec (a manufacturer of ATMs and computer software, mainly for bank automation); and Elekeiroz (a manufacturer of chemical products such as resins for the construction industry).

With the acquisition of Unibanco in 2008 the group's financial services business became the largest bank in Latin America, though still heavily focused on the domestic Brazilian market. Previously, in 1998 Itaú had purchased Banco del Buen Ayre in Argentina, making it one of the top ten full-service banks in that country. In 2014 Itaú-Unibanco acquired control of Corpbanca, with extensive operations in Chile and Colombia, as well as Citibank's operations in Uruguay. Today Itaú-Unibanco has a presence in almost all Latin American markets, with either full-service coverage (as in Brazil, Chile and Colombia) or investment and corporate banking only (in Mexico).

The internationalization of Itaúsa has been almost completely within Latin America, though each of its businesses does have clients in other parts of the world, particularly in the United States. The banking business is the only one with operations in other countries, and even in this instance the percentage of total activity outside Brazil is less than 10 per cent of the bank's total financial services activity. This is clearly a company with huge opportunity to move into overseas markets for its manufactured goods as well as for expansion of its financial services business. Figure 7.7 shows how Itaúsa operates in two very distinct value-added chains, and it implies that the group could move further into additional services and definitely outside Brazil.

FIGURE 7.7   Itaúsa value-added chain

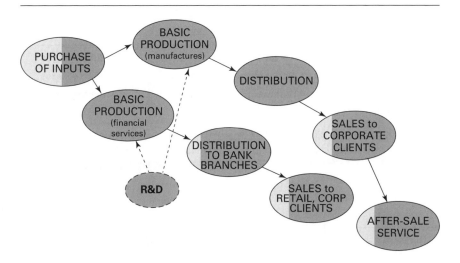

GEA from Colombia

GEA, originally known as the Sindicato Antioqueño, is the largest business group in Colombia, and it would be listed in the Fortune Global 500 except that the group structure does not list one company as a holding company for the rest. That is, there are three main divisions of the group, consisting of financial services (under the insurance affiliate, Suramericana de Seguros), cement (Argos) and foods (Nutresa, formerly Nacional de Chocolates) – and they operate through cross-holdings and cross-directorships in each other. The main companies in the group are shown in Figure 7.8.

GEA was set up in 1978 as a response by Medellín businessmen to a wave of takeovers of local companies by companies from Bogotá and elsewhere. Local leading companies, including Postobon (soft drinks), Coltejer (textiles) and Banco Comercial Antioqueño, had been acquired by Bogotá-based business groups, and the heads of 14 Medellín-based companies came to a formal agreement to invest in each other's companies and form a defence network that would preclude outsiders from taking control of any of them. At that time, two of the pillars of GEA (Nutresa and Inversura) had seen creeping takeover of shares by Grupo Grancolombia from Bogotá, and they in particular were strongly committed to the mutual defence scheme. Today there are about 150 companies in the GEA, grouped under the three industrial headings shown in Figure 7.8, along with the bank, Bancolombia.

FIGURE 7.8   Group structure – Grupo Económico Antioqueño

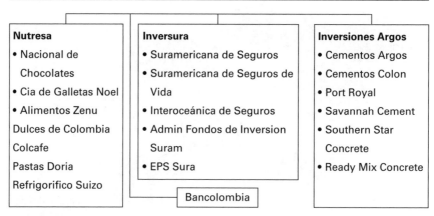

Major companies of the 150 total belonging to the Grupo Empresarial Antioqueño.

The group has functioned successfully within Colombia since that time, with ups and downs along with the general economic condition of the country. In the late 1990s and 2000s several of the group's companies made significant pushes to internationalize by establishing subsidiaries in other Latin American countries. Inversura, for example, owns insurance companies in Mexico, Peru, Chile and Panama, as well as in some smaller markets in Latin America. Argos has expanded by acquiring a large cement business in the southern United States, as well as others in Honduras, the Dominican Republic and Panama. Nutresa has chocolate or other food operations in all Andean countries of South America, Argentina, all Central American countries and an extensive network of subsidiaries in the United States. Figure 7.9 shows the geographic expansion of GEA, and the notable hole in that coverage, namely, Brazil.

The group's strategy is clearly one of diversified growth, with the three main product/service sets of companies not accounting for all of the major businesses in which GEA is involved (eg the bank, the textile company, Fabricato, and the aeroplane importer, Internacional Ejecutiva de Aviación). For each of the three main business lines the group has defined a strategy of being a market leader in the Americas, from the United States to Argentina, and this strategy has been partially realized in every instance. Clearly the main target market that remains in the region is Brazil – though GEA's market share in most countries outside Colombia is not the largest, so room for growth exists in those existing markets as well.

Aramex from the United Arab Emirates

Arab International Logistics (Aramex) is a large international express delivery and freight shipping company based in Dubai, United Arab Emirates. The company's stated mission is: 'to be recognized as one of the top five global logistics and express transportation service providers'. Aramex was founded in 1982 and has grown to encompass a network of delivery vehicles operating in more than 350 locations in 60 countries served by 14,000 employees. This is probably the most global and least known company discussed here.

Aramex began by offering express delivery service in the United Arab Emirates and nearby countries. Service was naturally expanded to other countries where existing clients had needs for letter and package delivery, including the United States and Europe. Rather than entering into local delivery service in the United States or European Union, Aramex has remained on the sidelines in those countries, operating through alliances with other companies inside those countries.

FIGURE 7.9 Grupo Empresarial Antioqueño affiliate network

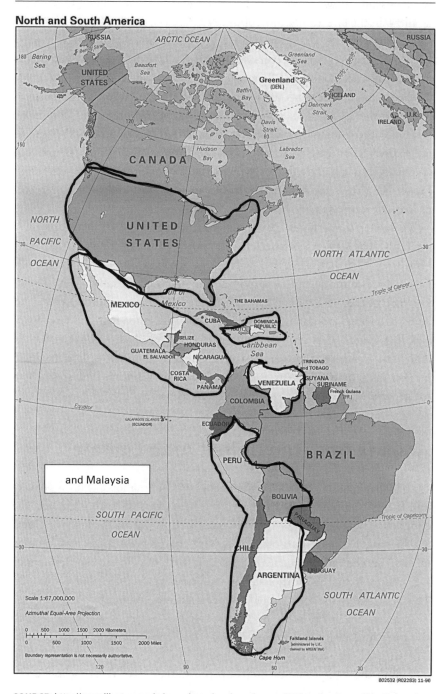

North and South America

and Malaysia

In fact, Aramex participates in the Global Distribution Alliance in which more than 100 logistics and transportation companies offer local service to their alliance partners in over 200 countries. This enables Aramex to compete with FedEx, UPS and DHL in markets such as the United States and the European Union without having its own proprietary network of delivery vehicles in those countries.

Aramex is following a clear strategy to build its network of delivery infrastructure in the Middle East, Africa and Asia rather than in the traditional Triad countries. Aramex has acquired Mail Call Couriers in Australia, Berco Express in South Africa, Avanti Couriers in Malaysia and OneWorld Courier in Kenya in the past five years. At the same time the company has proceeded to set up alliances with additional local delivery companies in other emerging markets and to establish a franchising model to include locally owned delivery companies under the Aramex brand name.

FIGURE 7.10   Aramex value-added chain

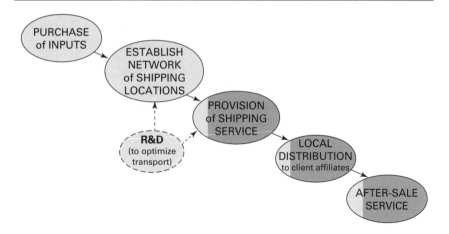

The company operates a very decentralized management structure, with local affiliates in each country maintaining a large degree of freedom in their activities, linked by the global information network to coordinate shipments.

Aramex's fit into a global value-added chain is shown in Figure 7.10.

A review of the international strategies of eight emerging market companies

From Aramex to Wipro, these emerging market giants are actively competing internationally. Most of them are operating regionally and mostly in other emerging markets, as shown in Table 7.2.

TABLE 7.2 Emerging market MNEs and their international expansion

Company/ trait	Home country	Key competitive advantages	Countries with operations	% intl sales
Aramex	United Arab Emirates	Knowledge of and relationships with clients in Middle East	60 countries in Middle East, Asia, and globally	>80%
FEMSA	Mexico	Strategic alliance with Coca-Cola; client relationships in Latin America; diversification; flexibility	Argentina, Brazil, Colombia, Costa Rica, Guatemala, Nicaragua, Panama, Peru, Venezuela, Philippines, United States	<20%
GEA	Colombia	Client relationships in Central America and Andean region; diversification; flexibility	Chile, Dominican Republic, Haití, Malaysia, Panamá, Peru, United States, Venezuela	<20%
Geely	China	Low-cost production; Volvo technology; flexibility	Australia, Indonesia, Sri Lanka, Malaysia, Russia, Sweden, United Kingdom, Ukraine, United States	20%
Itaúsa	Brazil	Client relationships in Latin America; diversification; flexibility	Argentina, Cayman Islands, Chile, China, Colombia, European Union, Japan, Mexico, Paraguay, Peru, Switzerland, UAE, Uruguay, United States	<20%
LAN/LATAM	Chile	Routes and client relations in Latin America; high-quality service	Argentina, Brazil, Colombia, Ecuador, Paraguay, Peru, United States	>50%
MTN	South Africa	Knowledge of African markets; client relationships in Africa	18 African countries; Afghanistan, Cyprus, Iran	60%
Wipro	India	Client relationships with global clients; low-cost service; previous diversification	mainly United States, European Union; Singapore	89%

Wipro and Aramex are clearly exceptions to the regional focus, since they operate globally. Wipro, however, is much more focused on the Triad countries, while Aramex is clearly focused on emerging markets. Geely's sales are primarily domestic, but with the acquisition of Volvo, it has a major presence in Europe and in the United States with that brand of cars.

Conclusions

The large MNEs based in emerging markets discussed in this chapter tend to have competitive advantages in non-traditional areas such as customer relationships, flexibility to shift business activities, and diversified portfolios of business lines. The companies tend to stay relatively close to home with their international expansion, although exceptions do exist in the case of Aramex, which really operates globally through its own affiliates and through alliances with other express delivery companies, and Wipro, which serves clients mainly in the United States and European Union, even though the company is based in India.

In some cases these companies are quite dependent on Triad-based partners – FEMSA in particular depends heavily on Coca-Cola, and to some extent LATAM depends on One World alliance partners American Airlines and British Airways.

None of these companies competes based on traditional Triad MNE capabilities of proprietary technology or marketing skills embodied in a globally recognized brand name. Because the software industry is not typically measured in terms of R&D intensity – even though its products often are very technology intensive – Wipro does not demonstrate such a capability, though technology probably is in fact a base of their competitiveness. Because most of these companies compete mostly in emerging markets, their names tend not to be known to residents of Triad countries. Even so, MTN ranked number 93 on the *Financial Times* list of the 100 best-known brands in the world in 2014 (and another dozen emerging market companies appear on the list, including Tencent, Baidu, ICBC and China Mobile (China); MTS (India); and Sberbank (Russia)).

Notes

1 The British firm subsequently went into bankruptcy in 2012, and Geely bought the assets in 2013, including a taxi manufacturing plant in Coventry, England, from which Geely continues to produce the MBH taxis.

2 Telkom sold its half-share in Vodacom in 2008. Today Telkom competes directly in the mobile phone market, with a market share of less than 5%, and retains its monopoly on fixed-line phone service in South Africa.

3 FEMSA was briefly discussed in Chapter 1, looking at its fit into the supply chains of partners Coca-Cola and Heineken.

References

Annual reports:

Aramex [Online] http://reports.aramex.org/annual/2014/

FEMSA [Online] http://www.annualreport.femsa.com/

GEA:no report exists. See, for example, [Online] http://en.wikipedia.org/wiki/Grupo_Empresarial_Antioque%C3%B1o

Geely: no report exists. See, for example, [Online] http://global.geely.com/

Itaúsa [Online] http://www.itausa.com.br/EN/Documentos/5687_RA13.pdf

LATAM [Online] http://memoria2013.marketinglan.com/LATAM_Annual_Report_2013.pdf

MTN [Online] https://www.mtn.com/Investors/FinancialReporting/Pages/IntegratedReports.aspx

Wipro [Online] http://www.wipro.com/documents/investors/pdf-files/Wipro-annual-report-2013-14.pdf

Innovation is key

08

What to expect in Chapter 8

While it cannot be unambiguously stated that innovation is the key competitive advantage of the 21st century, innovation certainly ranks very high among priorities. For countries, faster growth rates in this century have come thus far from production and export of natural resources.[1] Even so, over many centuries of economic development, as discussed in Chapter 3, we see that countries where innovations are spawned tend to be those that produce the greatest well-being for their citizens.

The most innovative countries in the early 21st century do tend to be in the Triad. Emerging markets generally are behind in generation of patents, scientific publications, R&D spending and other measures of innovation. However, in aggregate terms, China is second only to the United States in R&D spending and in production of scientific journal articles, so it clearly is already in a leading position (though not on a per capita basis). And other large emerging markets, India and Brazil, also are rising in the lists of innovative activity.

Still, the amount of innovation by companies in emerging markets, measured as above, is far behind that of similar companies from Triad countries. When one looks at the successes of emerging market companies, as we have been doing here, it is evident that they have some competitive advantages that are innovative. Maybe not a patented pharmaceutical product, but a method for managing conglomerate business activities. Maybe not a new IT product, but a skill in operating a supply chain and particularly a distribution network. Thus, the challenge may be less on the question of innovation, and more on how it is measured.

Regardless of the note that emerging market companies pursue non-traditional innovation, they still trail Triad companies in many regards, often because of cultural conditions in many emerging markets that deter innovation. The amount of entrepreneurship in different countries may be a good indicator of this challenge to innovation. One way for emerging market companies to respond to this challenge, and to benefit from the innovation that occurs in other countries, is to establish affiliates there, to participate in that activity. This is just what Geely from China did with its acquisition of Volvo, and JBL from Brazil did with its acquisition of US-based Swift foods.

Introduction

The threat of growing competition from firms based in emerging markets is very real for many Triad-based companies. And also from the opposite perspective, the opportunities for emerging market companies to compete internationally are growing rapidly, and those firms are looking for ways to build strong competitive positions. The combination of low-cost production and often protected domestic markets has positioned a large number of emerging market-based companies to compete against foreign MNEs domestically as well as in overseas markets. In addition, with the growing attractiveness of emerging markets as targets for sales, the companies based in those countries have a competitive advantage in knowledge about their home country markets relative to Triad-based MNEs.

But, back up and think about company competitiveness in general these days. One key source of competitiveness for companies around the world in the 21st century is innovation.[2] The ability to create new products/services and introduce them successfully into the market has always been one source of advantage for companies; and with the globalization of competition, it has become even more important today. It is harder every day to hide behind protection from a government or protection from a monopolized channel of distribution, and it is increasingly important to be able to create and introduce new products, processes and services.

This chapter looks at both company innovation and national innovativeness. While the discussion up to this point has largely focused on company activities, the environment in which companies operate is especially important when we look at innovation. If a government does not offer incentives to innovation, and if a society penalizes people for trying to innovate (eg launch a new company) and failing, then the environment in that country will not be favourable towards the activities needed to produce a substantial and continuing flow of innovations. What is more, if per capita income levels are low, and education does not provide adequate access to new knowledge in engineering, medicine and other scientific endeavours, then the society will tend not to produce these kinds of innovation. So country-level factors are particularly important in this context.

Measures of innovation

One factor that still largely distinguishes companies from the Triad relative to their rivals based in emerging markets is their ability to generate technology advantages based on R&D to create new products, services and processes. The innovative activity in this context has remained a feature of North America, Western Europe and Japan – while emerging markets such as Mexico, Brazil, India and China have produced very few companies that lead the world technologically. Just looking at national levels of R&D activity shows a stark contrast between emerging markets and Triad countries. Table 8.1 compares recent total annual spending by companies, government and universities combined for selected countries.

TABLE 8.1   National spending on R&D, selected countries, 2012

		National R&D expenditure by all sources		
Rank	Country	R&D as % of GDP @ PPP	Expenditures on R&D, billions of $US at PPP	Rank based on total R&D spending
1	Israel	4.20%	10.3	18
2	Finland	3.80%	7.7	22
3	Sweden	3.62%	12.9	16
4	Japan	3.48%	157.6	3
5	South Korea	3.45%	56.4	5
6	Denmark	3.08%	6.6	23
7	Switzerland	3.00%	10.4	17
8	Germany	2.87%	90.6	4
9	United States	2.85%	436.0	1
10	Austria	2.75%	9.9	19
11	Singapore	2.65%	8.8	20
12	Taiwan	2.38%	22.3	12
13	Australia	2.28%	21.8	13

TABLE 8.1   *continued*

		National R&D expenditure by all sources		
Rank	Country	R&D as % of GDP @ PPP	Expenditures on R&D, billions of $US at PPP	Rank based on total R&D spending
14	France	2.24%	51.1	6
15	Belgium	2.03%	8.6	21
16	Canada	2.00%	28.6	10
17	Netherlands	1.90%	13.7	15
18	Norway	1.85%	5.1	24
19	United Kingdom	1.84%	42.4	7
20	Ireland	1.75%	3.2	25
21	China	1.60%	198.9	2
22	Spain	1.42%	20.4	14
23	Brazil	1.25%	30.0	9
24	Russia	1.08%	26.9	11
25	India	0.85%	41.3	8

PPP = purchasing power parity.

SOURCE: data from
http://battelle.org/docs/default-document-library/2012_global_forecast.pdf?sfvrsn=2

It is clear from this table that the Triad countries (and especially northern Europe) dominate in their commitment to R&D, while the United States and China lead total spending by a large margin. No emerging market even reaches the top 20 countries in terms of R&D intensity, although almost paradoxically due to its large size, China ranks second overall in total R&D spending. This last point is quite important: even if China lags far behind in R&D relative to the size of its total economy, still the amount of R&D

taking place in China today dwarfs that of every other country except the United States.

These data on national R&D intensity include government spending, university spending and company spending on R&D. It is not clear from the aggregate information how much is spent by companies, and thus how much the companies are investing in building R&D advantages. In the United States, about two-thirds of R&D is undertaken by companies, and this is typical for the top seven countries in total R&D, but very different from most of the rest of the world. In most countries the government is the largest investor in this activity, with companies a distant second.[3]

In sum, while the Triad countries do tend to dominate R&D activity measured at the national level, still China is pursuing a huge amount of such activity, and thus is not at all behind in that regard. If we look at per capita spending on R&D, China and all emerging markets indeed fall far back in the pack – but still the aggregate amount of such activity is impressive and is large enough surely to position China as a global technology leader in the future. Even India and Brazil, not noted as R&D leaders in the world, rank eighth and ninth in total R&D spending among countries today. So while their intensity of such activity is not great, their overall spending certainly is.

Another measure of R&D activity is the registration of patents for new technology developed in a country. This is a narrower indicator of R&D activity, and it is measured here just using data from the largest source of patent registrations globally, the US Patent and Trademark Office. Table 8.2 gives a simple illustration of this situation, showing patents filed by country of origin as a measure of innovative activity.

China is the only emerging market ranked in the top ten, and arriving there only in the past five years. The list is dominated, not surprisingly, by the United States, Japan and Germany, though today South Korea and Taiwan are not far behind. In this measure of technological innovation, the Triad-based scientists clearly have a strong advantage over emerging market rivals – although Chinese patent activity clearly is catching up. This may be a surprising finding for those who believe that China is a 'copycat' country, with little ability to produce its own technological advances. The same was once said for Japan and for South Korea, both of which have demonstrated the ability to join the rest of the Triad countries in innovative activity during the past half-century.

This measure of patents is attractive for our purposes, because it focuses on the source of the patent, which generally is a large or small company. So this ranking of countries tends to reflect the innovative activity of companies

TABLE 8.2   US utility[1] patents by country of origin

Country/Year	2013	2012	2011	2010	2000
United States	133,593	121,026	108,626	107,792	85,072
Japan	51,919	50,677	46,139	44,814	31,296
Germany	15,498	13,835	11,920	12,363	10,234
S Korea	14,548	13,233	12,262	11,671	3,314
Taiwan	11,071	10,646	8,781	8,238	4,667
Canada	6,537	5,775	5,012	4,852	3,419
France	6,083	5,386	4,531	4,450	3,819
China	5,928	5,341	3,174	2,657	119
United Kingdom	5,086	5,213	4,307	4,302	3,667
Israel	3,012	2,474	1,981	1,819	783
Other... (eg Italy, Netherlands, Switzerland, Sweden)	...	...	...	...	
India	2,424	1,691	1,234	1,098	131
Russia	417	331	298	272	183
Brazil	254	196	215	175	98

[1] From the USPTO website: *Utility Patent* – Issued for the invention of a new and useful process, machine, manufacture, or composition of matter, or a new and useful improvement thereof, it generally permits its owner to exclude others from making, using, or selling the invention for a period of up to twenty years from the date of patent application filing ++, subject to the payment of maintenance fees. Approximately 90% of the patent documents issued by the USPTO in recent years have been utility patents, also referred to as 'patents for invention'.

SOURCE: data from US Patent & Trademark Office, http://www.uspto.gov/web/offices/ac/ido/oeip/taf/reports_stco.htm

there, though even so the patents may be obtained by local affiliates of foreign companies or other foreign registrants filing locally. Also, the patent registrations only cover technology that is patentable – which means that many kinds of R&D are not included, such as a lot of computer software, recipes for food products, methodologies for carrying out business services, and many kinds of intangibles that are generally hidden to protect them rather than using patents for protection. In fact, one of the key points to take away from this chapter is that emerging market companies are often leaders in developing non-patentable innovations – so their competitiveness in patent generation is not a good measure of their overall level of innovative activity.

A third measure of technological advances is scientific articles published by authors in various countries (see Table 8.3). These are articles published in academic journals that are reviewed by peer scientists (or social scientists, as the case may be). This measure indicates new knowledge that may be obtained and then used by companies who have access to the publications.

In this measure of knowledge creation, the country rankings are not that different overall, with China as the only emerging market in the top ten, although both China and the United Kingdom do rank much higher using this criterion. With all measures, the United States is far and away the leading producer of technological advances in the world in the early 21st century. The difficulty in using scientific articles as a measure of innovativeness of companies from different countries is that the knowledge generated by the scientists in academic journals is not necessarily transferred to companies, local or foreign. The missing link is to understand how likely it is that [local] companies will take advantage of the advances that appear in journals in any country.

In all three of these measures, what is being considered are advances in knowledge, rather than innovations of products or services in the marketplace. That is, in none of the cases is there a direct link between the spending, the patent or the article and a new product or service (or business process) that is launched in the market. Nevertheless, if we look at patents by the company/individual who files with the US Patent and Trademark Office, it does turn out that the main companies in the list are Triad-based companies, some multinational and some small and local companies. That is, the link between scientific advances and introduction of the science into the market does demonstrate a direct connection to company activity in those cases. If we look at the scientific articles, there is no direct connection to companies taking advantage of the advances, and indeed, most of the articles

TABLE 8.3 Scientific and technical journal articles published by country of author

Scientific and technical journal articles	2011	2009	2005	2000
United States	n/a	208,601	205,565	192,743
China	89,894	74,019	41,603	18,479
Japan	47,106	49,627	55,527	57,101
United Kingdom	46,035	45,649	45,658	48,216
Germany	46,259	45,003	44,194	43,509
France	31,686	31,748	30,340	31,427
Canada	n/a	29,017	25,862	22,701
Italy	26,503	26,755	24,663	21,409
S Korea	25,593	22,271	16,396	9,572
Spain	22,910	21,543	18,346	14,795
India	22,481	19,917	14,635	10,276
...				
Russia	14,151	14,016	14,425	17,180
Brazil	13,148	12,306	9,897	6,407

SOURCE: data from World Bank, http://data.worldbank.org/indicator/IP.JRN.ARTC.SC?page=1 &order=wbapi_data_value_2009%20wbapi_data_value%20wbapi_data_value-first&sort=desc

are published by academic researchers rather than company scientists or analysts. But it is true that the articles tend to be published in the United States, European Union and Japan, and that there is far less activity in emerging markets.

An interesting aspect of this scientific activity is that it is not limited to Triad-based companies. That is, companies from China or India or Honduras or Thailand can gain access to scientific advances just as their rivals can. However, the cultural distance from the Triad countries and their practices makes it much more difficult for an emerging market company to obtain the information and to implement it in a business context (eg Shane, 1993; Taylor and Wilson, 2012). So, for instance, when an article is published about a nanotechnology advance, it is much easier for a scientist who has experience in reading this literature and understanding the style of writing to interpret the advance and possibly to take advantage of it in a business context. Most of the people with this kind of experience are in, or have studied in, the most-developed countries.

One more measure of innovation that goes more directly to company activities is the annual survey done by the European Union of the 1,000 companies worldwide with the largest spending on R&D activity. This listing in Figure 8.1 very clearly shows that the self-reported spending on R&D is concentrated in Triad companies, with just one large Chinese firm, Huawei, in the list. (The list presented here stops with just the top 50 companies; the full list is available on the website noted as the source of this figure.)

This R&D list still limits our understanding of innovation to the extent that service companies are excluded, and we certainly know that firms such as McKinsey (management consulting), Goldman Sachs (financial services) and WPP (advertising) are highly innovative, large organizations. Since service-sector companies dominate economies in the 21st century, from the United States to China, we should find a way to capture the amount of innovation going on in those sectors where R&D is not identified clearly. So our definition of what to include in R&D is itself somewhat problematic.

All of these measures demonstrate activity that may lead to successful innovation – but there is no guarantee of success. That is, the creation of new knowledge through scientific research may lead to inventions of new products, processes or services, but it does not at all ensure that the new item will be successful in the marketplace.[4]

What is innovation, and how should it be measured?

Innovation refers to the combination of invention and subsequent commercialization. The Merriam-Webster dictionary defines innovation simply as: 'the act or process of introducing new ideas, devices, or methods [into the marketplace]' (**http://www.merriam-webster.com/dictionary/innovation**).

FIGURE 8.1 R&D spending by company

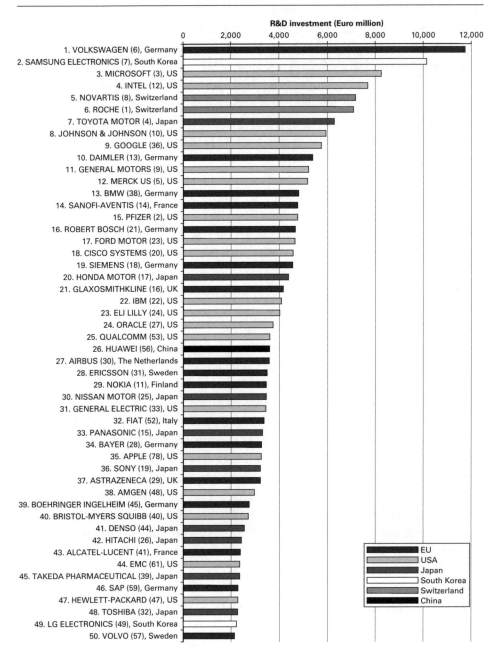

NOTE: The number in brackets after the name of the company indicates the ranking in 2010.

SOURCE: The 2014 world 2500 companies ranked by R&D. http://iri.jrc.ec.europa.eu/scoreboard14.html.
© European Union, 1995–2015

Both halves of the meaning – both creating the new items and marketing them – are important. Great success in inventing new things does not guarantee that the outputs will be introduced successfully into the marketplace. France ranks very high among countries in the patent list and the scientific article list – in Table 8.3 – but there are few French companies in the list of the top 1,000 innovative companies as shown by the EU survey in 2014 (while there are several Chinese and Indian companies in the list). We will look first at what innovation is, and then turn to the question of how better to measure it.

According to the definition above, innovations are new ideas, devices or methods that are introduced into the marketplace. Ideas as such are not particularly helpful to companies trying to build sales or reduce costs. An idea for a product such as a multifunction mobile phone is valuable because the idea is embodied in the phone, which in turn can be sold in the marketplace. Likewise, the idea of a methodology for creating and presenting an ad campaign is not valuable in itself; but the idea can be embodied in a methodology that is used to produce real ad campaigns, thus creating market value. In sum, devices (products) and methods (intangibles that are marketable) are the primary sources of successful innovation.

If we stick with this view of innovation, we are still missing the non-product, non-method business sectors, namely services. Perhaps services can be captured under the label of 'method', although it is difficult to see how a method could be differentiated for one bank versus another (other than customer relationship management, which was presented as a method). Or how a method would be differentiated by a new entrant into some personal service such as hair care, lawn mowing or house painting. These and other services would be perhaps better categorized as a type of product, the way a bank labels a home loan one of its 'products'. While this perspective is more aligned with service businesses, it still obscures the service sectors by using the word 'product', which implies a physical item.

In sum, the definition of innovation would be better stated if it were expressed as: *'innovation is the act or process of introducing new products, services, or methods into the marketplace'*. We will work with this more explicit definition of innovation, and then look for types of innovation that are pursued by different kinds of company and by companies from different kinds of country.

If we take this point of view, it raises the question of the appropriate scope of new products, services or methods that should be considered for measuring innovation. Are proprietary drugs and other patented products the only sources of key innovation? What about new services that are invented and marketed, with no measured spending in R&D by scientists, though perhaps significant spending in terms of a company's assignment of personnel and funds to create and launch new services? And what about processes such as customer relationship management, methodologies for providing consulting/advertising/accounting service to clients, and internal corporate management in highly diversified conglomerate companies? It may very well be that the main areas for innovation by emerging market firms turn out to be these less-visible but still very powerful types of innovation that produce sustainable competitive advantages.

In fact, if we review the competitive strengths of the various emerging market companies discussed in previous chapters, it becomes very clear that they have developed or are developing advantages based on 'innovations' such as customer relationship management in a particular institutional context, and sales strategies (methodologies) that fit markets with lower-income clients than the Triad countries, among other sources of advantage. The ability to take advantage of new technology developed in Triad countries and adapt it to emerging markets is another key strength that many of these companies are developing.

So, what is innovation? It really does need to include the advances realized by emerging market firms that give them the ability to achieve better customer relationship management, or better ability to manage a diversified conglomerate company – even though these innovations are not subject to patent protection, and they may not lead to scientific articles being published about them, or even spending in the traditional 'R&D' sense.[5] Corporate planners are not usually categorized as R&D workers, yet their contribution to a company's competitiveness may very well be in precisely this realm.

Perhaps a more appropriate evaluation of innovation will be a measure of companies' competitive advantages, dissected to see which ones are knowledge based (such as patented products or corporate methodologies for business processes), and which ones are not (such as financial size, natural resource availability or government protection). We could set up a system to measure the knowledge-based advantages in this way, as shown in Table 8.4.

Except for the first two lines in the table, all of the other innovation categories are outside the scope of what is usually measured, and what tends to be reported by companies in their annual reports and financial statements to shareholders and regulators. How difficult is it to see that the amazing competitiveness of companies such as General Electric or Siemens comes not from their patented technologies, which they often have in some business lines – but rather from their ability to manage a portfolio of businesses, including quite unrelated ones? Likewise, how hard is it to recognize that the competitiveness of Southwest Airlines or Enterprise Rent-a-Car relative

TABLE 8.4 Knowledge-based competitive advantages

Competitive advantage	Knowledge component	Value measure*	Examples
Patented product	R&D spending on product development	Product sales/year; # of product successes	Pfizer drugs; BASF chemicals; Samsung smartwatch; Apple iPhone
Patented process	R&D spending on process development	Efficiency relative to rivals	Amazon 1-click purchase; Priceline.com auctions
Customer relationship management (CRM) methodology	Computer-based record-keeping system for CRM	Billings from large clients; # of large clients; client feedback surveys	Lexus; Ace Hardware; Enterprise Rent-a-Car
Supply chain management methodology	Design of logistics management system; physical shipping methods	Cost of delivery for packages, letters; speed of delivery	UPS; Amazon; Wal-Mart; Inditex
Innovative financial products	Financial engineering	Value of derivatives sold; value of risks reduced	Citibank; Goldman Sachs; Merrill Lynch
Methodology for designing ads or providing management consulting or providing other business services	Computer-based record-keeping system of the methodology	Market ranking in sector; billings from large clients	McCann Erikson; Dentsu; McKinsey; Bain: KPMG; SAP
Ability to manage a conglomerate organization	Ability to integrate businesses; scanning capability for opportunities	# of sectors covered; % of sales in average sector	Grupo Luksic (Chile); General Electric; Mitsubishi; LG; Tata
Cultural/institutional knowledge of a particular market/group	Knowledge of government people; Knowledge of cultural ways	% of sales to government; % of sales to specific groups	Goya Hispanic foods; Todaro's Italian foods

* = the first measure of value in each case should be profitability relative to key rivals.

SOURCE: constructed by the author

to larger rivals is in the way they manage the delivery of service to their customers?[6]

For emerging markets companies, there are even more examples of these kinds of competitive advantage. In the context of managing multiple businesses it is clear in every emerging market that some or many leading companies are business groups such as Grupo Carso in Mexico or Astra International in Indonesia.[7] These groups may have one or more businesses in protected sectors, but the competitiveness generally comes from the group's ability to move into and out of sectors that become more or less attractive sources of profits – and to balance the demands of the various businesses in one organization.

This measurement system provides a much broader perspective on innovation, and may reflect the reality of what matters in the 21st century better than the other indicators above. It will require some effort to convince policymakers and others that this framework is both helpful for identifying valuable innovation and capable of being measured in such a way that innovations can be evaluated in comparison with each other. Nevertheless, this broader view is necessary if innovation is really to be understood adequately, and if policy and strategy are to be designed to promote it. It should not be hard to convince company managers that innovation matters, and that these additional kinds of innovation beyond patent-related R&D are solid bases for competitiveness today.

How do emerging market companies fare on broadly defined innovation?

Let's return to the list of the world's largest MNEs, and look just at those from emerging markets. Also, let's eliminate the companies in natural resource industries, where possession of the resource is a key advantage, rather than an internal company characteristic or skill. Table 8.5 shows the largest 50 non-resource companies based in emerging markets from the 2013 Fortune Global 500.

The list is presented with the traditional measure of annual sales, along with industry, nationality and market value of the firm. A new column is added showing some of the innovation-related competitive strengths of these firms. This list provides a simple demonstration that the largest emerging market firms outside of oil and other natural resources tend to be in financial services and electric power, plus a range of single businesses in China and conglomerates elsewhere. And that many of them are innovating in non-traditional areas.

TABLE 8.5 Top 50 non-resource emerging market companies in Fortune Global 500

Company	Country	Industry	Sales 2013 $US billions	MKT Value $US billions	Innovations
State Grid	China	electric power	298.4	156.3	Smart grid
ICBC	China	banking	134.8	237.3	Equator Principles (international social and environmental standards)
China Construction Bank	China	banking	113.1	202	Member of Global ATM Alliance (no transaction fees among member banks). Launched China Healthcare Investment Fund.
Agricultural Bank of China	China	banking	103	150.8	In 2012 ABC started a project to migrate to the Avaloq Banking System.
Bank of China	China	banking	98.1	131.7	In December 2010, the Bank of China New York branch began offering RMB products for Americans. It was the first major Chinese bank to offer such a product.
China Mobil Communications	China	telecom	88.8	213.8	Rural market reach (97% of population), even at Mount Everest. Information services targeted to rural market like 'Agricultural Info Service' which allows activities like sales and purchase of agricultural
China State Construction Engineering	China	engineering	76.7	16.9	By June 2011, CSCEC had won 8 State Scientific and Technological Progress Awards, 1 State Technological Invention Award, 19 State Good Design Awards, 327 Provincial Scientific and Technological Progress Awards, 127 National Construction Methods Awards.
Arcelor Mittal	India	steel	84.2	23.1	Best Process Innovation award in American Metal Market's (AMM) 2011 Awards for Steel Excellence. Created Protea, a groundbreaking low-cost, high-quality housing system.
China Railway Construction Corp	China	construction	74.5	10.4	CRCC has won 363 national awards in the fields of project contracting, survey, design, consultation etc. among them, 55 national science and technology progress awards, 74 national prospecting and designing 'four excellent' awards.
China Railway Group	China	railway engineering	76.7	10.2	
SAIC	China	autos	75	26.7	SAIC built an entire modern automotive component supply chain in Shanghai from scratch. The number and quality of locally produced auto parts rose significantly. SAIC operates a large R&D

TABLE 8.5 *continued*

Company	Country	Industry	Sales 2013 $US billions	MKT Value $US billions	Innovations
Reliance Industries	India	oil & gas, telecom, retail, textiles	70.3	50.4	Sustainability, Conservation, Management
China Life Insurance	China	insurance	63.2	79.9	Building a conglomerate
Banco do Brasil	Brazil	banking	69	37.9	Project with IBM to develop banking software in Fortaleza
Sinochem Group	China	chemicals	71.8	10.3	R&D in new pesticides, ODS alternatives, dye stuff, fertilizers, and oil exploration
China Southern Power Grid	China	electric power	66.7	30	R&D in Smart Grid, Transmission and Transformation, and Electric Vehicle Charging Technologies
China FAW Group	China	autos	64.9	15.6	China's leader in the R&D of cutting edge passenger and commercial vehicles, state-of-the-art engineering development and test centre in Changchun
Dongfeng Motor Group	China	autos	19.7	11.8	From 2000 to 2010, Dongfeng increased the number of patent and utility model applications from around 20 to nearly 500.
America Movil & Grupo Carso	Mexico	telecom, fin services, retail,	60.2	70.7	(America Movil data only) America Movil in 2013 launched the world's first 17,500km submarine cable system specifically designed for 100 gigabit per second (100 Gb) transmission
China North Industries Group	China	defence, civil construction	58	11.2	High-tech defence products (eg: precision systems, amphibious weapons, long-range weapon systems)
Banco Bradesco	Brazil	banking	78.3	71.6	Constantly expanding by acquisitions. Strategy focuses on relationship quality and flexibility.
CITIC Group (China Citic Bank)	China	investment management and banking	24.4	32.5	Attracting and utilizing foreign capital, introducing advanced technologies, and adopting advanced and scientific international practice in operation and management.
Shenhua Group	China	energy	39.7	70.8	The firm constructed the first coal-to-olefin plant.
Ping An Insurance	China	insurance	51.1	57	Many awards in Strength, Brands, and CG and CSR.

TABLE 8.5 *continued*

Company	Country	Industry	Sales 2013 $US billions	MKT Value $US billions	Innovations
China Post Group	China	post	50.9	27.2	(Nothing extraordinary)
Sabic (Saudi Basic Industries)	Saudi Arabia	chemicals and metals	50.4	74.8	Innovative Plastics
Aviation Industry Corp of China	China	aviation, defence	47.4	21.1	Has 33 institutes, 9 state-level labs, 30 key aviation science & technology labs, 16 state-certified enterprise technology centres and 32 provincial & ministerial level enterprise technology centres.
China Communications Construction	China	construction	45.7	12.9	National Normalized Construction Method. Also, ~365 patents, mainly utility models and invention related to construction. ~75 prizes in science and technology.
Koc Holding	Turkey	automotive, finance, foods, construction, IT	47.1	13.6	Four Koç Group companies were listed in the top-10 in the 'Companies with the Highest Number of Domestic Patent Applications in 2013'.
Baosteel	China	steel	35.4	13.4	Till 2012, Baosteel possessed 8,711 authorized patents (including 1,668 invention patents).
Sberbank	Russia	banking	36.1	73.3	Center of Macroeconomic Research established in 2008. Recent strategy focuses on tech breakthrough, financial performance, and mature organization.
China Huaneng Group (Huaneng Power International)	China	power	21.1	14.9	A unique management structure of technology innovation.
Bank of Communications	China	banking	43.5	56.7	Creation of the Pacific Credit Card Center in partnership with HSBC.
People's Insurance Co of China	China	insurance	41.3	24.4	Designated agent within China for most international insurance companies. JVs for more diversified product offerings.

TABLE 8.5 *continued*

Company	Country	Industry	Sales 2013 $US billions	MKT Value $US billions	Innovations
China United Network Communications (Unicom)	China	telecom	39.5	32.4	Founding member in the formation of Cloud Computing Industry Alliance in Beijing; only provider to sell SIM cards that provide native phone numbers on both sides of the border (mainland China & Hong Kong). R&D centres and innovation in both fixed and mobile telecom fields with many awards.
HeBei Iron & Steel	China	steel	21.2	4.1	Does R&D in steel manufacturing.
JBS	Brazil	beef, chicken & pork + beverages	38.9	10.4	Does R&D in livestock production, mainly through Swift subsidiary in US.
China Railway Materials	China	railway materials and steel products	37.2	0.1	Offering comprehensive end-to-end supply chain services in railway materials and steel.
State Bank of India	India	banking	35.1	28.1	Oldest commercial bank in India. Many awards, mainly in using technology and internet in banking.
China Guodian	China	electricity	36.8	6.4	R&D focus on emission reduction and energy savings and clean energy.
Sistema	Russia	conglomerate (telecom, banking, real estate, retail, media,	30	8.1	
Huawei Investment & Holding	China	electronics	34.9	12	R&D, 1st mover in end-to-end 100G solutions, and 17,765 patents granted as of Feb 2011.
Tata Motors & Tata Group	India	autos, chemicals, consulting	96.9	25	First Indian manufacturer to achieve competitive quality in manufacturing autos.

TABLE 8.5 *continued*

Company	Country	Industry	Sales 2013 $US billions	MKT Value $US billions	Innovations
Jiangsu Shagang Group	China	steel	34.6	5.4	Product high quality with certification, and diversity of products/specifications.
China Natl Building Materials Group	China	building materials	13.8	7.5	Sustainable development and green practices. Technology in construction material, improving industrial technical innovation, energy-saving and emission reduction, promoting industrial structure adjustment and optimization and upgrading.
Shougang Group	China	durable goods (steel)	34.3	13.7	Shougang finished applications for 52 patents and got national authority patents. Their products dominate almost one third of Chinese market within steel industry. They have built good relationships with overseas iron ore suppliers. Have experience in undertaking overseas.
Sinomach	China	heavy machinery and construction	34	5.7	With 25 state-level research institutes SINOMACH has won more than 3,500 state-level prizes and over 1,500 state-level patents and has participated in or helped coordinate promulgation of several hundred natl standards in China. SINOMACH does major tech equip devel, industrial planning, standards setting, technical consultations, engineering studies, quality monitoring and testing.
Wuhan Iron & Steel	China	steel	16.1	4.5	
Lenovo	China	computers	29.6	10.4	Combating piracy in China by allying with Microsoft to pre-load computers with a rebated Windows. Has several research centres and many patents.
Beijing Automotive Group	China	autos	33.4	4.8	Acquisition of Western technology. (Saab Automobile from GE), and trials in electric cars.
Teewoo	China	commodity trade and logistics	32.9	1.2	Modern logistics

SOURCES: data from *Fortune* magazine, Global 500 list for 2014 http://money.cnn.com/magazines/fortune/global500/index.html, company websites, and articles about the companies found through web search

The innovations for most of these firms come in non-patentable areas such as supply chain management and customer relationship management – but even so, many of the companies have patents and R&D centres in the traditional sense as well. The traditional R&D activity often comes through the acquisition of a Triad MNE, such as JBS's acquisition of Swift Foods in the United States, Mittal's acquisition of Arcelor in Europe, or Lenovo's purchase of IBM's PC division.

Where does innovation flourish and why?

Stepping back for a minute from the various lists above, it may be useful to think about the underlying conditions that may make innovation more likely or more successful in some places versus others. It is one thing to say that China, for example, spent just under $US 200 billion on R&D in 2012, and thus was the second-highest-ranking country for that measure of innovativeness. It is another to say that China really is a place where innovation flourishes. If we divide the amount of research and development spending by the huge population of China, the country ranking drops precipitously to below 50th in the world in per capita R&D.[8] Likewise, if we measure R&D spending as a percentage of GDP, China's ranking drops to 21st, as shown in Table 8.1. The net result of this restatement of the evidence points to a key issue: some countries are much more committed to innovation activity than others. And this fact leads to the question of: why?

The 'why?' question cannot be answered simply. Clearly, the amount of R&D spending depends very significantly on the country's level of economic development. The higher-income countries definitely have an edge over lower-income ones on this measure. But on the subject of having an environment that stimulates innovation, the picture changes a lot. For example, Anglo-Saxon countries are greater sources of innovation than Roman Catholic ones. Nordic countries are more innovative than countries in the Middle East or Africa. China and the Asian emerging markets are more innovative than countries in Latin America. There is clearly a cultural phenomenon involved here.

Again, there is no question that some societies/countries provide a welcoming environment for innovation and others do not. The literature in recent years has used the Hofstede (1984, 2009) and GLOBE (House *et al*, 2004) data on cultural characteristics of people in different countries to correlate cultural characteristics with innovation outcomes at the national level. Consistently, *individualism* as a cultural trait has correlated highly with innovation at the national level (Shane, 1993; Taylor and Wilson, 2012), and countries can be ranked by their scores on this item, as shown in the Hofstede scores in Table 8.6.

It is really striking that the Triad countries all appear above the centre point/median of the scale (a score of 50), and all emerging markets (except South Africa) appear below the centre point. The Anglo-Saxon countries cluster together at the top of the scale, while Latin American and Asian countries cluster mostly at the low end of the individualism scale.

The China-related countries (since Hofstede did not have access to mainland China information in his study) cluster towards the bottom of the individualism scale, even though the measures shown earlier put Taiwan, Hong Kong and Singapore as well as China itself consistently high in innovation. So, there must be some features other than individualism that contribute to a country's innovative capabilities. Taylor and Wilson (2012) suggest that one element may be the degree of nationalism or patriotism demonstrated by the people in a country. They found that institutionally collectivist countries (where individualism ranked low and society-level collectivism ranked high) had greater innovation rates than countries with family-based or local group-based collectivism. They labelled this type of collectivism 'nationalism' or 'patriotism'.

This empirical evidence certainly seems to indicate that innovation is more likely in countries that possess certain cultural characteristics such as a high degree of individualism, or a collectivism at the national level that could lead to a common purpose in which innovation is favoured. There are surely additional national characteristics that stimulate higher levels of innovation. Clearly, higher per capita income enables greater investment in R&D and other kinds of innovation (confirmed by Taylor and Wilson, for example). And there are likely other factors at the national level that contribute as well. Climate seems to be one: countries in more temperate/colder climates tend to be more innovative. Immigration might be another: countries that are more open to foreigners entering and taking up residence may be more innovative, as they receive a greater flow of ideas from abroad relative to more closed societies.

A different indicator of cultural acceptance of innovative behaviour is reasonably captured by measures of *entrepreneurship* in different countries. That is, countries that demonstrate greater entrepreneurial activity may be classified as more innovative (or open to innovation). Table 8.7 shows a comparison of countries ranked according to their entrepreneurial activity. Once again we see countries from the Triad, Nordic countries and Anglo-Saxon countries near the top of the ranking, and countries from Latin

TABLE 8.6   Selected country ratings on individualism from Hofstede's study

USA	91	Jamaica	39
Australia	90	Brazil	38
UK	89	Arab countries	38
Canada	80	Turkey	37
Netherlands	80	Uruguay	36
New Zealand	79	Greece	35
Italy	76	Philippines	32
Belgium	75	Mexico	30
Denmark	74	East Africa	27
Sweden	71	Yugoslavia	27
France	71	Puerto Rico	27
Ireland	70	Malaysia	26
Norway	69	Hong Kong	25
Switzerland	68	Chile	23
Germany	67	West Africa	20
South Africa	65	Singapore	20
Finland	63	Thailand	20
Austria	55	El Salvador	19
Israel	54	South Korea	18
Spain	51	Taiwan	17
India	48	Peru	16
Japan	46	Costa Rica	15
Argentina	46	Pakistan	14
Iran	41		

SOURCE: data from Hofstede (1984)

TABLE 8.7 Global Entrepreneurship and Development Index (GEDI)

Country	Rank (refers to situation in mid-2010)	Score	Change
United States	1	0.60	+2
Australia	2	0.57	+2
Sweden	3	0.56	+2
Canada	3	0.56	+1
Switzerland	3	0.56	−3
Iceland	6	0.55	+1
Denmark	6	0.55	−6
Belgium	8	0.52	+1
Netherlands	9	0.49	+5
Taiwan	9	0.49	−
Norway	9	0.49	−4
Singapore	12	0.47	−1
Austria	13	0.46	+0
United Kingdom	14	0.45	−2
Ireland	14	0.45	−1
Finland	14	0.45	−7
France	14	0.45	−3
United Arab Emirates	14	0.45	−4
Israel	14	0.45	+1
Germany	14	0.45	−1
Chile	21	0.43	+0
Slovenia	21	0.43	−8
Czech Republic	23	0.40	−1
Saudi Arabia	24	0.37	−1
Korea	25	0.36	−2
Hong Kong	25	0.36	+0

TABLE 8.7 *continued*

Country	Rank (refers to situation in mid-2010)	Score	Change
Japan	27	0.35	−4
Uruguay	28	0.34	+0
Spain	28	0.34	−1
Latvia	30	0.32	+0
Poland	30	0.32	–
Portugal	32	0.30	−1
Turkey	32	0.30	−2
Hungary	32	0.30	+8
Italy	32	0.30	−9
Croatia	32	0.30	−1
Greece	32	0.30	−6
Colombia	38	0.28	−7
Montenegro	38	0.28	–
Peru	40	0.27	−5
South Africa	41	0.26	−4
Lebanon	41	0.26	−4
Mexico	41	0.26	−5
Malaysia	44	0.25	−6
Argentina	44	0.25	−7
Tunisia	44	0.25	−3
Romania	47	0.24	−2
Macedonia	48	0.23	−5
Jamaica	49	0.22	+0
Jordan	49	0.22	−5

SOURCE: data from http://www3.imperial.ac.uk/newsandeventspggrp/imperialcollege/newssummary/news_23-4-2012-10-22-17

America, the Middle East and Africa near the bottom. Interestingly, Saudi Arabia and the United Arab Emirates rank in the top half of the distribution, well ahead of other emerging markets other than Chile. There is clearly a strong correlation between individualism and entrepreneurship, as seen from comparing Tables 8.6 and 8.7.

Conclusions about innovation and national/company characteristics

In trying to understand the competitive capabilities of emerging markets firms, we have entered into the realm of country characteristics, and particularly national comparisons of individualism and entrepreneurship, in this discussion. Looking at the level of entrepreneurship in various countries, the emerging markets fall far down on the list, with Chile in 21st place as the highest-ranking emerging market in the Global Entrepreneurship and Development Index. As far as individualism is concerned, once again the emerging markets are far below average, with only South Africa (65) ranking above the mid-point of 50 on the scale.

Returning to the direct measures of innovativeness, the evidence points to strong leadership by Nordic and Anglo-Saxon countries in most indices, with emerging markets particularly in Africa and Latin America falling far behind. It appears that, even if we allow for innovation to be construed as new knowledge that applies to business regardless of its relation to patents or other measures of scientific input, the emerging markets are weak on this dimension. This is not news to anyone who has studied world affairs during the past 150 years or so. What may be very interesting is the continuing dominance today of services in national economies, and the concomitant importance of non-patentable innovations in company competitiveness.

If our assertion is that innovation is a hugely important competitive advantage in the 21st century, then emerging markets firms are going to need to develop ways to innovate that are different from those that are common in the Triad countries. And if we accept the added assertion that innovation includes those items listed in Table 8.4, then everything after the two categories of patents should be accessible to emerging market companies. There is clearly room for these companies to succeed in innovating in areas such as conglomerate management, customer relationship management and supply chain organization.

An interesting aside is that, if the conditions for innovation and entrepreneurship are much stronger in Triad countries, particularly the

Anglo-Saxon and Nordic countries, then it makes sense for emerging market companies to establish affiliates in those locations, to participate in the innovation activity there and to carry it to the rest of the global company. Headquarters do not have to be based in Silicon Valley or in London's financial district; the companies just have to be flexible enough to locate the relevant activities where the relevant strengths are. After all, the famous criminal Willie Sutton, when asked why he robbed banks, responded 'because that's where the money is'. Emerging market companies looking for money need to have operations in New York and/or London. Likewise, if they are managing supply chains, they should be trying to learn from UPS, Amazon and other world leaders in this activity. If they want to produce pharmaceuticals, they need to be learning from the clusters of firms in New Jersey, Switzerland and Ireland, among other pharmaceuticals research centres.

The continued growth of service sectors, already constituting about two-thirds of world employment, will make non-patented innovation an increasingly greater part of total innovative activity around the world. This opens a large door of opportunity for emerging market firms to build competitive advantages in services. The best-known advantages identified for service sectors are the production of new services (as if they were physical products), and the processes for producing services (again, parallel to the example of products). In addition, there are methodologies for service provision that establish strong competitive advantages. These methodologies – typically for carrying out service provision to advertising, banking or consulting clients – are certainly not simple to build up as differentiated capabilities. However, they are equally certainly possible for emerging markets to develop, especially when the methodologies have to do with dealing with clients in emerging markets, where the main growth of the world economy is occurring.

Notes

1   One can talk about the 'resource curse' which implies that natural resources blunt a country's efforts to build competitive businesses and become too dependent on the oil/coal/other resource. This may be true for a number of countries, but not for major oil producers, including the United States, United Kingdom, Norway and Canada.

2   It used to be said that knowledge was a key competitive advantage late in the 20th century. Now, with internet access to more information and knowledge than has ever been available in history, the situation calls for the ability to

process that information and utilize that knowledge. So, *innovation* is the main form in which these inputs can be transformed into business value.

3   See, for example, National Science Foundation, *National Patterns of R&D Resources: 2011–12 Data Update*, http://www.nsf.gov/statistics/nsf14304/pdf/nsf14304.pdf, and also http://www.nsf.gov/statistics/seind14/index.cfm/chapter-4/c4s2.htm

4   This is an almost constant refrain heard in the pharmaceuticals industry. Large drug companies regularly spend billions of dollars on R&D, but their new drug pipelines are often very limited in terms of success stories. See for example, http://www.forbes.com/sites/matthewherper/2013/08/11/the-cost-of-inventing-a-new-drug-98-companies-ranked/

5   R&D is generally divided into three stages: basic research, applied research, and development. The first two focus more on scientific activities (eg laboratory science), while the third stage is clearly consistent with the kinds of innovative activity that most characterizes emerging market firms. See the US National Science Foundation definition at: http://www.nsf.gov/statistics/randdef/fedgov.cfm:

- Basic research: systematic study to gain knowledge or understanding of the fundamental aspects of phenomena and of observable facts without specific applications towards processes or products in mind;

- Applied research: systematic study to gain knowledge or understanding necessary for determining the means by which a recognized and specific need may be met; and

- Development: systematic use of the knowledge and understanding gained from research for the production of useful materials, devices, systems, or methods, including the design and development of prototypes and processes.

6   Try them out, if you have not experienced the difference in service quality yourself. Southwest and Enterprise do not offer a different service from their competitors, but they really differentiate the quality of the experience.

7   Astra International in Indonesia, for example, started in 1957 as a general trading company, specializing in groceries. In the 1960s Astra entered into the importing of asphalt and construction materials, to serve the massive infrastructure investment programme of the Sukarno government. The subsequent Suharto government asked Astra's owners to take over a car assembly business that had been purchased from GM, and so they entered the automotive industry in 1969. Two years later the group entered into an importing agreement with then-upstart Toyota, along with an assembly agreement to use the existing factory in Indonesia. Astra later entered into import distribution agreements with Isuzu and Daihatsu, and with Honda to import motorcycles (since 1970). Astra sold most of its participation in the Toyota assembly venture in 2003. It started Bank Summa in 1988, and then lost that investment during a major business downturn in 1992. The group was forced to sell controlling ownership to the Indonesian government in the mid-1990s, as the impact of the Summa

bankruptcy overwhelmed it with debt. Subsequent major shareholder Jardine Matheson (from Hong Kong) continued with the diversified business approach, and in 2014 the Astra Group was involved with car distribution, vehicle finance, agribusiness, heavy equipment distribution and some smaller activities.

8 This measure is not shown in the text or tables. It is constructed by dividing national R&D spending (of $US 198.9 billion in 2012 in China) by population (of 1.35 billion in 2012 in China). This gives China a per capita spending level of $US 147 in 2012. Contrast this with US per capita R&D spending of $US 436.0 billion/313.9 million people = $US 1,389/person, which is about 10 times higher. Or compare with a small Triad country such as Belgium, where 2012 R&D spending was $US 8.6 billion with a population of 11.14 million, which is $US 772 per person.

References

Battelle Institute (2014) *2014 Global R&D funding forecast*, Battelle, Columbus, OH [Online] http://www.battelle.org/docs/tpp/2014_global_rd_funding_forecast.pdf

Dutta, S, Lanvin, B and Wunsch-Vincent, S (2014) *The Global Innovation Index 2014*, Cornell University, Ithaca, NY [Online] https://www.globalinnovationindex.org/content.aspx?page=GII-Home

Hofstede, G (1984) *Culture's consequences: International differences in work-related values*, 2nd edn, Sage, Beverly Hills, CA

Hofstede, G, Hofstede, G J and Minkov, M (2010) *Cultures and organizations: Software of the mind*, 3rd edn, McGraw-Hill, New York

House, R J *et al*, eds (2004) *Culture, leadership, and organizations: The GLOBE study of 62 societies*, Sage, Beverly Hills, CA

National Science Foundation (2014) *Science and Engineering Indicators 2014*, ch 4: Research and development: National trends and international comparisons, NSF, Washington, DC [Online] http://www.nsf.gov/statistics/seind14/index.cfm/chapter-4

Shane, S (1993) Cultural influences on national rates of innovation, *Journal of Business Venturing*, 8, pp 59–73

Taylor, M Z and Wilson, S (2012) Does culture still matter? The effects of individualism on national innovation rates, *Journal of Business Venturing*, 27, pp 234–47

The Economist (2010) Innovation in emerging markets, *The Economist*, 15 April.

Large, small, family-owned and state-owned companies from emerging markets

09

What to expect in Chapter 9

The largest companies from emerging markets that are competing internationally are mostly SOEs. In addition, well over half of them are based in China. And these companies tend to operate in two major sectors: oil and banking, both of which are very sensitive topics of government concern today. Indeed, host government relations with both the SOEs and their home governments will be an increasingly important feature of international business as a result.

A second major category of emerging market multinationals is family-based groups. Beyond India-based Tata conglomerate and Mittal steel, other family-based groups are significantly smaller than the SOEs discussed here. The family-based groups are often quite diversified, achieving greater sales and earnings stability by spreading their business activities across several sectors. Such family-based firms are also very common in Triad countries other than the United States and United Kingdom, so they are not a particular phenomenon in emerging markets.

Another category of emerging market firms going abroad are small and medium-sized enterprises (SMEs). These companies, of course, are less known than the big multinationals, but they are by far more numerous both in the domestic context and in doing international business. The same logic that has been used to analyse the large companies and to recommend strategy for them applies to these SMEs. Namely, they need to understand their fit into global value-added chains and devise strategies to take advantage of that fit, as well as explore expansion into other markets and other stages along the value-added chain.

As time goes on, it will be interesting to see if the emerging market-based SOEs and large family-based groups develop more of the traditional competitive advantages of R&D/innovation and marketing skills. Whether they do or not, there still is a need to think carefully about the goals and motivations of these two types of company as they go overseas, since these differences are likely to produce persistent differences in behaviour relative to traditional MNEs.

This chapter looks at some broad issues related to emerging markets and companies based there, which we have not explored in any detail up to now. The fact that the majority of the largest companies in emerging markets are SOEs is a real concern for several reasons. The fact that the largest non-SOEs from emerging markets are often family-owned businesses is another feature that should be considered. And finally, if we talk about the importance of emerging markets in business today, we should also look at not-so-large companies and consider their role in global value-added chains and their relations with foreign multinational firms.

Government-owned companies (SOEs)

The largest companies based in emerging markets are mostly government-owned oil companies and banks, plus other natural resource and utility companies. Table 9.1 lists the 25 largest emerging market SOEs, almost half of which are oil companies, and almost two-thirds of which are based in China.

TABLE 9.1   Top 25 emerging markets state-owned companies in the 2014 Fortune Global 500

	Company name	Country of origin	Industry	Annual sales 2013 ($US bill)	% Govt ownership
1	Sinopec	China	Oil	457.2	73.96%
2	China Natl Petroleum Co. (PetroChina)	China	Oil	432.0	86.7%
3	State Grid	China	Electric power	333.4	100%
4	Gazprom	Russia	Oil	165.0	50%
5	ICBC	China	Bank	148.8	70.4%
6	Petrobras	Brazil	Oil	141.5	60.5%
7	Pemex	Mexico	Oil	125.9	100%
8	China Construction Bank	China	Bank	125.4	59.9%
9	PDVSA	Venezuela	Oil	121.0	100%

TABLE 9.1 *continued*

	Company name	Country of origin	Industry	Annual sales 2013 ($US bill)	% Govt ownership
10	Lukoil	Russia	Oil	119.1	92%
11	Rosneft Oil	Russia	Oil	117.1	69.5%
12	Agricultural Bank of China	China	Bank	115.4	82.9%
13	China State Construction Engineering	China	Construction	110.8	60.5% non free-float
14	China Mobile Communications	China	Telephone service	107.6	73.7%
15	Bank of China	China	Bank	105.6	67.9%
16	Petronas	Malaysia	Oil	100.7	100%
17	China National Offshore Oil	China	Oil	96.0	64.4%
18	China Railway Construction	China	Construction	95.7	63.3%
19	PTT	Thailand	Oil	92.6	66.0%
20	SAIC Motors	China	Autos	92.0	100%
21	China Railway Group	China	Railroad transport	91.2	56.1%
22	Indian Oil	India	Oil	81.3	87.3%
23	China Life Insurance	China	Insurance	80.9	68.4%
24	Sinochem Group	China	Chemicals	75.9	100%
25	China FAW Group	China	Autos	75.0	100%

SOURCES: companies from Fortune Global 500 list, 21 July 2014; company webpages for all other information

As an aside, if we look at the list of the largest non-SOE emerging market companies, only two are as large as the ones in the SOE list. This distribution of the largest emerging market companies implies a number of things. First of all, it means that government-owned and/or controlled companies will be an increasing factor in international business, as these emerging market-based companies expand their horizons overseas. Kowalski *et al* (2013) note that more than 6 per cent of world GDP and 11 per cent of global market capitalization of listed companies is constituted by the top 200 SOEs.[1] This dominance of SOEs thus implies that relations between home and host country governments will play a larger role in the companies' activities, as more of them are controlled by home governments.

We have already seen some of the political implications of this phenomenon as governments in Triad countries erect barriers to companies that are controlled by governments. Examples include the US government's refusal to allow Chinese electronics company Huawei to acquire 3Leaf Systems in 2010, and the rejection of Dubai Ports' attempted acquisition of the port management business for six major US ports, including New York, Philadelphia and Miami, in 2006. Both of these decisions were made on the basis of 'national security', in the first case relating to key technology that could have military applications, and in the second case to operation of seaports that could be needed for national defence.[2]

A second key feature of the distribution of the largest emerging market companies is that they are also concentrated in two important industry sectors: oil and banking. While one can argue that technology and innovation are crucial elements of a successful economy in the 21st century, it still remains true that oil for energy needs and banks for financing needs are fundamental building blocks of an economy. The average per capita income of an oil-producing country (including the United States and the United Kingdom) is far above that of other non-oil countries in the world.[3] Likewise, possession of large banks with huge balance sheets and international scope of activities provides a country with easier access to financing and some degree of economic power relative to countries without such financial institutions. Thus these two sectors are extremely important in economic development today, and they are populated by many state-owned companies from emerging markets.

The concentration of the world's largest companies in oil and banking is not new with the focus on emerging markets. Looking just at the Triad countries, the distribution is similar, with large banks such as JP Morgan Chase and BNP Paribas, and oil companies such as Exxon and Shell, leading the list.[4] The economic power of these enormous institutions which control key elements of functioning of the economy should not be underestimated. The global financial crisis of 2008–09 demonstrated the fundamental dependence of the world's economies on financial institutions, and the repeated oil crises of the 1970s and 1980s, along with oil price swings since then, demonstrate the world's crucial dependence on this sector as well. This is not to criticize or to praise the companies, but rather to highlight their importance, and to point out their significance to government policy-makers as well.

A third key issue related to the distribution of the largest emerging market companies is that they are associated closely with national economic and political power. That is, countries with oil resources control access to those resources, which can make other countries dependent on them, and less likely to take policy positions against the interests of the oil state. An outstanding example is Russia in 2014, when its takeover of the Crimea region of Ukraine and its attempted takeover of Ukraine were 'condemned' by other countries in the European Union and the United States – but very little was actually done to constrain Russia, owing to the oil and gas dependency on Russia in Europe.[5]

The possession of large banks and other financial institutions is not nearly as strong a political/economic tool, but still the large banking sectors in the United States and United Kingdom give those two countries disproportionate economic power based on their concentration of global financial activity. While there has been growth of emerging market financial centres such as Shanghai and Dubai, they are not challenging New York and London as the global leaders. Nevertheless, both Shanghai and Dubai are growing more rapidly than their Triad counterparts, and they could easily give China and the UAE disproportionate economic power in the years ahead.

Let's look further at each of these three issues, starting with the fact that these SOEs are the largest emerging market companies. This is probably not a particular concern when the SOEs operate in their domestic markets. When they export products, they may sell at unfair prices to serve political goals. When state-owned companies invest abroad, the questions are: what criteria are they using to undertake the investment, and how are they managing the overseas businesses? If decisions are based on market criteria (ie towards maximizing profits of the enterprise), there should be no difference between a state-owned and an investor-owned company's decisions. If decisions are made on the basis of national interest of the parent government, on the other hand, this could clearly diverge from the market-based interest of other companies in the market. It could also be different from the host government's view, since the host government also wants to gain from efficiencies of the company and not allow decisions to go against efficiency in favour of a foreign government's political interests.

In a non-defence context, just think about a government-owned electronics company moving its R&D activities to India or Brazil because the government-owner there wants to build up local R&D capabilities. If the move is made just to generate R&D work in the home country, and there are not comparative or competitive advantages to the firm in doing so, this would go against economic efficiency and would justify a government intervention in the host country to disallow a foreign government-owner to take such a step. It is quite difficult to disentangle the reasons for such a potential move. If Huawei or ZTE were to acquire a US or UK software company, and then move the acquired company's R&D to China, that might appear to be a political step – but it just as well could be an economic step to concentrate more R&D in one location, and to benefit from economies of scale and scope.

Or consider an emerging market car company that acquires a foreign competitor to obtain the technology and market access of that acquired firm, and then uses those capabilities along with government subsidies to outcompete foreign rivals at home and abroad. (Think of Dongfeng Automotive in China acquiring a major part of Peugeot Citroen in 2014.) The move to obtain technology may be a completely market-driven decision. However, the ability of the SOE to obtain home-government subsidies and/or other support may allow it to compete with a major advantage relative to private-sector car companies without such ties. In the case of Dongfeng, the acquisition of a 14 per cent interest in Peugeot Citroen was a continuation of the two companies' relations. They have operated a joint venture in China producing cars for the local market since 1992. Regardless of the long-term relationship, the knowledge and market access gained from this tie-up may enable Dongfeng to compete more successfully internationally, based partly on support from the Chinese government.

Dongfeng Motor Corporation was founded in 1969 as Second Auto Works, in Wuhan, Hubei Province, China. From the outset Dongfeng was one of China's Big Three carmakers, along with Shanghai Automotive and First Auto Works (which now are the Big Four carmakers, including Chang'An). The company is the China market leader in producing commercial vehicles, and ranks third in producing passenger vehicles. Annual sales in 2013 were approximately $US 62 billion, with over 3 million vehicles sold, and placing the company at number 113 in the Fortune Global 500. Dongfeng sold approximately 1 million cars under its own brand names and 2 million cars under the brands of alliance partners.

Dongfeng has operated alliances with several foreign car companies, acting as the distributor for those companies in China and assembling some foreign car models locally. The first such alliance was with Peugeot Citroen (PSA) from France in 1992, in which Peugeot Citroen cars were assembled in Wuhan from knocked-down kits (CKD). This venture was followed by similar agreements with Kia from Korea (in 2002), with Nissan and Honda from Japan (both in 2003), and then with Yulong from Taiwan (in 2010). In 2013 Dongfeng announced plans to build trucks in a joint venture with Volvo (majority owned by rival Chinese carmaker Geely).

More recently Dongfeng agreed to invest $1.1 billion to buy 14 per cent of Peugeot Citroen, establishing Dongfeng as one of three equal partners in ownership of major stakes in the French carmaker. This step is likely to be followed by further deepening of the relationship between Dongfeng and PSA, presumably bringing additional manufacturing technology and market access to the Chinese company. Since they have been in the alliance producing Citroen and later Peugeot cars in China for over 20 years, the two partners know each other quite well.

Dongfeng's strategy has been focused consistently on the domestic market, with little effort to export its own brands to other countries. Partner companies, of course, are able to use joint production with Dongfeng in China to reduce their costs and serve foreign markets as well as the Chinese market. The recent investment in Peugeot Citroen may enable Dongfeng to begin selling its own cars through PSA distributors in other countries.

State-owned companies may operate their foreign affiliates in normal times as profit-oriented businesses without causing concerns for the host government. However, in the case of a political confrontation between the two countries, this company could easily be brought into the political realm by either country's government. Thus, the political aspect of foreign government ownership of a company is a real concern for host countries large and small.

Government ownership of an international company is bound to create the appearance of favouritism, even when it might not exist in fact. A government-owned car company or bank will almost certainly be criticized in its efforts to expand internationally for being unfairly subsidized. This challenge is a real problem for the international expansion of state-owned companies, despite efforts in international organizations to establish rules for oversight of the SOEs when they go overseas.[6]

These concerns are often magnified due to the concentration of these companies in oil and banking. In the cases of Gazprom, Lukoil and Rosneft from Russia, the national political interest has clearly been served by the actions of these oil and gas companies threatening to hold up oil and gas supplies to European countries when the government desires.[7] In the cases of Chinese banks ICBC, China Construction Bank and the Agricultural Bank of China, no particular concerns have been raised – but these enormous government-owned banks easily have the financial capability to acquire any of the largest private-sector banks such as JP Morgan Chase or Société Générale. Because of the unequal power and the visibility of these SOE banks, it is unlikely that that any of them would bid to take over a major foreign bank – but conditions could change, and a financial crisis could make a target bank very weak and potentially accessible to one of these giants.

Reviewing the various issues and considerations involved with state-owned companies competing internationally, and taking account of the fact that state-owned companies dominate large parts of the economy in emerging markets, one can see the potential for conflict in the future. Governments of Triad countries are not going to want government-owned companies from emerging markets to gain significant positions in their economies – for competitive as well as political reasons. At the same time, huge and powerful SOEs in the oil and gas sector are not going to disappear, and this group of companies in particular will undoubtedly be the source of conflict in the years ahead. Fortunately, the majority of SOEs are not in this sector, and recent history demonstrates that the level of conflict is far lower in dealing with these non-oil companies.

Even moving away from oil and gas, the number of large state-owned companies around the world is not declining. Or in other words, there is no 'natural' tendency for SOEs to disappear as economic development progresses. Given this reality we are likely to see a proliferation of SOEs in emerging markets in the years ahead, from electric power suppliers to mining companies to banks. Generally these companies will continue to operate in natural resources and utilities rather than manufacturing, but in any case many of the largest firms in emerging markets will continue to be these SOEs.

Family-based business groups from emerging markets

As discussed in Chapter 5, diversified business groups, often based on a single or a couple of family owners, are a very common feature of the largest non-SOE companies in emerging markets today. The earlier discussion focused on the issue of diversification of these business groups. In this chapter we look more closely at the family owners of many of the groups. To illustrate the importance of this phenomenon, Table 9.2 shows the largest 50 family-based business groups in emerging markets.

TABLE 9.2 Top 50 emerging markets family-based business groups in 2013

	Company name	Country of origin	Industry	Annual sales 2013 ($US bill)	Ownership
1	Tata Group	India	Conglomerate	138	Tata
2	Mittal	India	Steel	132	Mittal
3	Reliance Industries	India	Chemicals	73.1	Ambani
4	Grupo Carso	Mexico	Conglomerate	64.5	Carlos Slim
5	Ping An	China	Insurance, banking, invest	64.5	CP Group
6	Hutchison Whampoa	China/HK	Conglomerate	53	Li
7	Odebrecht	Brazil	Conglomerate	43	Odebrecht
8	JBS	Brazil	Meats	43	Batista
9	Aditya Birla	India	Conglomerate	40	Birla/Pilani

TABLE 9.2   *continued*

	Company name	Country of origin	Industry	Annual sales 2013 ($US bill)	Ownership
10	Koç Group	Turkey	Conglomerate	42.6	Koç
11	Sistema	Russia	Conglomerate	34	Yevtushenkov
12	Interros	Russia	Conglomerate	more than 30	Potanin
13	Saudi Binladin	Saudi Arab	Construct; conglomerate	more than 30	Binladen
14	Pao de Azucar	Brazil	Supermarkets	27	Diniz
15	Zhejiang Geely Hold.	China	Autos	25.8	Li
16	Antarchile	Chile	Conglomerate	22.7	Angelini
17	Femsa	Mexico	Beverages	18.3	Garza Laguera
18	Rembrandt Group	South Africa	Conglomerate	18	Rupert
19	Cencosud	Chile	Retail stores	18	Paulmann
20	Gerdau	Brazil	Steel	16.8	Gerdau
21	Alfa Group	Russia	Conglomerate	16.6	Fridman
22	Grupo Alfa	Mexico	Conglomerate	15.9	Garza Sada
23	Cemex	Mexico	Cement	15	Zambrano
24	Grupo Luksic	Chile	Conglomerate	13.8	Luksic
25	Grupo Bimbo	Mexico	Bread	13.8	Servitje
26	Charoen Pokphand Gr	Thailand	Conglomerate	13.4	Dhanin
27	Haci Ömer Sabanci	Turkey	Conglomerate	12.1	Sabanci
28	Falabella	Chile	Retail stores	11.9	Falabella
29	Mahindra & Mahindra	India	Conglomerate	11	Mahindra
30	Votarantim	Brazil	Conglomerate	11	Moraes
31	San Miguel/Petron	Philippines	Oil; beer	10.4	Zobel
32	Orascom	Egypt	Telecom; conglomerate	more than 10	Sawiris

TABLE 9.2 *continued*

	Company name	Country of origin	Industry	Annual sales 2013 ($US bill)	Ownership
33	Shoprite Holdings Ltd	South Africa	Grocery stores	10.1	Weise
34	Organizacion Soriana	Mexico	Grocery stores	8	Martin
35	Camargo Correa Group	Brazil	Engineering snd construction	8	Camargo Corrêa
36	Wipro	India	BP outsourcing	7.3	Premji
37	Globo Group	Brazil	Media	7.2	Mourinho
38	Grupo Modelo	Mexico	Beer	7.1	Diez Fernandez
39	Sun Hung Kai	China/HK	Real estate	6.9	Kwok
40	Swire Pacific	China/HK	Real estate	6.6	Swire
41	Pick N Pay	South Afr	Grocery stores	6.3	Ackerman
42	Grupo Ardila Lulle	Colombia	Conglomerate	6.3	Ardila Lulle
43	Grupo Televisa	Mexico	Media	5.3	Azcarraga
44	Dogus Group (incl. Garanti Bank)	Turkey	Banking; construction	5.1	Sahenk
45	Dangote Group	Nigeria	Cement; sugar; salt	more than 5	Dangote
46	Al-Kharafi & Sons	Kuwait	Trading; construct	more than 5	Al-Kharafi
47	Gudang Garam	Indonesia	Tobacco	4.7	Wonowidjojo
48	Cheung Kong	China/HK	Property development	4.2	Cheung Kong
49	Godrej Group	India	Conglomerate	4.1	Godrej
50	Djarum; Bank Cen Asia	Indonesia	Cigarettes; banking	more than 4	Hartono
50	Avantha Group	India	Conglomerate	4	Thapar
50	Indofood	Indonesia	Food	4	Salim

SOURCE: companies identified from *Fortune* Global 500, 21 July 2014; and lists of largest business groups in BRICS; and websearch on other large countries.

About 90 per cent of these companies are diversified into at least two major business areas (defined as three-digit standard industrial classifications), and most are involved in even more sectors.

It has been argued in a number of places (for example, in Khanna and Palepu, 1997 and in Li *et al*, 2006) that emerging markets firms are often diversified into business groups because of the failure of local financial markets to provide adequate sources of funding for their operations and growth. There is no doubt that the financial markets in most emerging markets are relatively less developed than in many Triad countries. But the Triad countries are just as frequently characterized by business groups (La Porta, Lopez-De-Silanes and Shleifer, 1999). And that view is backwards in terms of causality in many cases. The emerging market groups generally succeed at some business and then discover opportunities for profitable business in other activities as well. Over time, then, the groups enter and leave businesses until they appear as diversified conglomerates, or sometimes more narrowly focused entities. Just as with General Electric in the United States, these groups expand, contract, and rebalance their portfolios of businesses over time as opportunities come and go. Their distinctive skill is at managing businesses well and identifying new opportunities more quickly and more agilely than competitors – as well as letting go of businesses that cease to be attractive.

In most of these cases the families behind the business groups have been in control for at least three generations. The exceptions are mostly in formerly communist countries (especially Russia and China), where private-sector business was marginalized until the 1990s. In those cases we see mostly first-generation families or individuals in control, and the challenge of passing the business on to future generations has not yet been faced. In more common cases such as Alfa in Mexico, the Garza Sada family has been in (the beer) business since 1890, and has gone through several generations of leaders and business sectors. Likewise, the Tata Group in India was founded in 1868 as a trading company that subsequently diversified into and out of dozens of businesses into its current conglomerate form.

The Tata Group from India is both common to the phenomenon of large private-sector companies based in emerging markets and very unusual as well. Tata is 'typical' in that it is comprised of multiple businesses under the overall group, with a range of products and services, from consulting and engineering to steel and cement manufacturing. The group began its existence as a trading company in Bombay in 1868. In 1874 founder Jametsetji Tata established the Central India Spinning, Weaving and Manufacturing Company, marking the group's first move into industrial production. Subsequent growth culminated with the construction and launch of the Taj Mahal Hotel in Bombay in 1903. By that time Tata was clearly an industrial and commercial conglomerate, with major businesses in three very diverse sectors.

The path created by Jametsetji Tata was followed by his sons, who set up Tata Iron & Steel in 1907 and then Tata Hydroelectric Power Supply Company in 1910. Further diversification took place over the years, until Tata & Sons had a dozen large businesses in different industrial and commercial sectors. A business in soaps and detergents was founded in 1917, and much later sold to Unilever in 1984. An insurance business, New India Assurance, was set up in 1919, and then nationalized in 1956; subsequently Tata re-entered the insurance business in 2001, forming a major joint venture with AIG. The Indian national airline was founded as Tata Aviation (later Air India) in 1932, and nationalized by the Nehru government in 1953. Tata Chemicals was established in 1939 and Tata Motors in 1945; these are Tata's main industrial bases in the 2000s. Tata Consulting Services was founded in 1968, and by 2013 had become the largest of Tata's businesses. In sum, the Tata Group has operated very much like other emerging market powerhouses, with wide diversification into different industries and a willingness to enter and leave businesses as conditions change.

A notable difference in Tata's operation as a major business group is its ownership structure. Most of the Tata businesses are controlled by Tata Sons, Ltd, which holds either majority or at least the largest block of shares in them. Tata Sons is controlled by several trusts owned by the Tata family. Then the major companies are listed on stock exchanges, from Bombay to New York, including Tata Automotive, Tata Steel, Tata Consulting Services, Tata Teleservices and Tata Chemical, plus another half-dozen businesses. This allows the companies to operate fairly independently, although ultimate control does rest with the Tata family through the trusts.

Interestingly, the two largest businesses in the Tata Group today are Tata Consulting Services, which provides back-office services including call centres and software development to companies worldwide, and Tata Teleservices, which provides broadband and telecommunications services in India to retail and corporate clients. In both cases Tata fits into a global value-added chain of products and services, offering services to largely corporate clients in the first case and largely retail clients in the second. In neither case does Tata provide end-to-end production, as it has in the automobile and chemicals sectors; these last two sectors have declined notably in Tata's overall portfolio during the 2000s.

The family-based groups sometimes demonstrate poorer financial performance than more focused companies (Almeida and Wolfenzon, 2006); but on the other hand, many times they have proven to be more successful and more durable than focused companies (Hainz, 2006; Khanna and Palepu, 2000). This theme of performance of the family-based groups is quite fascinating; for example, it is frequently the case that the best-performing family groups are under either the founder or the third generation of the family. The second generation frequently produces poor results in comparison with the earlier and later ones. In a review of literature on business groups, Khanna and Yafeh (2007) noted that groups in less developed countries tended to have a valuation premium in the market, while business groups in more developed countries tended to show a valuation discount relative to unaffiliated firms in the same industries. Given that family-based groups have not faded away over time around the world, it seems likely that performance is at least acceptable to investors, who otherwise would demand break-up of the groups to unlock value.

Large vs small companies

Although our emphasis throughout this book is on large and internationally competitive companies, we also should think about smaller emerging market companies that fit into global value-added chains, and which may become global leaders in the future. The idea here is to emphasize that emerging market companies fit into global value-added chains, and those that may start small can expand their way into becoming global leaders. For example, the Cisneros Group in Venezuela staked a major position in that economy by representing foreign brands in the local market. For a long time Cisneros was the Pepsi-Cola distributor for all of Venezuela, before defecting in 1996 to become the national Coca-Cola distributor. In the first instance Cisneros was a fairly small, local company that hitched its wagon to the international star, Pepsi-Cola. By the time of the decision to switch colas, Cisneros was already a large conglomerate. Along the way, the Cisneros Group also was the representative for Chrysler automobiles and a number of other important US brands. Building on this early set of distributor relationships, the Cisneros Group ultimately focused on media, where it represented DirecTV in Venezuela and the Miss Universe pageant as well. The point is that an internationally competitive business group developed out of a local company that represented foreign brands, and through these relationships built up its size and power.

Similar stories exist around the world where local distributors of cars (eg Imperial Holdings in South Africa; Astra International in Indonesia) or car parts (eg Grupo Alfa in Mexico; Coscharis Group in Nigeria) or soft drinks (RJ Corp in India) or fast-food restaurants (Americana Group in Kuwait) grow to country-leading size, and then find businesses in which they can become internationally competitive. With the resources that they build up in terms of learning from the multinational branded partner such as Coca-Cola or Burger King, and the financial strength that flows from successful operation of the franchised/licensed business, these firms are well-positioned to launch into their own businesses as part of the group.

The Coscharis Group was founded by Cosmos Maduka, a Nigerian entrepreneur from the countryside who was apprenticed to his uncle and learnt how to do car repairs and sell car parts. In 1975 he left his uncle's business and set out on his own at the age of 16 to buy and sell car parts. First he collaborated with his brother, and then with a friend, before going his own way and launching the name Coscharis in 1982. His initial business was to sell car parts for Japanese cars. Through a fortuitous decision of the government in 1982 to allow Coscharis a licence to sell imported car parts in Nigeria, Maduka's company was able to operate with very limited competition.

The car parts business continued to grow successfully over the years, and Maduka began to branch out – into sales of cars (BMW and Land Rover, and subsequently also Ford). Then in the late 1990s he began to move into other industries, first with IT products as the licensee of

Microsoft and Hewlett-Packard in Nigeria and then in several other sectors, including pharmaceuticals, beverages and real estate. In 2014 the company operated in seven industries, with most sales remaining in car parts, cars, motorcycles, and other downstream stages of the car industry.

Coscharis is a good example of a fairly early stage emerging market family-based group. The company is still run by the founder; it has diversified into unrelated industries; and its sales are still primarily in the home country, Nigeria. Coscharis has expanded into neighbouring African countries, including Ghana and Côte d'Ivoire, and potentially could pursue additional African countries that are further away, such as Kenya and South Africa. It has diversified, but sales remain largely in the car and parts industry. The majority of sales are resale of branded products from Triad countries (cars, parts, car accessories, and electronics). It remains to be seen if Coscharis will be able to grow and establish itself with either own-brand products or a service network that distinguishes the firm from local and multinational competitors. For now, the company clearly fits into the downstream end of the value-added chain for cars and car parts, and generally in that same stage of the chain for its other businesses such as pharmaceuticals (Biostadt distributor) and medical equipment (Rudolf Riester and Sonoscape distributor).

While none of the examples presented in this section are tiny companies, they all started out small and have grown to medium or large size through exploitation of opportunities in international value-added chains. Once established as significant players in an industry such as automobile sales or operation of a television channel, they find additional opportunities to expand in purely domestic businesses (eg newspapers, food production, or transportation service) as well as other internationally linked businesses such as restaurant chains, franchise hotels or contract manufacture for foreign MNEs.

It would be a very incomplete story if we did not also mention the informal sector in emerging markets, which is often estimated to be half or more of the total economy.[8] Informal companies tend to be small in size and very often not connected strongly to the formal sector, except as purchasers of inputs and consumers of formal-sector final products. In principle, informal-sector companies can enter into global value-added chains, but their competitiveness outside of limited local markets is extremely low. So, although we recognize the importance of the informal sector, and the idea of trying to incorporate it into the formal economy, we do not pursue this subject further in the present context.

Conclusions

This chapter serves to highlight the great importance of SOEs and family-based groups among leading firms in emerging markets. In China the SOEs dominate the list of companies going international; in India the family-based groups predominate; and in most other major emerging markets the large international companies are a mix of these two types. These companies possess a number of characteristics different from traditional US/UK multi-nationals, and it is important to note these features and their implications.

The SOEs such as the oil companies (PetroChina; Pemex; Saudi Aramco) and banks (several Chinese banks) are in many cases quite global in their reach, and they compete directly with the largest multinationals from Triad countries. The goals and motivations of these state-owned entities must be somewhat different from those of the private-sector oil companies and banks, because they have non-economic considerations as well as profits to deal with. This reality implies that regulators around the world will have additional considerations to take into account when allowing the emerging market SOEs to operate in other countries, from political risk to possible movement of economic activities to the home countries of these SOEs for non-economic reasons. And private-sector competitors have to deal with the potential government backing received by the emerging market SOEs, which may give them an (unfair) advantage.

The family-based groups are more common than not as a dominant business form in most countries, and emerging markets are not an exception. These groups are less common in China thus far, since the communist regime up until the 1990s did not allow much business to grow outside the government sector. Even so, it is expected that Chinese family-based groups will grow and become more important in the near future, as they historically have been in Hong Kong, Taiwan, Singapore and other China-related countries that were not centrally planned during the second half of the 20th century. The family-based groups permeate all sectors and countries, and they are very often much more diversified than the SOEs. The successful ones generally have demonstrated skills in entering promising businesses and leaving declining ones, operating as good portfolio managers rather than as technical experts in one sector or another. And they tend to demonstrate competitive strength in managing diverse, often unrelated business activities and sectors.

Small and medium-sized companies are the most numerous in any country, and emerging markets usually contain not just incorporated firms in this category of business, but also large numbers of 'informal', unregistered businesses that would constitute SMEs if they were recorded. The main point of our discussion is to identify the fit of the SMEs into global value chains, and thus to find opportunities for these companies to grow in the value chains.

Notes

1 Kowalski *et al* (2013).
2 A bid by a Chinese firm with links to Beijing's municipal government to buy the bulk of US aerospace company Hawker Beechcraft Inc fell apart because of the US government's national-security objections in 2012.
3 This is despite the 'Dutch disease' that points out the problem in the Netherlands that oil production and export pushes up wages and other costs, and makes other Dutch products less competitive in international markets.
4 To be accurate, Wal-Mart leads the list of the largest companies by sales, and several car companies as well as conglomerates General Electric and Berkshire Hathaway also figure in the list ahead of the banks. Even so, there are about a dozen oil companies and another dozen banks in the top 75 Triad firms.
5 See, for example, *The Economist* (2014).
6 Kowalski *et al* (2013).
7 A thoughtful analysis of the Russian oil and gas supply threat to Europe appears in Stegen (2011).
8 The size of the informal sector in emerging markets very often exceeds 50% of total employment. See, for example, International Labour Organization (2009), p 26; and Singh (2012).

References

Almeida, H and Wolfenzon, D (2006) Should business groups be dismantled? The equilibrium costs of efficient internal capital markets, *Journal of Financial Economics*, **79**(January), pp 99–144

Björnberg, A, Elstrodt, H-P and Pandit, V (2014) The family-business factor in emerging markets, *McKinsey Quarterly*, December, pp 1–6

Cuervo-Cazurra, A, Inkpen, A, Musacchio, A *et al* (2014) Governments as owners: state-owned multinational companies, *Journal of International Business Studies*, **45**, pp 919–42

Delios, A and Ma, X (2010) Diversification strategy and business groups. In *The Oxford handbook of business groups*, ed A Colpan, T Hikino and J R Lincoln, Oxford University Press, Oxford, pp 717–41

Hainz, C (2006) Business groups in emerging markets – financial control and sequential investment, CESIFO Working Paper No 1763, July

Hong, J, Wang, C and Kafouros, M (2015) The role of the state in explaining the internationalization of emerging market enterprises, *British Journal of Management*, **26**, pp 45–62

International Labour Organization (2009) *Globalization and informal jobs in developing countries*, ILO, Geneva [Online] http://www.wto.org/english/res_e/booksp_e/jobs_devel_countries_e.pdf

Khanna, T and Palepu, K (1997) Why focused strategies may be wrong for emerging markets, *Harvard Business Review*, **75**(4), pp 41–51

Khanna, T and Palepu, K (2000) Is group affiliation profitable in emerging markets? An analysis of diversified Indian business groups, *Journal of Finance*, **LV**(2), pp 867–91

Khanna, T and Yafeh, Y (2007) Business groups in emerging markets: paragons or parasites? *Journal of Economic Literature*, **XLV**(June), pp 331–72

Kowalski, P *et al* (2013) State-owned enterprises: Trade effects and policy implications, *OECD Trade Policy Papers*, No 147, OECD Publishing, Paris [Online] http://dx.doi.org/10.1787/5k4869ckqk7l-en

La Porta, R, Lopez-De-Silanes, F and Shleifer A (1999) Corporate ownership around the world, *Journal of Finance*, **LIV**(2), pp 471–517

Li, M, Ramaswamy, K and Petitt, B S P (2006) Business groups and market failure: a focus on vertical and horizontal strategies, *Asia Pacific Journal of Management*, **23**, pp 439–52

Singh, A (2012) Out of the shadows, *Finance & Development*, June [Online] http://www.imf.org/external/pubs/ft/fandd/2012/06/singh.htm

Stegen, K S (2011) Deconstructing the 'energy weapon': Russia's threat to Europe as case study, *Energy Policy*, **39**, pp 6505–13

The Economist (2014) Reducing Europe's dependence on Russian gas is possible – but it will take time, money and sustained political will, *The Economist*, 5 April [Online] http://www.economist.com/news/briefing/21600111-reducing-europes-dependence-russian-gas-possiblebut-it-will-take-time-money-and-sustained

Conclusions

10

Emerging markets really are both a threat and an opportunity to traditional Triad-based companies, regulators and consumers. The main point of this book is to demonstrate that emerging markets are where the action is in the 21st century, and that good leaders of companies should look to take advantage of the opportunities there. Whether it is as sources of inputs into a business activity (such as offshore assembly of manufactured goods or back-office services) or market opportunities not yet explored, these countries are the main source of growth in this century. And while this view is aimed largely at Triad company decision makers, at the same time we have talked about the strategies of emerging market-based companies. So, the logic of including an emerging market(s) into corporate strategy goes both ways.

By looking at a company's fit into global value-added chains, it is possible to evaluate the current competitiveness of either type of firm. And in addition we can look at the sustainability of a company's strategy and at opportunities to expand into upstream and downstream activities as well as into other countries. Consider two final examples of companies in this context: a quintessential emerging market family-based company – Hutchison Whampoa – and a Triad-based multinational that has evolved to take great advantage of opportunities in emerging markets – Nike.

One final emerging market example: Hutchison Whampoa

Hutchison Whampoa (HW) is one final example of an emerging market-based multinational enterprise that may give further support for the logic employed throughout this book, namely that the company can be seen as a part of a global value-added chain(s). Based on locating the firm in such value chains, its strategy can be evaluated and opportunities identified for extending the firm's reach both up and down the value chain and also across countries. In this instance, let's look at HW both early in the life of the company and in recent times, to demonstrate the flexibility that has allowed the firm to survive for more than a century.

The Hutchison part of HW was founded as Hutchison International, a wholesale trading company and importer of consumer products, in 1877 by John Duflon Hutchison. Hong Kong and Whampoa Dock was formed even before that, in 1863 by John Couper, as a port management company. The original Hutchison company focused on imports from Europe into the port of Hong Kong, which was open to international trade as a result of the British victory in the opium wars with China in the 1840s and 1850s. Figure 10.1(a) shows the value chain participation of Hutchison in the early days, while Figure 10.1(b) shows the recent combined company's situation.

Hutchison and Whampoa operated independently for one hundred years, before controlling interest in the port management company was acquired by Hutchison International under the leadership of Douglas Clague in 1965. He pursued an aggressive path of diversification, acquiring additional businesses in retail food and drugs, supermarkets, real estate and other activities. In 1975 the group proved to be overextended and encountered a disastrous financial crisis; Clague was forced out when HSBC purchased a 20 per cent interest in the group at that point and demanded new leadership (from Bill Wyllie). The new management team in 1977 purchased the outstanding

FIGURE 10.1   Hutchison Whampoa (a) early value-added chains

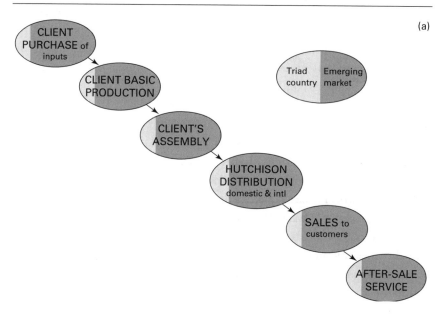

FIGURE 10.1   Hutchison Whampoa (b) recent value-added chains

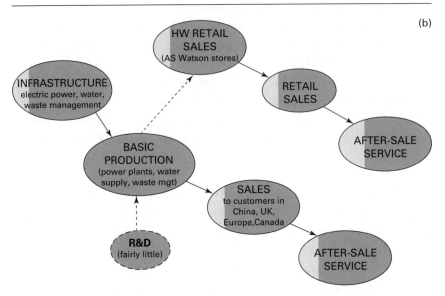

(b)

shares of Whampoa that Hutchison did not already own, and the group was renamed Hutchison Whampoa.

HSBC listed the company on the Hong Kong Stock Exchange in 1979 and sold its own 22 per cent share to Hong Kong business magnate Li Ka-shing that same year. Since that time and under the leadership of Li Ka-shing, HW has become a Fortune 100 company with widely diversified businesses ranging from the ports management and trading activities from a century earlier to newer businesses in telecommunications, hotels and energy. In this case the company has remained involved in its original businesses (ports and trading), while expanding heavily into electric power generation, telephone service provision and video service. And different from most of our family-based company examples, HW was originally controlled by one family (Hutchison), and is now controlled by another (Li Ka-shing). Under both the Hutchison family and the Li family, HW has operated a diversified set of activities and has moved into and out of various businesses.

In recent years HW has expanded its traditional ports management activity from Hong Kong and a handful of nearby ports to operate in 26 countries, such that this business is truly global today. At the same time HW entered into the telecommunications business – an area that quite a few family-based groups entered once mobile phones became technologically viable and national governments began to deregulate the telephone service business starting in the 1990s. Also, since the 1980s HW's retail store division has grown dramatically, with its AS Watson stores now numbering more than 11,000 in 25 countries. Major HW divisions also operate in hotels, oil and gas, and infrastructure. In 2014 the dominant businesses in the HW portfolio were infrastructure (electric power, water, and waste management companies), retail sales and telecommunications.

In light of the value-added chains that currently play the largest roles at HW – infrastructure and retail sales – the opportunities suggested by Figure 10.1 are to expand geographically in those two businesses. HW is very active in China and the United Kingdom, but not as active in other Asian countries such as Indonesia and India, which should provide major market opportunities. In general the geographic opportunities that make most sense are those linked to Hutchison Whampoa's traditional markets, along with new countries where an existing competitor may be in weak condition and ripe for a takeover that would enable HW to turn around that business. In terms of stages of the value-added chain, this group is really involved all along the chain, and it does not make sense to move into raw materials (inputs) or into equipment manufacturing. HW is a service provider and infrastructure operator, so these are the kinds of business activity that it could make sense to move into.[1]

One final Triad example: Nike

Nike started out in 1964 as the brainchild of a University of Oregon distance runner, Phil Knight, and his former coach, Bill Bowerman. Knight had graduated and was looking to start a business when he visited Japan and went to the Onitsuka athletic shoe company headquarters. He brashly negotiated an agreement to market Onitsuka Tiger running shoes in the United States, and then returned home to try to figure out how to do it. He went to his former coach, and they agreed to set up a company which they called Blue Ribbon Sports. Within a few years they had installed a number of retail stores in the western United States to sell these running shoes. Then in 1971 they decided to make their own shoes, becoming a manufacturer and then separating from Onitsuka in 1973. They called their initial line of running shoes 'Nike', after the Greek goddess of victory. In 1979 the company itself was renamed Nike.

From the outset Nike focused on building running shoes that would help their wearers perform better. Bowerman designed a waffle-shaped outsole for track shoes, to better grip the running surface, which was patented in 1974.[2] Nike continued on this path of innovation when they launched running shoes with air-filled cushions in the soles in 1979. Nike running shoes with air bubbles visible on the side of the soles were popular during the 1980s, leading to the first widely promoted model, the Air Max, in 1987. In 1984 Nike signed basketball star Michael Jordan to their endorsement list, and the Air Jordan lines of shoes was launched. The Air Jordan line still leads Nike sales 30 years later.

Even before Jordan, Knight began recruiting famous US athletes to wear the shoes and appear in commercials and other advertisements. In 1972 tennis star Ilie Nastase was the first athlete recruited by Nike, followed by Steve Prefontaine (distance runner) in 1974, Jon Anderson and Henry Rono (marathon runners) in the late 1970s, Jimmy Connors (tennis) in 1979, Jordan in 1984 and in 1987 baseball/football star Bo Jackson. Today Nike sponsors dozens of athletes in sports, ranging from running to basketball, football, tennis and golf.

After a serious jolt in the 1980s, when Reebok surpassed Nike in athletic shoe sales, Nike refocused its attention on design and innovation.[3] New lines of shoes were created for additional sports segments such as aerobics, and for a key additional market segment, women. In 1999 Nike began to offer custom-made shoes to clients who order shoes online, specifying their preferred colours, sizes, fabric and other characteristics. NIKEiD allows customers to largely design their own unique athletic shoes, within the limits of construction capabilities of Nike factories overseas.[4]

Nike's innovation efforts in recent years have produced the FuelBand, a wristband that keeps track of the wearer's running speed, energy used and steps taken, using an Apple iPhone or an Android phone. A shoe developed in 2012, the Flyknit Racer, is an extremely lightweight running shoe with a patented knit upper and lightweight waffle sole that feels almost like a sock rather than a shoe. In sum, Nike says in its advertising: 'We create products, services and experiences for today's athlete while solving problems for the next generation.'

The company also diversified into a wide range of athletic clothing, from sweatsuits to ski boots to sunglasses. Even so, about 80 per cent of Nike sales remain in athletic shoes, with a much wider range of sports than the original running shoes. Today there are Nike shoes for running, basketball, soccer, football, tennis, aerobics, golf, skateboarding and snowboarding. And probably more, if you keep in mind the ability of the consumer to design his/her own shoes on NIKEiD.

In the production process Nike focuses on design and innovation of athletic shoes and other athletic wear (Figure 10.2). The production of Nike

FIGURE 10.2 Nike's value-added chains

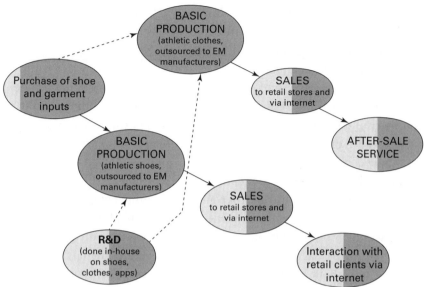

shoes and clothes is and has been 100 per cent outsourced to offshore contract manufacturers in China and another dozen countries since the early 1980s. Nike does do quality control evaluations of these independent manufacturers, to ensure quality production and also to avoid accusations of using sweatshop labour or other practices viewed as illegal or unethical.[5]

Looking at these value-added chains leads one to consider the opportunities for Nike to spread its shoe and apparel assembly operations to additional low-cost countries, where additional savings may be achieved. At the other end of the value-added chain, it may be desirable for Nike to put more owned stores into more (emerging) markets, since the Nike store concept has proved successful in several countries. Also, the use of sales on the internet has become a solid contributor to Nike's overall revenue, and additional innovations to the online sales structure could lead to additional revenue sources. Since Nike is so successful in athletic clothing, and not just shoes, it makes sense for the company to consider moving into additional athletic products and perhaps services, such as sports equipment. Each of these potential targets for continuing to build the business arises from consideration of the value-added chains in Figure 10.2.

These final examples demonstrate not only the benefit of looking at a company as part of global value-added chains, but also of looking at the value-added chains themselves, to see where HW or Nike could move to extend its business activities to additional stages of the chain and to additional locations around the world. With its solid base in China and emerging Asia, HW has a very strong position to expand into other Asian emerging markets. With its strength in athletic clothing, Nike may choose to move further into athletic equipment.

In both of these cases, and in several of the other examples in this book, the author does not have detailed inside knowledge of the companies. But as an observer, the outsider can identify business opportunities as done here. As an insider one can take the logic much further, by knowing the constraints and occasional serendipitous opportunities that arise and can be pursued. The examples of Standard Bank, LAN Chile, FEMSA, Crescent Petroleum, SABMiller, Morris Group and several other companies described in the book benefit from that knowledge. And as readers aim to use this thinking in their own companies, we will see how valuable the perspective is in coping with the challenges and opportunities of business in the 21st century.

As we talk about a rapidly changing business environment, where companies rise and fall perhaps even more dramatically than in the past, it is very helpful to have an anchor concept such as the global value-added chain to orient our thinking. No company dominates an entire value-added chain globally, while many small and large companies belong to value-added chains, from the oil industry to the mobile phone industry. Since we are focusing on emerging markets, the allocation of parts of almost any value-added chain to these countries provides a huge opportunity to traditional Triad companies at the same time as it opens a huge challenge to existing market leaders with new competitors arising from China, India and elsewhere.

Thinking back to the discussion of emerging markets through history, you realize that the United Kingdom and United States themselves were once emerging markets, and in the recent past Korea and the Czech Republic were emerging markets (while today they are clearly emerged, and are members of the OECD). Who will be the next to emerge? If personal incomes are the main measure of economic development, for example, then the Central and Eastern European countries clearly will be next, since they are already at personal income levels which are more than half of those in the United States and European Union. If we look at the most rapidly growing emerging markets, clearly China is at the forefront. However, starting from a very low per capita income base in the 20th century, China will probably take the rest of the current century to catch up. Even so, I wonder if we will consider China an emerging economy in 10 more years, when it is the largest economy in the world; it will have approximately half a billion people in middle- or upper-income categories; its companies will rival the US companies for leadership among the world's largest; and its technology development will continue to gain on the United States for world leadership.

A very striking feature of the largest emerging market companies is their nature either as state-owned or state-controlled enterprises (SOEs), or as business groups often based on a single or couple of families. The majority of the largest oil companies around the world are SOEs, many based in emerging markets. Probably well over half of the top 50 non-SOEs in most emerging markets are family-based companies, very often diversified into various businesses. This kind of family-based business is not a phenomenon limited to emerging markets; the largest companies in Japan and Korea are keiretsus and chaebols, just as the leading companies in France and Germany have control or strong minority positions of single families (eg Carrefour, Peugeot, Pinault, Bouygues, Michelin and Auchan in France; BMW, Bosch, Tenglemann, Aldi, Karstadt and Bertelsmann in Germany).[6] Both state-owned companies and family-based groups will be a major part of the global economy for the rest of the 21st century, and competitors need to better understand the motivations and features of these firms.

It would be a real mistake for one to think about emerging market companies as low-tech or as weak in marketing/branding. The reality of the 21st century is that with the economic opening worldwide through the 1990s, companies can quickly obtain brands by purchasing them (eg Volvo, bought by Geely in China; Miller Brewing, bought by South African Breweries; Arcelor Steel, bought by India's Mittal; CSX and P&O transport companies, bought by Dubai Ports World; Sara Lee baking, bought by Bimbo from Mexico – just to name a few). Likewise, they can obtain technology by acquisition of companies or by hiring scientists and engineers for their own research labs, as Geely has done in Germany and Australia. So, while emerging market companies may have more experience in dealing with intrusive governments and weak infrastructure in their home markets, they are very capable of acquiring traditional competitive advantages in the Triad countries.

This phenomenon of acquisition of capabilities by emerging market companies has been extended even further with the growth of sovereign wealth funds. These government-owned financial organizations invest the wealth accumulated by a national government from, say, exports of oil. The world's largest sovereign wealth funds today manage the oil-generated wealth of the governments of Norway, United Arab Emirates, Saudi Arabia, China and Kuwait. In addition, sovereign wealth funds from Singapore, Australia and South Korea are enormous investors in international markets.

Traditionally, such funds invested in portfolios of government bonds, bank deposits and some shares of companies. In recent years some of them have begun investing in controlling ownership of companies, thus making sovereign wealth funds from emerging markets another category of potential competitors for traditional Triad companies with their R&D activities and their brands and marketing skills.

This is not much different from the situation facing US companies in the 1800s, when they had to claw their way up to compete with European, particularly British, rivals. Over time the US companies did develop technology and brands that are world leaders today. The challenge today is for emerging markets companies (and their Triad competitors) to build these capabilities through acquisition or in-house efforts, and to be flexible and responsive enough to deal with the unexpected technology changes and government policy shifts that will come along the way.

Notes

1 In June 2015 Li Ka-Shing restructured his business empire, folding Hutchison Whampoa into Cheung Kong Group. So today the company exists as Cheung Kong Group, with all of the HW pieces included.

2 See, for example, http://salempress.com/store/pdfs/gevents_20c_pgs.pdf, which describes Bowerman's invention of the waffle-sole shoe.

3 Actually, it would be more accurate to say that Nike focused on marketing. Reebok had supplanted Nike as the lead seller of athletic shoes in the mid-1980s, specifically serving the markets for aerobics and also for women. Nike found itself with declining sales, and made a major thrust into marketing by hiring an ad agency and moving into the market segments noted above. At the same time Nike renewed its focus on innovation, where it has led the athletic shoe business since the early years.

4 NIKEiD is available at website: http://www.nike.com/us/en_us/c/nikeid

5 Nike was accused of exactly this practice of using sweatshop labour in the late 1990s at its contracted manufacturing sites in Asia. See: http://www. theguardian.com/environment/green-living-blog/2012/jul/06/activism-nike. Nike responded with a continuing effort to eliminate this practice and to provide not only worker-friendly but also environment-friendly production of its products around the world.

6 Even in the United States there are many very large family-based companies across many industries. For example, Wal-Mart, Ford Motor Company, Cargill, Motorola, Tyson Foods and Weyerhauser, just to name half a dozen. Still, in the United States more than half of the companies in the Fortune 500 are widely traded on a stock exchange, usually the New York Stock Exchange or NASDAQ.

GLOSSARY

adaptability A competitive advantage of emerging market companies, based on their ability to adjust quickly to changes in the competitive environment, such as new government regulations, new technology, economic crisis, and so on.

affiliate A company related to a parent company, such as a foreign subsidiary of an emerging market company.

American Depositary Receipt (ADR) A derivative instrument whose value is based on shares of a company. An emerging market company may issue ADRs in the United States in dollars, with underlying value equal to a specified number of shares denominated in pesos (local currency), for example.

Apartheid The period from 1948 to 1994 when South Africa was ruled by a white minority government that discriminated severely against non-white South Africans.

assembly operations A manufacturing process in which parts and components of a final product are combined to produce that final product. For example, cars are often assembled from chassis, body, window glass, wheels and tyres, plus many other parts, in assembly plants in low-cost locations.

back-office service (back-office support) Record-keeping for a business that is often carried out in a low-cost location where repetitive labour costs can be minimized. Such service includes accounting records, storing and accessing data files on company customers, products and so on.

banking assets These are assets on the balance sheets of banks, principally loans. Any other credit extended by a bank would be an asset, as well as investments in securities and other assets.

banking liabilities These are liabilities on the balance sheets of banks, principally including deposits. Other bank liabilities include loans received from other lenders and securities issued by a bank.

barriers to entry Aspects of a business that make it difficult for a new firm to enter that business. These include barriers ranging from government protection of existing companies to proprietary technology that is difficult to copy or replicate. These are often seen as the competitive advantages of the existing firms in the business.

BRIC Four emerging markets identified by Jim O'Neill of Goldman Sachs in 2001 as being ready to burst out as key markets of the 21st century. They are Brazil, Russia, India and China.

business group This is a set of companies or divisions that are owned and controlled by a single or small number of owners, such as a family. The group often is diversified across industries, such as General Electric or Mitsubishi.

business process outsourcing   Business processes such as accounting record-keeping, inventory management, human resource record-keeping and other functions may be contracted out (outsourced) to an unrelated supplier of such a service.

call centre   A function typically carried out in a low-cost location such as Bangalore, in which a company locates people who respond to customer phone calls for technical support, response to complaints, and other requests.

capital inadequacy   Banks face rules on the minimum capital (outstanding stock shares and available cash and liquid securities) that they must maintain. When a bank fails to meet the regulatory requirement for such minimum amounts of capital, it is subject to legal penalties due to capital inadequacy.

capital intensive   A business or industry may be categorized as capital intensive if it requires large investment in physical capital such as a mine or a car manufacturing plant. This term refers to the relative cost of plant and equipment compared to labour and sometimes knowledge (or R&D).

cash-and-carry   A type of store in which retail purchases of a goods are made, typically paying in cash and taking immediate delivery of the goods. This style fits stores like Walmart and Target as well as small retailers of similar goods.

chaebol   Korean business groups that are very large, diversified and that dominate many sectors in South Korea. These include Samsung, SK, Hyundai, GS and LG.

cloud computing   A means of data storage and access that is done in non-resident locations managed by third-party providers of this service. The service may extend to data processing as well as storage.

code-shared flights   A form of strategic alliance among commercial airlines in which they agree to jointly list their flights, offer passengers the ability to transfer bags automatically, and book through one airline for service by any of the alliance members. The codeshare refers specifically to a given flight that is listed for two or more airlines.

collectivism   A cultural feature of societies in which interests and goals of the group are seen as more important than goals/interests of the individual. Key values include the priority of group goals and social harmony/cohesion. On Hofstede's scale, the most collectivist societies are Latin American and Asian countries such as Venezuela and Argentina, Indonesia and China, while the least are the United States and United Kingdom.

commodity   A product that has standard features that are not differentiated. Minerals and metals, oil, and many agricultural goods are commodities.

competitive advantage   A capability or strength possessed by a company that enables it to outcompete rival companies. Competitive advantages arise from barriers to entry, and they are also often called (company) resources. They include characteristics such as proprietary technology, superior customer relationship management, economies of scale and even government protection.

conglomerate   An organization comprised of multiple subsidiaries or divisions that operate in related and unrelated businesses. Major examples include Tata group, General Electric and Mitsubishi.

conglomerate management   A competitive advantage that a company may demonstrate in competition with other conglomerates and/or with more focused rivals in individual businesses.

consortium   An association of several companies that are owned by different owners who collaborate in order to reduce costs or expand markets. The idea is that they can pool their resources to obtain more competitive results than any of the participants by itself.

contract manufacturing   A legal arrangement under which one company manufactures another company's (branded) products, providing just the physical production facilities and receiving payment for units produced.

contractual agreement   A legal arrangement that commits one company to provide a product or service to another without involving joint ownership or other additional links.

convenience store   A retail store format that sells 'convenience' items such as snacks, soft drinks, coffee and a variety of other items depending on the context. The largest networks of such stores are 7–Eleven and Circle K. They are often associated with petrol (gasoline) filling stations.

cost-based production   Manufacturing that is competitive because of low-cost conditions that allow production costs to be lower than in other places or companies. Asian countries, particularly China, have become leaders in providing low-cost production for a wide range of manufactured goods.

crowd funding   A financing arrangement in which a project/investment is described by the borrower, and then multiple lenders or investors are sought (typically via the internet) to each put up part of the funding needed for the project or investment.

customer relationship management (CRM)   A methodology or plan for dealing with a company's customers/clients that can give one company a competitive advantage over others. CRM elements include a record-keeping system, methods for interacting with customers, and key account management plans.

de novo company (greenfield investment)   In general the establishment of a new company, as contrasted with the acquisition of an existing company. In the case of foreign direct investment, greenfield investment occurs when the company sets up a new company overseas, rather than buying an existing company from someone else.

distribution channel   The part of the value-added chain that occurs after producing the product or service up to final sale to the ultimate customer and perhaps after-sales service. A distribution channel for shoes could involve shipping the shoes to wholesalers, who subsequently ship the shoes to retail stores, which sell to individual customers. An alternative channel would be via an internet webpage that allows customers to purchase the shoes, and then physical delivery of the shoes to the customer via the post office, or UPS, or amazon.com.

diversification   Expansion of a company into new businesses (product diversification) or new locations (eg international diversification).

diversified business   A company or business group that operates in multiple product lines and/or multiple geographic locations. McDonald's is geographically diversified into more than 100 countries. Berkshire Hathaway is diversified into more than a dozen industry sectors.

diversified business group   A corporate organization that operates in multiple industry sectors under a control structure managed by one lead company or family. Carlos Slim's Grupo Carso in Mexico is controlled by his family and operates in half a dozen industries, including telecommunications, retail stores, banking and construction.

downstream   The part of the value-added chain that occurs after obtaining the raw materials involved. This term is used especially in the oil sector, where downstream means oil refining, distribution, operation of petrol filling stations and production of petrochemicals.

economic opening   A regulatory change in which government control over the economy is reduced and private-sector business is encouraged. This is generally used to identify times when a national economy moves from communism to capitalism (eg Russia in 1991) or from highly inward-looking industrialization to more open-market policies (eg Mexico in 1986; Spain in 1986; China in 1978).

economy of scale   An ability of a company to reduce unit costs of production by producing a larger number of units of a product. Producing one car would cost probably more than $US 10 million; but producing 10,000 cars of the same type in a factory would probably cost more like $US 8–10,000 per car. Economies of scale are often a key competitive advantage of large companies.

electronic banking   Provision of banking services such as deposit-taking, funds transfer and lending via telephone or internet.

emerging market knowledge   A competitive advantage of companies that have experience operating in emerging markets and thus knowledge of how to compete successfully in that environment.

enterprise resource planning (ERP)   A methodology for keeping track of activities in a company, ranging from customer accounts to human resources to inventory management. Major electronic systems for ERP are offered by the two largest suppliers globally: SAP and Oracle.

entrepreneurship   The process of starting up a new business, including definition of the business activity, obtaining the inputs needed to carry out that activity, and marketing it to the target customers. Typically, entrepreneurship refers to creation of small businesses, which in turn form the largest segment of economies around the world.

family-based group   A company or group of companies led by one or even two or three families. Often the group name is the family name, as in the cases of Tata, Odebrecht, Koç and Swire Pacific.

family-owned business   A company or business group that is owned by one or a small number of families. The majority of the largest companies outside of the US and UK around the world are either state-owned enterprises or family-based groups/companies.

financial crisis While there have been many financial crises in history, in recent times the main one was the financial crisis of 2008–09, which began in the US real estate market and proceeded to affect financial markets around the world. The crisis occurred when US real estate-based assets lost in many cases half or more of their value, and then investors in those assets were either bankrupted (eg Lehman Brothers) or severely hurt (eg all other major US investment banks). The crisis then spread to the non-banking sector, leading to bankruptcies of GM and Chrysler and subsequently to long-lasting spillovers in Europe and elsewhere.

fixed-line telephone Traditional telephone service provision, which takes place through physical lines made of copper or optical fibre as opposed to mobile phone service that takes place without wires via microwave transmission.

footwear assembly The production of shoes, which includes taking the materials such as leather or synthetic fibres and machining or hand-assembling them into finished shoes. This production process today often takes place offshore in low-labour-cost locations such as China and Indonesia.

fossil fuels These are energy sources obtained from long-term decomposition of living plants and animals (fossils), which produce hydrocarbons over millions of years. These fuels include oil, natural gas, and coal.

franchisee A company that obtains the right to use another company's name and business model to sell products or services can operate under a legal contract called a franchise. The franchise permits the franchisee to use the brand name of the hotel, restaurant or other item in return for payment of a fee and various additional conditions. This kind of contract is common in hotels (eg Sheraton, Hilton), fast-food restaurants (eg McDonald's, Burger King) and convenience stores (eg 7-Eleven, Circle K).

GDP Gross domestic product, the main measure of annual output of a country's economy.

GDP growth rate The rate of change of GDP from one year to the next. This is a common measure of economic health of a country – a faster rate of growth implies a better-functioning economy.

generic drugs Pharmaceutical products sold without a brand name. Once a patent expires, any patented drug can be produced by third parties; for example, Tylenol is now sold as paracetamol by various generic drug companies, in competition with the formerly patented Johnson & Johnson product.

global supply network (global supply chain) A set of stages and participants in the process that goes all the way from producing raw materials needed to make a product or service, to producing it, to transporting it, to selling it to customers, and finally to after-sales service. The 'global' label refers to the fact that many supply chains cross national boundaries, and often they involve emerging markets.

global value-added chain This is the same idea as the global supply network, focusing more on the incremental value that is contributed by each participant in the process.

globalization   The process of increasing interconnection among people and companies around the world. With the advent of the internet and the decrease in the cost of travelling across national borders, along with rising global incomes, the process has advanced very dramatically since about 1990.

holding company   A corporate form in which one company owns and controls other companies in a group. The holding company is often completely focused on the management and oversight of the portfolio of companies in the group, while the other companies operate in the industry(ies) targeted by the group.

individualism   A cultural feature of societies in which interests and goals of the individual are seen as primary, before the interests and goals of the society overall. Or, in other words, the individual is seen as the target whose interests the society wants to optimize, while the society is seen more as the sum of all the individuals. Key values include individual independence and self-reliance.

informal institutions   These are features of a society that contribute to the development of business systems and activities, alongside of formal institutions such as government, legal structure and even religions. They include elements such as family structures, cultural traditions and social norms.

informal sector   This part of an economy is the unrecorded, 'underground' part of total economic activity. In many emerging markets a large informal sector operates a wide range of production and service provision activities that are not recorded, not taxed and thus not recognized explicitly. Examples of informal activities include illegal drug trafficking and money laundering – but also 'normal' business activities such as street markets where retail products are sold, provision of retail services from haircuts to home care, and other typically small-scale retail activities.

information technology   The part of business activity involving data/information management by computer and transmission of that data by telephone or internet. IT today is an integral part of most multinational companies, and it is the target of such companies as Apple, IBM, Cisco, Huawei, Bharti, Telefónica and many other companies coming from one of the two sides (computers or telephones).

innovation   The creation of new knowledge (ie invention) combined with the commercialization of that knowledge in some business form. Creating new knowledge and getting it successfully to market is considered one of the key competitive advantages of the 21st century.

institutional knowledge   This is a capability to deal with government regulators, competitors, suppliers and customers in a given market, and generally an ability to deal with the local institutions that surround the marketplace. This contrasts with technological knowledge or skill.

internet purveyors   Providers of access to a company's products via the internet. So, for example, W.W. Grainger provides access to Morris Group International's products along with products from many other suppliers through Grainger's website. A better-known example is amazon.com's provision of access to millions of companies' products and services through Amazon's website.

iPhone value chain   This is the global supply chain of inputs, assembly and final sale of Apple's iPhone as described in Chapter 1. It is an excellent example of how multiple companies in multiple countries participate in the production, distribution and sale of the product, the iPhone.

joint venture   This is a form of strategic alliance in which two or more companies each partially own a subsidiary or project that they operate together. Dow Corning is a joint venture owned partly by Dow Chemical and partly by Corning.

keiretsu   In Japan the largest business groups, typically based in one family, are called keiretsus. They are the descendants of the zaibatsu industrial powers of previous centuries. Today less than a dozen of them – including Mitsubishi, Mitsui, Sanwa and Sumitomo – still constitute more than a quarter of the total Japanese economy.

knocked-down kit (CKD)   This is an assembly arrangement for manufactured goods in which parts and assemblies are shipped to a manufacturing location as a CKD, and then they are assembled into the final product for sale to local customers. CKD value chains are often used in the car industry, so that a target country market can be served with 'local' production that involves just final assembly of the car sub-assemblies and components. The process can involve completely knocked-down kits (CKD) or partially, semi-knocked-down kits (SKD).

knowledge intensive   A business or the production of a product is 'knowledge intensive' if it requires above-average investment in R&D or in general if knowledge of a technology or methodology for carrying out some business process is key to competitiveness. This is different from R&D intensity, because it includes not only scientific knowledge but also institutional knowledge and knowledge of business processes.

knowledge-seeking   In the context of FDI, knowledge-seeking investment occurs when a company wants to obtain proprietary knowledge about producing a particular product or service, and the company invests overseas to obtain that knowledge. This kind of FDI has occurred in New Jersey with foreign pharmaceuticals companies setting up operations to participate in drug development there. It also has occurred in Silicon Valley as foreign IT companies set up operations to learn from the local clusters of computer, software and telecom companies.

licence Raj   In India, since the end of colonial times in 1947 the government has played a large role as regulator of the economy, requiring permissions for a very wide range of business activities. Getting such authorization from a government official, which has frequently taken long periods of time, produced the label of the 'licence raj' to refer to the bureaucrat who held back companies with red tape. The bureaucracy has been reduced somewhat in the 2000s, but government restrictions on business remain a major hurdle for many industries.

life science   The scientific analysis of plants and animals. Life science companies are generally pharmaceuticals companies that develop products to deal with diseases, other medical applications, plant growing, bio-engineering and other areas.

local purchasing requirement   To encourage the development of local producers in many sectors, governments around the world have established local purchasing or local-content requirements. The local purchasing requirement demands that a company must buy some value or percentage of its inputs from local suppliers. The local-content requirement states that a certain value or percentage of the final price of a product must be obtained locally.

logistics   This is the management of the flows of inputs, assemblies and products in a supply chain from purchase of initial inputs to sale of final products or services. Logistics generally refers to the physical transportation of the products involved, but it also extends to management of the whole supply chain.

low-cost labour   Low wages in a particular location/country may persuade companies to establish labour-intensive activities there to benefit from this cost advantage relative to other locations. China has been particularly well known for the past quarter-century as an excellent place to do offshore manufacturing due to low-cost, good-quality labour availability. India likewise is well known in this same time frame as a place to do offshore service provision such as back-office processing, operation of call centres, and generally business process outsourcing, due to low local labour costs.

low-tech   Products or industries are considered low-tech if they require less than the overall industry average spending on technology or R&D for companies to compete. Most services sectors are considered to be low-tech, as are manufactures of many commodity products.

macroeconomy   The overall economy of a country can be considered the macro-economy, especially when discussed in terms of aggregate measures such as total income, unemployment and inflation. The microeconomy then is the same country's economic activity observed from the level of the individual company or the individual decision maker (consumer, producer, investor).

maquila   This is the Spanish word for 'offshore assembly'. In Mexico maquila is very common for automobiles, clothes, and some electronics products that are assembled in Mexico and subsequently sold in the United States.

market capitalization   The value of a publicly traded company is most often measured as its market capitalization, the value of its outstanding stock shares in the market.

marketing intensive   A business or industry may be characterized as marketing intensive if it requires relatively high spending on advertising compared with others. Similarly, it would be marketing intensive if the business/industry requires greater than average expense on non-advertising activities in marketing, such as building distribution channels or investing heavily in CRM. Many consumer products industries such as cosmetics and processed foods are considered to be marketing intensive.

methodology A framework or process for carrying out some business activity. The methodology used by McKinsey, Inc to provide management consulting to its corporate clients is called the McKinsey Way, and it includes a sequence of steps to take in designing a consulting analysis, a database of information about previous client experiences and consultants who worked with them.

mixed oligopoly An industry structure in which a small number of firms dominate the industry or business, and they are a mix of privately owned and government-owned companies.

mobile communications equipment The telecom equipment used to operate a mobile phone network, from network switching gear to mobile phone towers to routers.

Mongol Empire The largest (geographically) empire in the history of the world, stretching from China to Hungary, and from India to Russia. Under Genghis Khan, his sons and his grandson Kublai Khan the empire lasted for most of the 13th century and then collapsed.

multinational enterprise (MNE) A company that operates in at least three countries, hence is multinational. The MNE must have operations in the different countries, rather than just exports there, such that it has a presence in multiple countries.

NAFTA The North American Free Trade Agreement, signed by Canada, the United States and Mexico in 1993. This agreement lowered or eliminated tariffs and non-tariff barriers on trade in most products among the three countries. It should be noted that trade restrictions were very few even before NAFTA, and the agreement did more to signal the commitments of the three countries to free economic activity among them than to reduce already-low tariffs.

nanotechnology R&D or technological work that uses matter on a scale of nanometres (one billionth of a metre). It includes research on organic chemistry, molecular biology and semiconductor physics, among other areas.

national champion A company that is seen by a country, particularly by a national government, as a leader for that country in international competition. Often national champion companies are given support by the government to help them compete with foreign rivals.

nationalization The forced sale of a foreign company's subsidiary to either the host government or another local owner. This occurred frequently in the 1970s, as emerging market governments tried to exercise sovereign power and control the activities of foreign MNEs. The nationalization could occur with compensation to the foreign owner, or as an expropriation without (fair) compensation.

network A web or chain of companies involved in an industry where they provide complementary or sequential parts of a value chain. The network of companies that produce the Apple iPhone discussed in Chapter 1 is a good example.

network equipment Electrical/electronic gear that is used to connect computers. It includes routers, switching gear, modems, networking cables, hubs, repeaters and so on.

offshore assembly   This is a manufacturing process that takes inputs from one (eg home) country, ships them abroad to a low-cost location, and uses local labour and other factors to put together the final product, which is then sold in the home country or elsewhere. Offshore assembly of clothing, cars and electronics products is very common today.

open-door policy   In China in the late 1980s the government began to allow private-sector business, including foreign companies, to operate. This opened the door to extensive development of the private sector and to foreign MNEs entering and operating in the Chinese market.

open-market policy   As contrasted with a high-regulation economic policy or a regime in which the government owns or controls most business, an open-market policy means that the market is allowed to operate and that companies can compete for business.

outsource   To contract out to a third party the production or assembly of a product. Outsourcing just means using an external party to carry out part of the company's production process; it may occur domestically or offshore.

patent   A legal commitment given by a government to the creator of a new product or process. The patent allows the holder a monopoly on use of that product or process for a period of time, generally about 15–20 years. Patents protect companies that invest heavily in R&D, so that they can benefit from their discoveries for a long enough time to recoup the investment and to generate both a return on it and an opportunity to pursue further R&D.

per capita income   The income generated in a country during one year divided by the number of people living in the country. So it is average per person annual income.

peripheral equipment   In the computer industry particularly, the computer is the basic product, and then add-on equipment such as a mouse, a printer, a modem and so on are peripheral equipment around the central product.

populist   Government policy is populist if it aims to support local people at the expense of both foreigners and corporate entities. That is, populist policy is often anti-business as well as anti-foreign. This type of policy has been particularly evident in Venezuela and Argentina in recent years.

portfolio investor   This type of investor buys securities in a company or financial institution without taking any control over that entity. So a portfolio investor could buy shares of a natural gas company such as BG Group [bought by Shell in 2015], whereas Shell was a direct investor that purchased controlling ownership of that company. Portfolio investment may be in stocks, bonds, bank deposits and other financial assets.

preferential treatment   Policy application to some firm(s) that gives that firm a more favourable outcome than others. Putting tariffs or ownership restrictions on foreign entrants into a country provides preferential treatment to local firms.

price control   Limit on how high a price may be set on a particular product that is regulated. In many emerging markets, prices are kept low through such controls on milk, bread, petrol and other basic consumption items. Such controls distort markets, as they tend to encourage black markets that operate outside the controls.

private branch exchange (PBX)   One kind of network equipment is the PBX, private branch exchange. This is a switching gear that enables a local network of telephones to operate within, say, a company or organization.

privatization   The sale of a government-owned company (SOE) to the private sector. The sale may occur to one purchaser, or through a stock issue on an exchange, or in various other forms. The government may retain partial ownership in a privatized company.

proprietary network   A set of companies or computers or telephones that operate under a single owner. So Federal Express's network of aeroplanes, trucks, depots and other transport service elements is a proprietary network, just as any company's internal telephone system may be a proprietary network.

proprietary pharmaceuticals   Drugs that are patented and available only under the legal permission of the patent owner. These are the drugs that include blockbusters such as Valium, Crestor or Lipitor, which major pharmaceutical companies strive to create and to protect with patents.

proved reserves (proven reserves)   The amount of oil in an oilfield that has been proven by exploratory efforts to be recoverable in the field. This is usually measured in barrels or millions of barrels. The terms also apply for natural gas and coal deposits.

purchasing power   The ability of an individual's income to buy products. This usually refers to per capita income, sometimes adjusted for price and exchange rate differences across countries. Rich countries have greater purchasing power, poor countries less.

purchasing power parity (PPP)   A comparison of prices of products across countries. Parity exists if products cost the same in different countries, once passed through the exchange rate. So if purchasing power parity existed fully, a Big Mac hamburger should cost the same everywhere.

R&D intensive   A business or industry may be characterized as R&D intensive if its spending on R&D is above the global average. That average was about 2 per cent of sales in 2013. We usually think of pharmaceuticals, computers and software, and telecommunications as being R&D-intensive sectors.

retail banking   In commercial banking the retail segment of the market is the set of services offered to clients such as individuals, families and small businesses. Typical retail banking services are deposit-taking, consumer lending and funds transfers.

rules of the game   The laws, rules and practices that define how a business may operate are called the rules of the game. The game is business, and the rules limit companies (players) to activities within those limits.

service sector　The service sector is broadly anything that is not manufacturing or an extractive industry. Alternatively, services are items that are not tangible, often require interaction between buyer and seller, and are transactional rather than storable. Services – from banking to hotels to lawn mowing to education to healthcare – make up more than three-quarters of most economies today.

small and medium-sized enterprises (SMEs)　Companies with at least a few employees and sale of less than perhaps $US 10 million per year might be considered as SMEs. The idea is that they are larger than micro-enterprises of one or two people with small sales, and smaller than large companies with hundreds of employees or more and millions or billions of dollars in annual sales. No precise definition of SMEs exists, and it would differ somewhat from country to country.

software　Instructions provided in some machine-readable form to guide a computer to perform a task. Software includes the word-processing program used to write this sentence. Software is intangible in the sense that it is not a physical product.

software implementation　A service provided to software users to instruct them on how to utilize a particular software program. This is particularly common with ERP software from SAP and Oracle, where they or third parties provide implementation assistance to purchasers of the software.

sourcing　Obtaining products or services from outside suppliers. The firm carries out some business activities internally and then sources additional inputs, services, distribution and so on from third parties. Sourcing may be done domestically with other companies, or it may be done to obtain inputs from other countries.

sovereign wealth fund　An investment vehicle owned by a national government or its agency. These funds have become major international investors in the cases of several oil-exporting countries such as Norway, Saudi Arabia and the UAE, as well as in other countries such as Singapore (Temasek).

standard of living　A measure of economic development. Standard of living is often measured as per capita income. The intent is to place a country in the global scale of living standards, using either per capita income or some other measure of well-being such as wealth, comfort, or availability of goods and services.

state-owned enterprise　A government-owned company. SOEs are particularly important in the oil and banking sectors, as well as in formerly communist countries in general.

statist　A political-economic system in which the government greatly controls the economy. This can be done through communist ownership of the means of production, or by extensive regulation. A statist system can be contrasted with an open-market (capitalist) system.

stock listing　When shares of a company are registered on a stock exchange, this is called a listing. In order to be listed, the company must comply with all of the rules of listing on the exchange, such as minimum capital requirements, acceptable corporate governance, and presentation of specific financial statements following prescribed reporting rules.

strategic alliance   Any form of collaboration between two or more companies may be considered a strategic alliance. Usually companies will form an alliance when they want to share costs and/or risks, or when they want to jointly present to the marketplace a broader portfolio of products or services or just locations. Joint ventures are one form of strategic alliance, and franchising and licensing are others.

supply chain management   The administration of a production and distribution process, from purchase of inputs to delivery of final products to customers. This is operation of the value-added chain, focusing on the coordination and optimization of the whole process.

switching gear (network switching gear)   Machinery used to route telephone calls or data transfers through a telecommunications network.

systems integration   The process of linking together software and hardware in a computer information system. SAP and Oracle ERP programs provide integration of multiple business activities and records for a medium or large enterprise.

technological catching-up   The process of modernizing for an emerging market, focused on gaining access to up-to-date technology. The acquisition of current technology may occur through education, alliances with companies that possess the desired technology, acquisition of people or companies that possess the technology or other methods.

technology intensity   The relative importance of technology in a business or an industry. R&D spending is usually used to measure this attribute, so R&D intensity is a similar concept.

telecom equipment   The hardware used in telephone and internet communications. This includes everything from handsets to large-scale network switching gear, routers, cables, and communications satellites.

Triad   Originally, the Triad countries were the United States+Canada, the European Union, and Japan. Subsequently the countries included have expanded to other Asian industrialized countries such as Australia and New Zealand. The Triad is intended to invoke the most advanced industrialized countries, as contrasted with the less developed countries or emerging markets.

turboprop   A propeller-driven aeroplane. These planes preceded jet aeroplanes and were the main form of commercial air transport during 1928–58, when the Boeing 707 jet was introduced.

upstream   The part of the value-added chain that occurs before downstream processing of a raw material. This term is used especially in the oil sector, where upstream means oil exploration and production.

utilities   Public utilities include a variety of services provided to the public. The most common utilities are electric power service, water and sewage service, natural gas or oil for home heating, and formerly telephone service (which is now often offered on a competitive, non-government basis).

value-added chain (or value chain)   The process of obtaining inputs, processing them, assembling a final product, delivering it to the point of sale, and selling it to customers. When the chain crosses national borders, it is called a global value-added chain. Services as well as products can be understood as value-added chains.

vertically integrated   A company is vertically integrated if it carries out multiple stages of the value-added chain within the company. That is, an oil company that both produces oil and refines it is vertically integrated. A company that just operates petrol filling stations is not. A company that produces agricultural products and operates restaurants is vertically integrated.

WTO (World Trade Organization)   The WTO succeeded the General Agreement on Tariffs and Trade (GATT), which was established after the Second World War to tries to negotiate multilateral reductions in tariff barriers to trade. Since 1994 the WTO has pursued the same objective, adding to it the idea of reducing non-tariff barriers to free trade as well. It is based in Geneva and has 160 member countries in 2015.

INDEX